NEGOTIATING CITIZENSHIl

Migrant Women in Canada and the Global System

While the designated 'rights' of capital to travel freely across borders have increased, the citizenship rights of many people, particularly the most vulnerable, have tended to decline. Using Canada as an example of a major recipient state of international migrants, *Negotiating Citizenship* considers how migrant women workers from two Third World regional settings – the West Indies and the Philippines – have attempted to negotiate citizenship in an age of neo-liberalism and globalization.

In this book, Daiva K. Stasiulis and Abigail B. Bakan challenge traditional theories of citizenship, which either base citizenship on membership defined in narrow national terms or insist that the nation-state is no longer determinant. Drawing on a variety of sources and approaches, the authors show how citizenship is a contested process, where 'gatekeepers' based in specific nation-states, and the uneven world system, create barriers to citizenship rights. Offering a unique perspective on current debates, *Negotiating Citizenship* demonstrates that the transnational character of migrants' lives – their labour strategies, family households, sense of community, diasporic consciousness, and political practices – presents important challenges to inequitable and exclusionary aspects of contemporary nation-state citizenship.

DAIVA K. STASIULIS is a professor in the Department of Sociology and Anthropology at Carleton University.

ABIGAIL B. BAKAN is a professor in the Department of Political Studies and the Department of Women's Studies at Queen's University.

Negotiating Citizenship

Migrant Women in Canada and the Global System

Daiva K. Stasiulis and Abigail B. Bakan

UNIVERSITY OF TORONTO PRESS
Toronto Buffalo London

© University of Toronto Press 2005
Toronto Buffalo London
Printed in the U.S.A.

Reprinted 2006, 2010, 2013

First published in hardcover in 2003 by Palgrave Macmillan

ISBN-13: 978-0-8020-7915-2
ISBN-10: 0-8020-7915-6

Printed on acid-free paper

Library and Archives Canada Cataloguing in Publication

Stasiulis, Daiva Kristina, 1954–
    Negotiating citizenship : migrant women in Canada and the global
system / Daiva K. Stasiulis and Abigail B. Bakan.

    Includes bibliographical references and index.
    ISBN 0-8020-7915-6

    1. Women alien labor – Canada.   2. Alien labor, Philippine – Canada.
3. Alien labor, West Indian – Canada.   4. Women domestics – Canada.
5. Nurses – Canada.   6. Citizenship – Canada.   I. Bakan, Abigail B.
(Abigail Bess), 1954–   II. Title.

HD6072.2.C3S73 2005   323.3'224   C2005-903082-8

University of Toronto Press acknowledges the financial assistance to its
publishing program of the Canada Council for the Arts and Ontario Arts
Council.

University of Toronto Press acknowledges the financial support for its
publishing activities of the Government of Canada through the Book
Publishing Industry Development Program (BPIDP).

In memory of our grandmothers,
Marta Sakkeus and Lena Blynn

Contents

Acknowledgements

This book is the culmination of a long period of research, teaching, advocacy and activism on the part of its authors. It is also the product of the generous support provided by an extensive network of individuals and institutions. The Social Sciences and Humanities Research Council of Canada and the Advisory Research Committee of Queen's University provided financial support for the research. We are grateful to Jennifer Nelson and Briar Towers at Palgrave, and Virgil Duff, for their perseverance and encouragement in the publication of the manuscript. Mukesh, V.S. of Newgen provided meticulous copy-editing of the manuscript. Expert research assistance at various stages of the study was provided by: Ceylan Cesur, Claudine Charley; Maria Leynes; Anne-Marie Murnaghan; Lorie Scheibelhoffer; and Marcia Williams. The Department of Sociology and Anthropology at Carleton University and the Department of Political Studies at Queen's University, and the many vibrant, articulate students who have participated in our classes, provided rich environments for testing our ideas about women's work, globalization and citizenship.

In the Philippines, Hong Kong and Singapore, we were welcomed into the homes and offices of numerous people and people's organizations who generously offered their time and knowledge. Particular thanks are owed to Gabriela, Migrante, Batis, BAYAN, Kanlungan and the family of the late Flor Contemplacion. In Canada, invaluable advice and information were provided by migrant, domestic workers and nursing associations. In Toronto, these included INTERCEDE, the Philippine Solidarity Group, the Coalition for the Defense of Migrant Workers' Rights in Canada, the Philippine Nursing Association, the Black Nurses Association and the Coalition of Visible Minority Women. The Montreal-based *Association des aides familiaux du Québec* allowed us to follow the experiences and conditions of domestic workers in Quebec. In Vancouver, we benefited from the generosity of the West Coast Domestic Workers' Association in giving us access to their files and documents. We owe much in terms of the insights we gained and support of our scholarship to Cecilia Dioscon and the many courageous activists associated with the Philippine Women's Centre in Vancouver. We are immensely grateful to all the domestic workers and nurses who agreed to participate in this study and who offered some of their precious non-work time to tell us about their experiences. We are also indebted to government officials in Canada and the Philippines, placement agency owners, hospital human resource managers and all those who were willing to speak to us and share their views regarding the negotiation of citizenship.

Several friends and colleagues have helped us in numerous ways. Pura Velasco was our intrepid guide and advisor in the Philippines and has been a major source of inspiration, advice and feedback throughout our research. Yasmeen Abu-Laban provided critical feedback and suggestions about the citizenship theory informing our work. We benefited from Pearl Rimer's breadth of knowledge on childcare.

Some of the arguments in this book have appeared in earlier versions elsewhere. Specific citations appear in this work accordingly, and we are grateful to the publishers for permission to use this material. Our intellectual debts are made explicit in our extensive endnotes and bibliography.

Our families fostered supportive conditions for writing this book while having to put up with our absences and the pressures associated with its preparation. Ignas Stasiulis provided Daiva with shelter and sustenance in Toronto, and Maia Stasiulis reminded her daughter of the strength and resilience of all the migrant women who had arrived in Canada as domestic workers to make a better life for their children. Adam McNally and Rachel Kellogg managed various stages of growing up with grace and strength, and endured their mother Abbie's long working hours at the same time. David and Mildred Bakan, and Clare and Mary Kellogg were ever present as a source of inspiration and encouragement.

Throughout, Radha Jhappan and Paul Kellogg have not only lent to this project their valuable skills with respect to critical scholarship, editing and technical support, but also their sympathetic ears, forgiving hearts and unstinting patience.

This work is written equally and jointly by the authors. Any errors or weaknesses are our responsibility.

1
Introduction:
Negotiating Citizenship

In 2000 there were over 130 million documented migrants worldwide, an increase from the 1965 figure of 75 million. This number swells to 150 million if the estimated number of undocumented migrants are included.[1] Most migrants originate from the poorest regions in the world, and an augmenting percentage are women. The implications posed by the growing numbers of female migrant workers from Third World states for our understanding of citizenship is the subject of this study. In an age of globalization, when national borders are commonly considered to be a minor factor in the world system – permeable to multinational corporations, technology and international organizations – the experiences of poor women of colour seeking to migrate in order to support their families often escape analytic scrutiny.

While the designated 'rights' of capital to travel freely across borders have increased, the citizenship rights of people, particularly the most vulnerable people, have tended to decline. Taking Canada as an example of one of the most economically advanced states in the world, and a major host state to international migrants, this study considers how migrant women workers of colour from two Third World regional settings – the West Indies and the Philippines – have attempted to negotiate citizenship rights in an age of neo-liberalism and globalization.

Several dimensions of the study suggest a unique perspective in the context of current debates. Unlike many contributions, we maintain that globalization has neither abrogated nor lessened the role of the nation-state. Instead, globalization expresses and has exacerbated an imperialistic hierarchy of states on a world scale, where multinational corporate interests based in the most economically advanced regions exert extraordinary pressures on the least developed. National citizenship has traditionally been defined in terms of social membership in a particular nation-state, or national citizenship. As such, citizenship includes the legal recognition on the part of states to allocate certain rights and responsibilities among a given population that are defined as having membership in, or belonging to a particular nation-state collectivity. But not everyone who resides in the territory over which a nation-state has legal jurisdiction is defined as part of that collectivity. The trend towards increased international mobility has meant that there are ever-increasing numbers of non-citizens who are working and residing in migrant-receiving states. Moreover, citizenship itself is increasingly subject to social and legal differentiation, producing new forms of gradational or hierarchical citizenship. While citizenship appears to be an inclusive, universalistic concept, in reality all state citizenships are not equivalent; nor are all state citizenships allocated in equivalent ways.

Citizenship includes legal status, demanding formal national state certification, but citizenship is not reducible to legal status alone. Citizenship exists on a spectrum, involving a pool of rights that are variously offered, denied, or challenged, as well as a set of obligations that are unequally demanded. The terms and conditions of citizenship rights and responsibilities are the product of active and ongoing negotiation. This process of negotiation involves numerous actors, where human agency on the part of non-citizens and citizens operates through a combination of individual and collective strategies within a matrix of relationships and institutional practices over space and time. Human actors operate within certain defined boundaries contoured by the global system, where gatekeepers closely regulate and monitor restrictions to citizenship. For poor women of colour from Third World states who migrate to advanced First World states in search of citizenship, or at least some elements of citizenship associated with membership in First World states, the challenges and barriers are extreme. Moreover, in all states in the global system, specific class divisions – and within and across classes, gender and racial oppression – comprise essential factors that influence and are influenced by the process of negotiated citizenship. At the same time, the transnational character of migrants' lives – their labour strategies, family-households, political practices, sense of community and diasporic consciousness – offer important challenges to inequitable and exclusionary aspects of nation-state citizenship.

In this study, we develop this perspective on citizenship in the global system in detail, and place our theoretical framework in the context of the contemporary debates about the challenges posed to national citizenship by the processes of globalization and especially the international mobility of peoples. Chapter 2 lays out five central tenets to aid in comprehension of the negotiation of citizenship in the context of globalization. The remaining chapters of the study apply such an approach to a particular case study of negotiated citizenship – the migration of West Indian and Filipino women workers to Canada to work in the caring industries of live-in domestic service and hospital-based nursing.

The selection of this case study is reflective of several considerations. The West Indies and the Philippines represent two Third World sources of large-scale migration internationally, and large-scale immigration to Canada. Women workers from both the Philippines and the West Indies have been recruited to Canada to service particularly the childcare needs of families in Canada as live-in nannies, and more recently care needs of elderly and infirm family members that have become increasingly privatized under neo-liberal government policies. Federal Canadian government immigration policy has been specifically shaped to this end. The demand for childcare services has increased as Canadian women have swelled the ranks of the public, paid labour force, yet Canadian governments have continued to fail to provide a national childcare programme. The interface of West Indian and Filipino non-citizen migrant women workers, employed to care for the children, other family members and the homes of Canadian citizen professionals, offers a unique window into the matrix of negotiated citizenship.

Filipino and West Indian migrant women workers have also worked in a second care-providing industry in Canada, as nurses in the health care sector. While nurses of colour face specific racial and gendered barriers to citizenship rights, the distance between public health care professional service and private domestic service is great. By including in our case study two distinct points of origin of migrant women workers, destined to fill two distinct occupational settings, the complexity of negotiating citizenship across various barriers and conditions is brought into sharp relief.

To consider this case study from the perspective of negotiated citizenship, we have used a multidimensional methodological approach. At the centre of the study is an original survey of domestic workers and nurses who have migrated to work in Canada from the West Indies and the Philippines. Interviews with domestic workers and nurses were conducted in Toronto, Ontario – the city with the largest percentage of migrant workers in the country – based on questionnaires for each labour sector. The questionnaires were specifically developed to address citizenship negotiating strategies, and living and working conditions associated with citizenship rights in Canada. Interviews were also conducted with gatekeepers, on the other side of the citizenship divide.

These included the directors of placement agencies operating in the private domestic service sector, and representatives of nursing regulatory bodies and hospital human resources managers in Toronto. We also travelled to Manila, Philippines in 1995, where we met with government officials, nursing college administrators and migrants' rights advocates to consider the perspective of those who remain in one of the main Third World sending states for domestic workers and foreign nurses in Canada. Our research also brought us to Dallas, Texas to a conference of the International Nanny Association, to London, England where we interviewed administrators with the Nursery Nurse Examination Board, and to conferences of black nurses and Filipino nurses in Toronto.[2]

The original data presented in this study is hence extensive, collected over the course of most of the 1990s. We have also compiled statistical data on migration, domestic service and health care covering both long-term trends and recent developments. Our effort in this process is not, however, simply to transmit information in a descriptive manner. We have structured the material in a narrative of analysis that attempts to highlight the specific constraints and the creative struggles of migrant women as they negotiate to gain the minimal rights to equality of treatment and decent standard of living that are normally associated with the discourse of citizenship in a liberal democratic context. Global realities, national state regulatory bodies, gatekeeping mechanisms and gatekeepers, families with all their various complexities in both the First World and the Third World, imperialism, sexism and racism, all figure into the analytical framework centred around the negotiation of citizenship.

Specifically, in the remaining chapters of the study, we attempt to unpack a story of negotiated citizenship, through the experiences of migrant women who are legally constituted upon arrival as non-citizens in Canada. Both private domestic service and public nursing service, as two major sources of employment of these migrant women, are closely considered. However, the conditions of the former reveal with particular transparency the contradictions of Canada's place in the global system, and the intersection of gender, race, citizenship and class within Canada. The domestic service sector therefore figures more centrally in the analysis.

The book is organized to reveal how the global, national and local contexts of capitalist and imperialist power relations intersect to produce particular life outcomes for women migrant workers. Chapter 2, entitled 'Negotiating Citizenship in an Era of Globalization', lays out the tenets of our theoretical understanding of contemporary citizenship as a set of rights, obligations and forms of agency that reveal tensions between the universalistic discourses of modern citizenship and the discriminatory impact of border policies of modern democratic states. A central feature of our framework is the global arena within which citizenship rights are now being negotiated, with sending and receiving states, private interests, citizens in receiving states, and migrants themselves being key actors in this negotiation.

Chapter 3, titled, 'Underdevelopment, Structural Adjustment and Gendered Migration from the West Indies and the Philippines', considers the conditions that compel women from these areas to leave everything that is familiar to them, often at considerable cost, and seek an uncertain future in countries such as Canada. The impact of structural adjustment programmes in aggravating conditions of poverty and underdevelopment in the West Indies and in the Philippines, and the resultant pressures towards out-migration, comprises one dimension in this chapter. The social construction of foreign domestic workers in Canada, and in particular the historical development of specific legislation regarding the recruitment and regulation of live-in domestic service, comprises another. These two processes combine to re-create the citizen/non-citizen divide that marks the features of the global system in microcosm within the private Canadian household. Canadian-citizen women in demand of childcare, turn to the employment of non-citizen women of colour to satisfy this demand. The families and childcare needs of West Indian and Filipino women are absented from the matrix of considerations in the formally recognized process. In return for acceptance of extraordinarily restrictive working and living conditions spurned by those with other options in the Canadian labour market, foreign domestic workers are compelled by law to live in the homes of their employers for a minimum of two years in a three-year period. Over this time period, under a federal policy dubbed the Live-in Caregiver Programme, foreign domestic workers are only allowed temporary residence status. Violation of the labour contract can be met with a deportation order. These workers are among the most vulnerable to conditions of exploitation and abuse of any workers in Canada. The incentive to tolerate such conditions, however, is the possible attainment of permanent, or landed immigrant status, which provides a portal to many valued citizenship rights and benefits, at the end of the compulsory term of live-in domestic labour.

In Chapter 4, 'Gatekeepers to the Domestic Service Industry in Canada', we continue to explore the barriers to citizenship imposed on foreign domestic workers. One particularly influential group of gatekeepers, private domestic placement agencies, is considered in detail.

The analysis combines the results of intensive interviews with the most established private agencies in the city of Toronto, with a general analytical framework that focuses on the social construction of the non-citizen foreign domestic worker. Blatantly racialized and gendered stereotypes facilitate and restrict the recruitment and placement of foreign domestic workers in the homes of Canadian families. While domestic placement agencies present themselves as ostensibly neutral stakeholders in meeting the needs of both employers and employees, the structural and ideological bias towards the citizen/employer, invoking particular representations of the 'legitimate citizen' and the 'fit nanny', are readily expressed in the research findings.

Chapter 5, 'Marginalized and Dissident Non-Citizens: Foreign Domestic Workers', turns to the survey findings drawn from interviews with West Indian and Filipino domestic workers. Unlike other studies of foreign domestic workers in Canada and internationally, which either describe general trends or focus on a single ethnic or national group, our research was shaped to allow us to explore the experiences of women of colour from two distinct regional and ethnic backgrounds. Though the sample size is not large enough to claim general representation, the findings suggest that the main distinction among the two groups is constructed by the greater restrictions on West Indian women relative to Filipinas. We maintain that distinct migration paths forged by the two groups have at least in part been produced by gatekeeping mechanisms at the level of the state and private domestic placement agencies, which have tended to disfavour West Indian women applicants as a result of a past history of organized resistance to oppressive conditions. Filipino household workers, however, are now similarly organizing, and restrictions on foreign recruitment have risen. When overall working and living conditions are considered, both West Indian and Filipino live-in domestic workers manifested similarly oppressive conditions. The survey findings suggest that the class division between citizen employers and non-citizen employees bears the most profound impact on the experiences of foreign domestic workers, whether they originate from the West Indies or the Philippines.

In Chapter 6, 'Marginalized and Dissident Citizens: Nurses of Colour', our focus turns to another caregiving occupation filled by West Indian and Filipino women workers. Though migrant nurses are considerably less constrained in their mobility and other human rights than domestic workers, nurses of colour have encountered intense racism in Canada, historically and in the present. Neo-liberal restructuring policies have severely limited resources in the health care sector in general, and to nursing care in hospitals in particular, across Canada.[3] Ontario, the largest province in Canada, host to the greatest proportion of foreign workers, and the focal point of this study, is among the regions in Canada that have been particularly hard hit. While nurses from the West Indies and the Philippines were once actively recruited to fill a shortage of labour, the 1990s and early 2000s witnessed a dramatic reversal of this trend. In an atmosphere of cutbacks and declining services, hospital management strategies have attempted to challenge the collective unity among nurses by turning to increased racial stereotyping in job assignments, promotion, and responses to patient complaints. A series of challenges taken up by nurses against racism in Ontario hospitals are described in this chapter.

In addition, the chapter examines the perceptions of the migrant nurses themselves as reflected in the survey. A question-by-question comparison between domestic workers and nurses was found to be inappropriate, and we have not attempted to force the findings into such a constricted framework. However, the findings do indicate some general similarities and differences. Migration strategies among West Indian and Filipino migrant nurses, similar to those of domestic workers, are suggestive of the broader patterns of migration access through the gates of the Canadian border. As in the comparison between the two groups of domestic workers, West Indian nurses faced greater barriers relative to Filipino nurses and hospital management strategies adopt divisive tactics that disfavour West Indian nurses. Working side by side with Filipino nurses, West Indian nurses expressed more frequent experiences of overt racial discrimination traceable to management tactics. Both Filipino and West Indian nurses, however, identified ongoing patterns of discrimination in the hospital sector.

In Chapter 7, 'The Global Citizenship Divide and the Negotiation of Legal Rights', we turn to a consideration of one form of resistance to barriers that limit citizenship rights for migrant women in Canada. The focus of this chapter returns to the experiences of domestic workers. While we maintain that legal citizenship is no guarantee of access to full and equal citizenship, a point clearly displayed in the experiences of foreign nurses, neither do we wish to underestimate its significance. In this chapter we examine legal strategies that have challenged the absence of formal, juridical rights to citizenship afforded to foreign domestic workers.

The final chapter, 'Dissident Transnational Citizenship: Resistance, Solidarity and Organization', concludes the study and focuses on collective, international solidarity movements for migrant rights. We trace some of the activities of the Filipino community in particular, which has played an inspiring role in maintaining ongoing international campaigns in support of migrant Filipinos seeking citizenship rights in various countries in the global system. Placing our case study in the wider context, we suggest that our theoretical approach may shed some light on other instances of the complex matrix of relationships of nego-tiated citizenship. We are convinced that the experiences of migrant women who have struggled so tenaciously to obtain and retain their rights, and have laboured tirelessly to care for the needs of citizens in Canada, have many lessons to teach us. We know there are many, many other dissident non-citizens who have similar stories to tell and lessons to transmit.

A brief note on terminology is in order. We are aware of the risk of over-simplification involved in the use of such dichotomies as First World/ Third World, North/South, developed/developing, and so on to designate the economic status of given states in the global economy. Our use of these terms in no way suggests that we accept a Eurocentric ranking of states according to ethical or cultural criteria. Nor do we endorse a static evolutionary schema of development, with a teleological goal of a 'mod-ern state'. In the absence of preferable terms we employ these dichoto-mous concepts in the knowledge that they retain heuristic value in identifying protracted processes of geo-political structural domination. In particular, our use of these terms reflects our understanding that the development of Third World states such as the Philippines, Jamaica, and other West Indian states, has been blocked and/or distorted as a result of their economic and political relations with 'developed' imperialist states and through an international system of economic and military competi-tion that forces external priorities on the internal management of human and material resources.

Also in regard to terminology, we employ the term 'women of colour' to refer to the collectivity of women who are subject to a multitude of forms of blatant and more subtle, systemic and more individual forms of racism largely on the basis of skin colour or other 'visible' differences. Racism in a settler society such as Canada, directed at migrants whose geographical origins may be half a globe apart, occurred in the context of European empire expansion, enslavement and oppression for profit of entire populations of several continents. We prefer the terms 'people of colour' and 'women of colour' to those such as 'visible minority'; the ori-gin of the latter term is in Canadian state-bureaucratic processes attempt-ing to classify 'others', whereas 'women of colour' has been coined by women who themselves have encountered the reality of racism. In this book we focus on the experiences of two distinct national/ethnic minori-ties, West Indians and Filipinos, whose experiences of racism in Canada are shaped by common factors on a global, regional and national level. At the same time, we have no intention of imposing a reductive commonality; we compare and contrast the specific negotiating strategies of women workers in these groups. The socially and politically constructed experiences of racism are centrally significant to the experiences of women migrant workers; the term women of colour is valuable in explaining this significance.

A further note needs to be added regarding the impact of 'September 11' on current citizenship debates. The research for this study was undertaken largely prior to the attacks in New York and Washington that occurred on September 11, 2001, and the subsequent 'war on terrorism'. However, as taken up in Chapter 2, efforts on the part of gatekeepers to regulate Third World citizenship in First World states, which were apparent prior to '9–11', have been appreciably intensified since that time. In Canada, Bill C-11, a new Immigration and Refugee Protection Act (IRPA),[4] was tabled in the federal House of Commons prior to the attacks on the World Trade Centre in New York City and the Pentagon in Washington, DC. This bill proposed a series of changes that greatly reduced access and rights to permanent residence in Canada on the part of new immigrants and refugee claimants, particularly those who lacked financial resources. Critics insisted that the bill if enacted into law would encourage racialized criteria that challenged the rights of immigrants and refugees of colour to obtain Canadian citizenship, and the rights of appeal to negative decisions based on racialized criteria. After September 11, the IRPA was enacted into law, in part on the grounds that it introduced necessary control and security measures preventing terrorists from gaining entry to Canada and access to Canadian residence. In a statement presented in March 2001, Amnesty International indicated its concerns that under the new legislation, 'there may be some people who are not protected from return situations where they may be arbitrarily detained, tortured, disappeared or executed'.[5] There is no minimizing the horror of the events of September 11. However, the increased scrutiny of immigrants and refugee claimants by governments that adopt racialized and otherwise discriminatory criteria to police the borders has not created a safer world. Instead, innocent people, particularly people of colour from Third World regions, have been increasingly treated with undue suspicion; the risks to Third World non-citizens of racial profiling and treatment as suspected criminals without grounds is grave indeed. The processes we identify in this study that serve to restrict access to citizenship rights for some of the most vulnerable migrants in the world system have only become more restrictive in the post-September 11 period.

Though our study is ambitious in scope, our aims are modest. We hope to enable some of the complex issues that have otherwise been blurred in the citizenship debates to come into greater focus. If, at the same time, the lives and experiences of dissident and marginalized non-citizens and citizens are given greater notice, concern, respect and solidarity, our goals will have been well met.

2
Negotiating Citizenship in an Era of Globalization

Contemporary international migration poses a major challenge to modern conceptions of citizenship. It generates complex and multi-faceted relationships of individuals to territories, nation-states, labour markets, communities and households. Perhaps more than any other process associated with globalization, international migration highlights the tensions between the universalistic claims of modern nation-state citizenship and its particularistic, and thus inequitable workings. Migration and immigration policies of liberal democratic states are implicitly and often explicitly discriminatory in class, racial, regional and national origins, linguistic, gender and other terms. Moreover, their discriminatory character is legitimated by international law and its interpretation within national jurisprudence that affirms and treats as self-evident the centrality of immigration control to the doctrine of strong, national, territorially based sovereignty.[6]

The discourse of modern citizenship, by way of contrast, has long been associated with values of freedom, democracy and equality of treatment.[7] Citizenship has 'come to offer beacons of hope – a reviving of past achievements and a mapping of future progress – in a world where democracy, community, human rights, and identity are under relentless siege'.[8] Yet policies regulating migration have largely undermined the emancipatory potential or equalizing promise of the 'evasive grail of citizenship'.[9] Thus, selective criminalization of certain types of migrants and the privileged treatment of others in migration processes and policies create and reinforce the hierarchical nature of national citizenship. They affect which migrants are treated as 'fit' candidates for host-society citizenship, which enter with probationary status and can be 're-fitted' at their own expense, and which are rendered completely ineligible through their exclusion or intensive policing. In other words,

11

invidious distinctions made between migrants in migration policies, which are based on North–South relations, their class positions, race/ethnicity, gender, or other markers of differences including disability and sexual orientation, are reproduced through a hierarchy of citizenship statuses; these relations operate in the lived experience of citizenship among disadvantaged migrants as a simultaneous process of inclusion and exclusion. While migration policies are not the only mechanisms that render citizenship antipodal in the sense of extending both important entitlements, and yet severe forms of 'repressive and exclusionary praxis', they are nonetheless powerful ones in the current historical moment.[10]

In this chapter, we provide some tenets for a theory about contemporary citizenship to assist in comprehending the citizenship experiences of women from the South migrating to a First World state in the North, to work in caregiving occupations.[11] Theories examining the nexus between citizenship and international migration reflect the forms of evidence, case studies and exemplars marshalled to substantiate particular trends or tendencies. Conclusions about the expansive or exclusionary nature of rights in liberal democracies for migrants, and whether 'post-national' or other non-national forms of citizenship have superseded nation-state citizenship diverge markedly. These widely varying positions reflect different geopolitical locations that ground more general accounts, as well as varying degrees of access to national citizenship and transnational benefits of various groups of migrants. Thus, theorizing on the inclusionary or exclusionary character of citizenship will bear the mark of whether the focus of analysis is primarily on the mobility and human/citizenship rights of those migrants actively sought out by states and corporations such as transnational capitalists and knowledge-based highly skilled workers, or those whose presence is welcomed more cautiously, temporarily or not at all. Included in the latter category are seasonal agricultural workers, undocumented service and factory workers, migrant family members, asylum seekers, sex trade workers, mail order brides and domestic workers. Our framework is informed by, and informs, case studies of South to North migration of female care workers, and especially private household workers, but it is attentive to the differential access of various groups of migrants to the promises of citizenship. It draws attention to the role of modern citizenship in accessing a wide range of rights, but as importantly in creating and reproducing inequality among individuals and groups in the context of contemporary globalization.

A central feature of our framework is the global arena within which citizenship rights are now being negotiated, with sending and receiving states, private interests, citizens in receiving states and migrants themselves being key actors in this negotiation.[12] Recently, 'post-national' citizenship theorists have suggested that national citizenship has been superseded by global, cosmopolitan or transnational citizenship regimes.[13] Instead, we argue that nation-states remain the most important governance site for allocation and regulation of citizenship rights, responsibilities, and burdens. However, the power relations that underlie national citizenship are not confined to dynamics within the nation-state and instead reflect and reinforce global relations of power such as the hierarchy of states in the overarching world system of states, and the increasingly transnational character of resistance in civil society. This chapter highlights five significant features or tendencies in contemporary citizenship.

First, citizenship, even within states that pride themselves on being democratic and multicultural, reflects tensions between claims to universalism, and the tendency towards exclusion and inequality based on the value accorded to a certain ideal type of citizen. The preference given in citizenship to subjects bearing particular valorized combinations of race, gender and class is expressed in contemporary immigration policies. The logic of national immigration policies is both tuned to maximizing the needs of the neo-liberal corporate sector, with business forming the major partner in immigration policy-making, and minimizing the security and integration costs to national states of autonomous migration. Regional attempts in North America and Europe to coordinate or indeed harmonize migration policies suggest that migration controls are now 'integral components of neo-liberal regional integration projects'.[14] Nonetheless, far from having withdrawn from the management of migration flows, individual states continue to defend their iron grip on control over national borders, and the criteria for national membership as intrinsic to their state sovereignty.

Second, the exclusionary and hierarchical tendencies of citizenship have deepened with the expansion of neo-liberal policies and corporate globalization, driven by the interests of powerful transnational actors. The international reorganization of productive and reproductive labour spurred by neo-liberal policies and globalization, has sharpened the 'global citizenship divide' between citizens in the North, or First World, and poor migrants from the South, or Third World. The maintenance of the status and entitlements of First World citizens of a particular class, is contingent on the imposition of diminished access to rights and of heightened expectation of obligations among poorer Third World migrants in receiving states.[15] The inequitable and relational character of citizenship is manifest in the relationship between predominantly female migrants from the South, who are 'imported' to care for the young, elderly, sick and disabled in the North, and their largely female citizen-employers.

Third, the neo-liberal realignment of the public/private divide, stemming from the retraction in public institutions such as hospitals and other care facilities, has located more care areas and activities in the private sphere such as the family household. This realigned public/ private division reflects and reinforces the global citizenship divide between citizen-employers of migrant caregivers and disenfranchised migrant household workers. While the retraction of systems of social provision has rendered citizenship more exclusive and 'thinner' in general, for low-wage migrant workers in labour-importing countries across the globe, the citizenship on offer is partial, provisional and precarious.

Fourth, despite countervailing trends, formal citizenship in advanced industrial countries remains a sought after goal by non-citizen migrants, a goal commensurate with that of defending and extending democratic rights and opportunities for a decent life. Advanced capitalist countries in North America, Europe and the Pacific (Australia, New Zealand) have long enjoyed a qualitatively distinct position in relation to the material and political experiences of the world. They 'have been largely spared the traumas of twentieth-century wars on their territories [while waging and encouraging wars elsewhere and have] known relative prosperity and stability for many decades'.[16] To illuminate the disparate experience of citizenship for people in the First versus the Third Worlds, Joseph Carens has compared citizenship in western liberal democracies to 'the modern equivalent of feudal privilege – an inherited status that greatly enhances one's life chances'.[17] However, holding the passport of an advanced country is no guarantee of full and effective enjoyment of citizenship rights, as these states are in fact increasingly polarized by class divisions. Nonetheless, the First World state's ability to deny Third World migrants access to naturalization becomes a legal and internationally sanctioned means of discrimination and withholding many basic human rights, and increasing oppression based on race and gender. Denial of citizenship guarantees also intensifies class exploitation, creating pools of labour cheapened and made vulnerable to abuse by threats of deportation, and by pitting recent immigrants against poor and working class citizens. Poorer migrants from underdeveloped countries, situated on the wrong side of the 'global citizenship divide', are compelled to fight for and negotiate many individual rights routinely provided to legal citizens.

Finally, this chapter explores the question of whether from the vantage point of migrants, nation-state citizenship is being superseded or supplemented by other forms of citizenship as several post-national theorists now suggest. Holston and Appadurai, for example, contend that the nation-state has exhausted its capacity to serve as a successful arbiter of citizenship as either a rights-bearing form of membership or type of participation.[18] Underlying their post-nationalist position is the view that in an era of mass migration, the transnational flow of capital, ideas, goods, images and persons is driving a wedge between national projects and spaces on the one hand, and the 'localization of global forces' and emergence of class differentiated life-worlds in urban centres, on the other.[19] Economic globalization has led to an 'unprecedented growth of economic and social inequalities [such that] the differences between residents have become too gross and the areas of commonality too few to sustain this compact. As a result, the social imaginary of a nation of commensurable citizens disintegrates.'[20]

Yasemin Soysal, in her book *The Limits of Citizenship: Migrants and Postnational Membership in Europe*, provides an influential and more optimistic post-national account. For Soysal, non-citizen residents in several European countries share similar rights with national citizens, thus suggesting that rights and membership have become de-territorialized and are based on universalistic principles of personhood rather than bonds of national affiliation. As we argue in this chapter, and substantiate throughout the study, globalization highlights important dimensions in the transformation of modern citizenship, particularly its foundations in not merely the state, but also a civil society that is becoming more transnational, and in power relations, ethical precepts, and forms of agency that transcend the boundaries of nation-states. The transnational existence of many migrants, evident in their continued citizenship affiliation in their home countries, their globally dispersed households and networks, international labour markets, internationalist politics, and strategic reference to human rights suggests that these global forces have significantly altered the spatial envelope for individuals' rights, entitlements and affiliations. Notwithstanding these significant transnational dimensions to the negotiation of modern citizenship, we contend that there exist formidable obstacles to enshrining and enforcing universal standards in migrant rights and moving to a global, or even regional, regime of transnational rights or de-territorialized citizenship. The five tendencies in modern citizenship sketched earlier will now be more fully elaborated.

Inclusions and exclusions of national citizenship

Citizenship is a form of nation-state membership that combines universalistic and particularistic criteria. These criteria, which appear to be contradictory to one another, actually are complementary and interdependent in the citizenship matrix. The universalism of citizenship stems historically from the idea of national sovereignty that emerged in the French Revolution, meant to eliminate any claims to independent, absolutist rule and loyalty from the nobility, clergy or the estates. European national citizenship thus 'helped liberate the individual from parochial feudal ties and the inertia of the soil'.[21] At the same time, the original 'citizenry', associated with the Greek *polis* was inherently exclusive, associated with males only, and those who were propertied. Within modern capitalist democracies, the contradiction between formal equality and inclusion, and material inequality and exclusion has actually increased. As Ellen Meiksins Wood summarizes:

> The separation of civic status and class position in capitalist societies thus has two sides: on the one hand, the right of citizenship is not determined by socio-economic position – and in this sense, capitalism can coexist with formal democracy – on the other hand, civic equality does not directly affect class inequality, and formal democracy leaves class exploitation fundamentally intact.[22]

This contradictory dynamic is apparent, if buried and only implicit, in the classic framework introduced by T.H. Marshall. Marshall maintained that citizenship brought at least formally equal rights to individuals in an ever-expanding set of spheres (civic, political and social) and opened up access to a growing number of oppressed or marginalized groups (workers, women, racialized minorities). For Marshall, the advent of social rights in the twentieth century signified that equality through the concept of citizenship served to ameliorate inequality deriving from class divisions.[23] In this, Marshall falls prey to the ideological promise of liberalism, and fails to see the inherent inequality of capitalism. Citizenship with its 'urge towards a full measure of equality' is counterposed to the capitalist class system, a system of inequality.[24] For Marshall, however, the equalizing dynamic of citizenship in modern nation-building, is intrinsically linked with a particular, bounded political community. The contradictory element of citizenship reasserts itself, with the particularity of the nation-state imposing the exclusionary boundaries.

> The universalism of the human right to citizenship could only be brought to fruition in the world of 'nation-states', in a framework of a multitude of particularistic states. From the beginning of modern nation-state building, inclusion in one nation-state meant exclusion from another.[25]

Marshall refers obliquely to the national, and thus particularistic, dimension of citizenship when he argues, 'Citizenship requires a bond of a different kind, a direct sense of community membership based on loyalty to a *civilization* which is a common possession'.[26] The 'single civilization' invoked by Marshall may at one level refer to an enhanced and egalitarian quality of life afforded by social welfare and a general reduction in poverty, risk and insecurity in western, developed countries.[27] Yet taken in the context of Britain and its empire, when Marshall was writing, it is difficult to avoid the colonial, Eurocentric and racialized connotations of 'civilization' which dichotomized the world into those peoples who were civilized, and colonized, barbaric 'others' who were deemed unfit for citizenship.

It is this latter definition of civilization, and by extension citizenship, that became institutionalized in Britain in a series of immigration statutes. Beginning in the 1960s, British laws curtailed and circumscribed the conditions of entry and political incorporation for those peoples from Britain's international empire in Asia and the Caribbean who sought the material advantages of 'civilization' by migrating to the 'mother' country. Similarly, every other European empire created its own colonial system of hierarchical citizenship. This meant that the question of who was admitted and permitted rights within the colonial 'motherland' became a 'problem' for the bureaucracies of all colonizing and former colonizing states.[28] Countries such as the United States, Canada, Australia and New Zealand whose constitutional foundations existed in their historical origins as 'white settler societies', adopted similar nation-building ideologies and policies to their colonial sponsors, drawing a link between citizenship and conformity to the standards of a particular western form of 'civilization'.

In practice, this meant that the historically late attainment of citizenship for indigenous peoples, whose numbers had been greatly reduced through outright colonial policies of genocide, was predicated on the loss of their traditional rights, lands and identities as sovereign peoples.[29] Immigration selection policies in settler states were fashioned to reproduce the racialized and ethnocentric tastes and notions of political and cultural suitability imported from the colonizing countries' ruling classes.[30] For instance, Thomas Jefferson argued against encouraging the immigration to the United States of the 'servile masses of Europe' on the grounds that they would transform the 'homogeneous' and 'peaceable' American people into a 'heterogeneous, incoherent, distracted mass' unfit for republican self-government.[31] Where even less acceptable groups, such as the so-called 'non-preferred races' from other continents, were sought by business interests for the superexploitation of their labouring and servant potential, state authorities attached conditions of entry that prevented these unwanted 'aliens' from attaining formal citizenship and substantive rights. Moreover, the United States was founded on the acceptance of African American slavery and genocidal policies against indigenous Native Americans. From its inception, the creation of purportedly 'universal' citizenship in modern European and settler nation-states, premised on Marshall's communal membership in a 'single civilization', required that particular identities of nationality, religion, race and ethnicity be recognized, while others be subordinated or excluded. The racialized basis for inclusion within citizenship is obvious in some countries, such as Germany, which until 2000 explicitly based its membership rules on blood ties or *jus sanguinis*.[32] However, it is also integral to the nation-building objectives of immigration policies within immigrant receiving countries such as Canada, the United States and Australia whose citizenship laws favour birthright or *jus soli*.

Globalization and neo-liberal citizenship

Many writers continue to define the essence of social citizenship in terms of its 'universality' and autonomy from market criteria for eligibility.[33] T.H. Marshall's assumption, however, outlined in his 1949 lecture 'Citizenship and Social Class', that modern and especially social citizenship undermines the inequality of capitalist social relations, has increasingly come under scrutiny. Several theorists have criticized Marshall's evolutionary perspective on the emergence and irreversibility of citizenship and social rights as part of some broad and immanent societal development.[34] There is widespread support for the view that the specific conditions brought about by economic globalization and informed by neo-liberalism have amounted to a major transformation in the 'regime' of citizenship in countries with developed social welfare states.[35] Ordinary citizens in developed countries are increasingly and painfully made aware of the uniqueness of the post-1945 historical juncture that brought about the structures associated with the Keynesian welfare state. In spite of wide variations in ideologies and forms of state intervention across advanced capitalist countries, and the militaristic conditions of the Cold War, the governments of advanced capitalist states provided at least rhetorical support for high, stable employment and income policies, and dedicated public revenues to the expansion of social services. Fiscal and monetary policies were forged according to the Bretton Woods system, including the hegemony of US foreign policy and the extension of global institutions such as the World Bank and the International Monetary Fund. Though these institutions operated at the expense of the people of the South, and of many groups within advanced industrial states who in race/ethnic and gender terms departed from the ideal model of the citizen, nonetheless, the postwar expansion of the economy was accompanied by discourses articulating notions of state support for inclusive citizenship.

This political environment provided fertile ground for the growth of movements of the poor, women, indigenous peoples, immigrants, racial and ethnic minorities, environmentalists, and gays and lesbians seeking integration into a broader and more inclusive framework of citizenship on the grounds of the right to equality of treatment. Notwithstanding the greater interest of some of these movements in fostering change within civil society rather than the public state sphere, one feature they shared was a political culture supportive of the use of state authority for promoting social and re-distributive justice.[36] The marginalization of specific oppressed groups at a time of strong popular support for universal inclusion, provided a space for the demands by social movements for increased citizenship rights. For example, even though the expansion of the welfare state in western countries was often premised on assumptions that the heterosexual, male-dominated nuclear family was the only legitimate form of family household, it nonetheless permitted many women and non-traditional families to claim state support for issues that had previously been deemed private and beyond the purview of state intervention.[37]

In contrast, by the late 1970s a rather different ideology was gaining ascendance. This emerged first among western states such as Britain under Margaret Thatcher and the United States under Ronald Reagan. This new hegemony was an incendiary mix of economic hyper-liberalism, dedicated to the enthronement of free market solutions, reduced social spending, and social neo-conservatism, with its emphasis on moral regulation and punitive, disciplinary policies. What was striking was not only the election of ideologically committed New Right governments, but also the adoption by nominally left and centrist liberal governments with broadly similar neo-liberal rationales for introducing policies advocated by the New Right.[38] What was not new, however, was the association of this agenda with hierarchical citizenship of modern capitalist states. Earlier examples of citizenship had also been compatible with the denial of rights to women, the enslavement of captured African agriculturalists, child labour and colonial conquest. What the New Right governments revealed was precisely how temporary and exceptional had been the claim to universal equality as a defining feature of modern citizenship. Political rights may remain; formerly excluded groups (women, indigenous peoples, minorities) may gain in formal political inclusion. Yet under neo-liberal citizenship, the scope of political rights and parliamentary democracy becomes restricted as 'market regulation takes over from direct regulation by state agencies and the judgement of the market is brought to bear on the conduct of states'.[39]

Two major imperatives informed the ascension of neo-liberalism. The first was the claim that government indebtedness was out of control, and that powerful international markets had forced governments 'to adopt austerity programmes whose only rationales appear to be deficit cutting and competitiveness'.[40] The second imperative was the need to offer incentives to attract global investment. The ideologically committed New Right governments argued for the reorganization of the state and its relationship to civil society to meet the demands established under the twin discourses of deficit reduction and global competition. This project entailed scaling back the post Second World War welfare states through major cuts to spending on public education, health care, housing and welfare. Their agenda also targeted programmes geared to specific constituencies, including affirmative action and pay equity policies, and programmes and facilities for the elderly, people with physical and mental disabilities, single mothers, battered women and so on. The New Right programme reflected a shift away from a more inclusive and pluralistic conception of citizenship in liberal democracies – one that recognized it as legitimate to compensate for the different life experiences and burdens of discrimination based on race, gender, immigrant status, age and disability – to a purely market-based conception.

Under the neo-liberal agenda, the marketplace rather than the nation became the ideal community of allegiance, and the citizen was to be entrepreneurial, as the 'citizen-as-customer'. Rights and access to previously public goods were now to be predicated on an unequal command of property and ability to pay.[41] The economic inequality of capitalism, never absent but better hidden behind an ideologically constructed notion of universally inclusive citizenship during the postwar years, now returned to reassert its command without apology. Neo-liberal citizenship is less a relationship between a collective membership with the nation-state that promises – even if for many it failed to deliver – access to a range of social, political and civil rights, and more a way of life defined by individuals' competitive initiative and capacity to succeed in the global economy. By prioritizing the pursuit of international trade and profitable investment above all else, governments have succumbed to an insatiable demand for cuts in corporate and wealthy individuals' taxes, privatization, social service cutbacks, means-testing, the introduction of user pay fees, wage rollbacks and downsizing in state bureaucracies. These forms of negative governance combine with what the United Nations Development Programme has identified as undesirable types of growth – 'jobless growth, ruthless growth which benefits only the rich, anti-democratic voiceless growth and unsustainable futureless growth' – to exacerbate divisions between the rich and the rest, including the growing ranks of the poor.[42]

The embrace by states of the objectives associated with corporate globalization has elevated the citizenship rights of global economic actors such as transnational corporations and global financial markets. This has been accompanied by the expanded power of multinational companies and supra-national and regional organizations and arenas (such as the World Trade Organization, the International Monetary Fund, the North American Free Trade Agreement and the Free Trade Area of the Americas) that bypass principles of democratic accountability in parliaments and national legal systems of states, or find states bending to co-operate with the terms they have set.[43] Ordinary citizens are asked to behave as shareholders and assess the government's performance in terms of its credit rating and the paradoxically denationalized national economy's 'competitive advantage', rather than in terms of social measures of collective well-being.[44]

These trends, associated with neo-liberalism and corporate globalization, have sparked heated debate about the meaning and nature of modern citizenship. The picture painted thus far, of developed capitalist countries in a neo-liberal hypnosis needs to be qualified. Neo-liberal measures such as the dismemberment of the welfare state and undermining of trade unions have encountered growing resistance. In contrast to the dominant eighteenth-century inspired theories of democracy in the United States and Great Britain, European advanced welfare states, strong unions and social movements are assumed to be an integral part of the social contract on which modern democratic states exist.[45] Within these countries, social movements, social democratic and environmentalist parties and institutions oppose unrestrained global capitalist development.[46] Nonetheless, it is notable that the leaderships of western social democratic parties in France, Germany, Britain, Spain, Canada, Australia and even Sweden have moved sharply to the right. All have accepted the unfettering of the market, through measures such as the elimination of non-tariff barriers to trade and privatization, as conditions for their participation in the global economy.

The current directions in state intervention have also fundamentally altered the ideal type subjectivity expected of citizens in liberal democratic states. Citizens are urged by their governments to become more self-disciplined, multiskilled, entrepreneurial and resilient, in riding the roller coaster vagaries of business cycles, technological changes, and restructuring of the labour market and public institutions such as hospitals and schools. What is striking about the rhetorical justification for the restructuring of national and local economies is the harnessing of the two 'contradictory attitudes of fatalism and voluntarism'.[47] Citizens are told that they must adjust to the challenges of global competition; at the same time, they are informed of the opportunities available once governments, institutions and citizens cooperate to meet these challenges. In order to live up to these challenges, everyone – regardless of their occupation, education or actual social condition – is urged to embrace values of competitive individualism and infinite flexibility.

The transformation of citizenship to fit the neo-liberal agenda has also involved what Janine Brodie identifies as a fundamental shift in the dominant philosophy of public management to embrace the ideals of privatization, individualization and familialization.[48] Government is equated with inefficiency, while private business and non-state sectors are assumed to provide services in a more cost efficient and/or humanistic manner, and to offer a greater array of choices to citizen-consumers.[49]

The public/private divide and the care gap

Feminists and other critical scholars have drawn attention to the gendered character and exclusions of citizenship, which are now widely recognized and well documented.[50] Women were not mere latecomers to citizenship, as suggested by Marshall's evolutionary scheme. Rather, women's exclusion and subordination were predicated on a specific sexual division of labour that accompanied industrialization in western capitalist societies associated with the public/private divide – the division between public and private life, activities and responsibilities. The social contract permitting men to participate and dominate within public life and the paid labour force depended upon a 'sexual contract' whereby financially dependent women were expected to provide unpaid domestic, sexual and reproductive labour in the private family household.[51] While liberal citizenship is rooted in the separation between the public and the private, whereby state power is circumscribed and does not stray into areas of private and individual areas of decision making, feminist and some Marxist analyses have tended to critique this divide as rendering women's oppression invisible and legitimate. This is because 'the private realm is exempt from liberal principles and political accountability, but also because activity and work in the private realm are not valued' and are regarded as insignificant to citizenship.[52]

The public/private divide has been identified to display gendered consequences for women's citizenship in the ideological and material demarcations drawn between the family and state, market and state, market and family, and state and community.[53] The development of the postwar welfare state, and the accompanying social movements, were critical to the emergence of more meaningful citizenship rights for women in that at least some of its provisions provided a realignment of the public/private divide that was fairer to women.[54] Public policies extending support for maternity and parental leave, childcare, and aid to victims of domestic violence have allowed some groups of women to strive for citizenship on terms more equitable with men through their partial release from the demands of the private realm.

Not all women, however, have been positioned similarly with respect to the public/private divide historically or in the present day. Their location within and across these spheres, and respective access to citizenship entitlements, has been circumscribed by interwoven dynamics of class, colonialism, race, ethnicity, sexuality and/or disability.[55] Thus, racialized, immigrant and working-class women in North America and Europe have historically had higher labour force participation rates than white upper- and middle-class women. As a result, these groups of women have prioritized as a source of oppression racialized/ethnic and class subjugation over gender dynamics in the private family household. Many of these women worked during the late nineteenth and early twentieth centuries as domestic servants in middle- and upper-class homes, their location in their employer's private family household subjecting them to disadvantageous contractual obligations, and sexist and heterosexist familial forms of regulation.[56] Regarded as dependents of male property owners rather than as autonomous subjects, domestic servants not surprisingly belatedly received enfranchisement as citizens.[57]

Like their nineteenth-century counterparts, contemporary international migrant domestic workers face a near universal exile from many basic citizenship rights in their employing states. Similar to previous women's rights campaigns, their battles to achieve access to citizenship involve struggles to renegotiate the meanings and positioning of the public/private divide. Also, in the tradition of the anti-racist civil rights movement in the United States in particular, which developed from the late 1950s through to the early 1970s, the modern movements incorporate the ideology of equal rights, and build on this to challenge exclusionary practices. However, in contrast to most earlier women's rights movements for enfranchisement in Europe and North America, the dissident citizenship struggles of migrant women explicitly raise issues of race and class. They also reveal how the interests of better-resourced female citizens have become pitted against those of their subordinated non-citizen employees in accessing cheap and flexible migrant household labour. In the process, the public/private divide is revealed to be a shifting and contested political construction. It is shaped by global capitalism and interwoven dynamics of race/ethnicity, class, and neo-colonialism, as well as gender.

In First and Third World countries, the neo-liberal realignment of the public/private divide has led to the increasing transfer of demands on time, labour and responsibility to the private sphere. This has intensified the pre-existing sexual division of labour, where private reproductive and domestic care is borne disproportionately by women. As research conducted from the 1970s to the 1990s has demonstrated, despite women's advances in formal education and the labour force, the sexual division of labour in the home has remained remarkably unchanged. Even where male contributions to housework and childcare have increased, domestic work and caregiving remain primarily 'women's work'.[58] The embrace of notions of individual and family responsibility thus mystifies the gendered consequences of neo-liberal citizenship, whereby the 'obligations' of female citizens are socially expanded. In care areas where the state has withdrawn, women become the unacknowledged shock absorbers, whereas in care areas that were never or inadequately covered by the state, there is continued reliance on women's unpaid labour.[59]

A caring gap thus emerges as the labour force participation of married women with children has increased and the number of people requiring such care, for example elderly or disabled adults, has grown. Increasing the quality of life of needy citizens through new medical technologies and de-institutionalization, having expanded in the postwar years, has now been abandoned as a state project. With the decline in public services, dependent adults are now considered a 'burden', placed on private families.[60] Given the increased demands on female citizens who must juggle paid employment with domestic responsibilities, some are turning to poorer and more vulnerable populations to help them carry out their obligations in the private sphere while continuing to participate in the public sphere.[61] Some female citizens are thus able to attain greater equality with men as citizen-workers because they are accompanied by the 'ghostly, often racialized figure of the domestic worker/nanny/caregiver', who is positioned on the other side of the globalized citizenship divide.[62]

But the introduction of waged workers in private family households in turn transforms the character of these households into a hybrid public/private space – less private yet without some of the benefits of public regulation, such as clear and consistent employment standards for the migrant household workers. As Hurtado, who examines the many incursions of repressive state regulation in the intimate aspects of the lives of women of colour suggests,

> Women of Color have not had the benefit of the economic conditions that underlie the public/private distinction ... There is no such thing as a private sphere for people of Color except that which they manage to create and protect in an otherwise hostile environment.[63]

The ability to afford the privatization of formerly public services – in health care and elder care – is thus affected by people's citizenship status, which is in turn tied to their positions in global and local hierarchies of class, gender and race. Alongside the shift in the ideological and institutional divide between the public and private spheres, the rise in neoliberal citizenship has brought about a growing deficit in citizenship entitlements for those most in need of these rights, among whom are non-citizen poor migrants from the Third World.

The north/south citizenship divide

It is no coincidence that expressions of support for heightened border control among advanced states are proliferating at a time when the pressures to migrate from developing to developed countries are augmenting. One form of inequality that has clearly grown is that dividing states located in the economic North from those located in the economic

South. The evidence for the growing gap in wealth between richest and poorest countries is incontrovertible. In its 1996 *Human Development Report*, for instance, the United Nations Development Programme 'estimated that, between 1960 and 1991, the share of global income of the richest 20 per cent of the world's people rose from 70 to 85 per cent while that of the poorest declined from 2.3 to 1.4 per cent'.[64]

Another aggregate measure of the growing gap between rich and poor nations is net flow of capital. Whereas in 1979, a net US$40 billion flowed from the Northern hemisphere to the developing nations of the South, by the late 1980s, the flow had reversed. In 1988, UNICEF reported that:

> [t]aking everything into account – loans, aid, repayment of interest and capital – the southern world is now transferring at least $20 billion a year to the northern hemisphere. And if we were also to take into account the effective transfer of resources implied in the reduced prices paid by the industrialised nations for the developing world's raw materials, then the annual flow from the poor to the rich might be as much as $60 billion each year.[65]

Advanced capitalist economies where wages are considerably higher[66] and welfare states more established, offer a potential pool of rights attached to citizenship significantly greater than those available to the vast majority who live in Third World nations. Concurrent with and hastened by internal threats to First World social citizenship through dismantling of the protective shield of the welfare state, have been efforts to shore up access to citizenship rights from demands by poorer developing state migrants to a share in the wealth and opportunities of developed states.

The economic, political and environmental pressures to migrate from Southern states have been steadily increasing. The compulsion to migrate overseas is anchored in legacies of colonialism, imperialism, landlessness, poverty and unemployment. These forces have been exacerbated by more recent forces of globalization and liberalization and by structural adjustment policies implemented by national political and landed elites working together with the World Bank and International Monetary Fund (IMF) in the wake of debt crisis. Despite the variety of reasons given by individuals for working overseas, the overriding structural reasons for emigration, even among professionals, are poverty and underemployment.[67] Many heavily indebted governments of developing countries have aggressively promoted and organized labour export, making their migrant workers an icon to their export-oriented development.[68] Indeed, remittances from their nationals working abroad have come to represent central pillars of many economies, and central sources of household income.[69] The financial significance of migrant worker earnings for the states and populations of developing countries is enormous when one considers that migrant remittances, estimated to exceed US$100 billion a year, is the second leading source of foreign exchange in the world, surpassed only by petroleum.[70]

In the economies of the South, the IMF-prescribed structural adjustment programmes create intense poverty for the poorest sections of society, women and men alike. However, women and men have dissimilar relationships to family maintenance and waged employment, implying gendered responses to the extreme conditions imposed. The material basis for the legitimacy of regimes imposing wage rollbacks and drastic cutbacks in services depends on the skills, intensified work and sacrifices of women to stretch dwindling resources in their households, and on the decision of many to work overseas in order to send home foreign remittances. As Cynthia Enloe maintains,

> the politics of international debt is not simply something that has an *impact* on women in indebted countries. ... When a woman from Mexico, Jamaica of the Philippines decides to emigrate in order to make money as a domestic servant, she is designing her own international debt politics.[71]

Economic dislocations associated with neo-liberal policies, exacerbating previous patterns of underdevelopment as a result of centuries of colonialism and neo-colonialism, are the underlying forces for much of the recent migration from Third World to advanced economies. The economic basis for these population flows often exists even for those categorized as refugees. Civil wars, the splintering and creation of new states, and other political upheavals are commonly cited as the causes for refugee flows. However, as Henk Overbeek observes,

> Political violence is often triggered by worsening economic conditions, and economic hardship often results from the exercise of repressive political power, thus relegating the distinction between the political and economic migrant, or between the forced and the voluntary migrant to the realm of ideology and manipulation.[72]

In navigating the inequities between the First and Third worlds, poorer Third World migrants entering more affluent countries encounter citizenship as a mechanism for reproducing inequality between those deemed to be legitimate and deserving candidates, and illegitimate 'others'. Poverty is the first marker of non-citizenship status; but these migrants are constructed as possessing other symbolic deficits insofar as they are likely to be racialized, or perceived to be racially inferior to the dominant racial population. The increasing 'feminization' of migration, the growing proportion of women relative to men, also indicates disadvantages based on gender oppression, as women are accepted, legally or as undocumented workers, in the most undesirable employment sectors, including prostitution and domestic labour.

Efforts to obtain First World citizenship are not a zero sum game, where the non-citizen enters without citizenship rights in search of obtaining them. Indeed, countries which export labour use their homeland 'citizenship to discipline migrants as cheap and flexible labour'.[73] While residence in affluent states, even of relatively long duration, fails to guarantee many social, political and civil rights widely enjoyed by citizens, contemporary migrants may be frustrated in their efforts to benefit from the citizenship rights attached to their state of origin while they are abroad, such as protection against employer abuse. In addition, they are frequently subjected to obligations to the state where they hold formal citizenship, such as the payment of exorbitant fees to their home state migration bureaucracies and mandatory remittances.[74]

Advanced capitalist states have not been opposed to immigration per se, even that originating in developing countries, but to autonomously organized migration that bypasses the highly selective immigration apparatuses and policies of these states.[75] Wealthier states have responded to the perceived threat of autonomous migration from poorer countries by becoming more aggressive in policing migrants' and asylum seekers' access to their territories. If and when migrants gain entrance, civil, political and social rights are highly regulated and unequally apportioned.

New regional and international bodies and agreements have formed to co-ordinate policies on global migration, raising questions about the relinquishing of control over national immigration and refugee policies to supra-state bodies, or to the hegemonic states within these fora. However, the new loci for interstate co-operation, and the dramatic expansion in information gathering and sharing have arguably increased the surveillance and border regulatory powers of the individual nation-state vis à vis border crossers.[76] In contrast to earlier postwar agendas of attracting migrant and immigrant labour for industrial growth, multilateral state discussions now take as their priority the curbing of unwanted migration – as illegals, asylum seekers, designated 'criminals' or 'terrorists', and so on – while selectively promoting the circulation of desired human capital.[77] The harmonization by the most prosperous countries of immigration, refugee and naturalization laws in more restrictive directions, is 'a form of "global apartheid" designed to protect these countries' from opening their doors in the face of mounting pressures to migrate from less affluent societies in Africa, Asia, Latin America and poorer countries of Europe.[78] Moisi, for instance, describes the emerging situation in Europe as an effort to present 'a white, wealthy and Christian "Fortress Europe" pitted against a largely poor, Islamic world'.[79] Similarly, policy proposals for a 'North American security perimeter' that would aid in the creation of a 'Fortress North America' harmonizing restrictive and security conscious Canadian and US immigration and refugee policies, received widespread purchase following the September 11, 2001 attacks in New York and Washington.[80]

Racialized policing of state borders

The tendency to construct national identities in more racially and ethnically homogeneous terms deepens in an era of global restructuring, ideological attacks on inclusive citizenship, and neo-liberal erosion in citizenship benefits. The trend towards more restrictive immigration and refugee policies in the North has also been linked to an ideological construction of 'a growing nostalgia for a simpler world in which people felt secure in homogeneous communities where neighbours shared "traditional" values'[81] and to the insecurity felt by many victims of global economic restructuring.[82]

Virtually all industrialized countries have recently witnessed a rise in movements, parties and public currents that reflect inward-looking protectionist, xenophobic and even neo-fascist sentiments.[83] The aftermath of the September 11, 2001 attacks on the World Trade Center and the Pentagon saw the rush to adopt antiterrorist legislation greatly expanding the surveillance and detention powers of law enforcement, the implementation of 'racial profiling' in border practices, and a dramatic increase in violence directed against Arabs, Muslims and people of colour in the United States, Canada and Europe. Fear and anxiety of possible future terrorist attacks among the US and Canadian public following September 11 led to a period of somewhat greater support for more stringent border control, electronic surveillance and security practices, to the detriment of civil liberties and multiracial justice.[84] However, there has also been a growing tide of resistance to the blatant racial profiling and criminalization of dissent. The setting of the direction of policies governing rights of entry into liberal democratic states occurs within a contested arena that involves a wide array of pro- and anti-migrant/refugee movements. There are internal divisions within states – between legislative, administrative and judicial branches, and/or between various political parties – in their orientation towards migrant/refugee rights.[85] While migration and refugee policies are a contested terrain, there is a secular trend towards more restrictive and selective immigration, refugee and border crossing[86] laws and policies within advanced states. Objectives of these policies invariably defined in terms of 'national interests' privilege first and foremost, the interests of regionally and globally oriented businesses, and minimally the interests of migrants or nongovernmental organizations concerned with migrant and human rights.[87] Security and control issues, while always a part of border (immigration and deportation) policies of migrant receiving nations, have received increased prominence in order to regulate and exclude autonomous migration. Efforts to control autonomous and undocumented migration have 'spilled over' to negatively affect the rights and experiences of immigrants and established minority communities with permanent resident status.

A few examples in North America and western Europe are instructive and are supported by recent anthologies and case studies documenting trends across Europe, North America and Japan.[88] The United States has led in efforts to regulate and stem undocumented migration primarily from Mexico and other Latin American countries. The enactment by the US Congress in 1986 of the Immigration Reform and Control Act (IRCA) followed a three-pronged approach designed to: legalize and provide amnesty to undocumented immigrants; discourage undocumented labour through employer sanctions; and increase the number of border enforcement agents.[89] Initially, between 1986 and 1989, border apprehension statistics seemed to suggest the effectiveness of employer compliance and the IRCA's deterrent effect. By 1990, however, the Immigration and Naturalization Service (INS) 'was apprehending as many illegal Latino entrants as it had in pre-IRCA days'.[90]

In the 1990s, US immigration authorities increased their efforts to deter illegal migration by imposing physical barriers at the US–Mexico border, including barbed wire, steel fences and a human wall of border patrol agents. The militarization of the border with Mexico and systematic denial of the most basic rights for undocumented migrants raised the alarm that through these acts the United States was violating human rights.[91] Immigration advocates decried the symbolic and legal significance of the 1986 IRCA which created a special category of US residents with significantly fewer rights than the population as a whole, unable legally to work or receive social benefits, and subject to apprehension, incarceration and deportation at any time.[92]

The US federal and some southern states attempted to control undocumented immigration by reducing access to social services. The Republican government of Pete Wilson in California led the way with Proposition 187, which if implemented, would have led to the denial of education, health care and other public benefits to undocumented immigrants and their children. In a state that receives an estimated 43 per cent of all undocumented migrants to the United States, the bill was approved by 60 per cent of the state's voters. Although most of the provisions of Proposition 187 were subsequently struck down by the federal court, it did succeed in stimulating political campaigns in other states such as Florida and Texas, and in the US Congress, to strip undocumented immigrants of their constitutional rights and access to basic social services. By 1994, there were no less than 150 pieces of immigration control legislation pending in Congress or the Senate.[93] During the Cold War era, immigration and refugee policies were subordinated to foreign 'national security' concerns, usually couched in an ideology of anti-communism. At least prior to September 11, discourses on immigration policy reflected in these bills encapsulated 'soft security' issues, constructing threats to the 'American culture' and serving as a scapegoat for everything from economic insecurity to environmental degradation and population growth.[94] Since September 11, border security has been redefined to focus on the real and imagined threat to human life, property and the safety of all Americans in the United States and abroad posed by global 'terrorists' and 'terrorism', especially originating in Arab countries.

The anti-immigrant US congressional bills have also moved significantly beyond policies designed to exclude undocumented migrants to campaigns and legislation to curtail services to legalized permanent resident immigrants. Calls for lower immigration quotas, and the elimination of family reunification principles have followed. These policies include proposals to deny public school education to children of undocumented parents, even though such proposals would be in open violation of past US Supreme Court rulings, and the repeal of the Fourteenth Amendment of the US Constitution in order to deny (*jus soli*) citizenship to children born in the United States of undocumented parents.[95] In spite of a vigorous activist community working in defence of migrant and refugee rights, the US national debate on 'immigration reform' in the wake of Proposition 187 has been cast primarily within a restrictionist framework. The legislative drive has been to seek ways to make immigration legislation more exclusionary, while allowing for exceptions such as the highly skilled labour needed by corporations in the information technology sector.

The human rights of refugees seeking asylum in the United States have also been jeopardized. For example, the Coast Guard has been used to interdict Haitian and Chinese refugees to prevent them from gaining access to the refugee admission process. The 1996 Antiterrorism Bill introduced new provisions drastically curtailing asylum rights for those arriving without documentation.[96] The more recent spate of antiterrorism legislation in the United States and many other countries including Canada and Britain that followed September 11, permits prolonged indefinite detention of terrorist suspects without charge. The broad and vague definition of 'terrorism' has been used to severely undermine the right to seek asylum in these countries. Some refugee legal experts have viewed these efforts to opt out of or 'relativise' international conventions of refugee protection as evidence of the minimal encroachments on territorial sovereignty of international refugee laws.[97] More generally, Human Rights Watch has identified a regression in commitment to protect refugees over the last 50 years among the industrialized states in Europe, North America and Australia that had first established the international refugee protection system.[98]

Increased policing of undocumented migrants and asylum seekers by US immigration authorities has also had a 'spread effect' in augmenting discrimination and hostility against Latino, Asian, and especially since September 11, Arab and Muslim and other communities of colour. Random identity checks and government sanctioned raids in Latino and Asian neighbourhoods, homes and workplaces, for instance, result in the violation of the civil rights of permanent residents and US citizens.[99] Reports of racial violence and discrimination against Latinos greatly increased in the year following the passage of Proposition 187 in California.[100] Human Rights Watch US, drawing on research in six large American cities, reported in November 2001 that since September 11, there had been a 1700 per cent increase in hate crimes against Arabs, Muslims and those perceived to be Arab or Muslim.[101]

In Canada, a tradition of supporting high immigration levels has been maintained by arguments about the economic, demographic and humanitarian benefits provided by immigration. Nonetheless, with some notable exceptions, virtually all reforms in immigration and refugee policies enacted in the 1990s and into the new millennium have been in more restrictive directions.[102] These have included measures to reduce the proportion of immigrants being accepted on grounds of family unification, an increase in the proportion of migrants entering Canada with temporary visas, and restrictions on sponsorship of overseas relatives for low income families. In a policy widely criticized for 'selling passports to the rich', legislative changes have increased the minimum required investment for business migrants. Changes in refugee policy, such as the unprecedented setting of refugee quotas in 1997, and the introduction of additional bars to access the refugee determination system in 2001 under the IRPA, reflect this approach.[103] Reductions in access to Canada for Third World poor women via the foreign domestic worker programme are also a feature of this increasingly restrictive immigration policy, thus encouraging a mushrooming in the numbers of undocumented live-in caregivers.[104] Restrictive policy reforms by the Canadian immigration authorities have been accompanied by official discourses which link immigrants and refugees to crime, welfare fraud and threats to national security.[105]

In the Canadian context, the attainment of legal–juridical citizenship status is, far from becoming less significant, becoming more salient as a portal to access and exercise many civil, political, social, economic and reproductive rights. Thus, the newest Canadian immigration legislation, the IRPA, inaugurated the term 'foreign nationals'. In this legislation, permanent residents are included under this rubric, thus breaking with Canadian immigration policy tradition by placing the latter on a par with those who enjoy no legal status at all in Canada.[106] As the Canadian Council of Refugees has argued, this neologism emphasizes the foreignness of permanent residents. Its significance, however, extends well beyond terminological shifts. The IRPA introduces new measures that strip permanent residents of several of the rights they previously enjoyed and thus erects a further boundary between permanent residents and formal citizens.[107] The events of September 11 also spurred the Liberal government to quickly introduce one of the provisions of the new legislation, the 'Maple Leaf Card', a state-of-the-art security 'fraud resistant' national identity card, stating details of permanent residents' appearance and residence status information. The new identity card, initially rationalized as a means of providing easier recognition for transportation companies and the rights of permanent residents, became folded into the Canadian governments' broader antiterrorism plan.[108]

Several countries in Europe have followed a similar pattern to the United States and Canada in rolling back the rights of non-citizens and resident foreigners. In France, a relatively more liberal attitude towards immigrants prevailed under the social democratic Mitterand government in the early 1980s, which saw an amnesty for illegal migrants, expansion of rights of association for foreigners and suppression of police powers such as arbitrary identity checks. Since the early 1990s, reversals have happened in many of these gains for migrants.[109] Proposals made in

1992–93 to significantly reform and limit the civil rights of immigrants and asylum seekers and withdraw social benefits from undocumented immigrants echoed earlier Proposition 187 debates in the United States. And similar to the history of such policies in other liberal republics, these restrictive measures were confronted with obstacles in French constitutional law.[110] A 1997 draft immigration law, tabled by French interior minister Jean-Louis Debré, sought to introduce many of the same measures rejected in 1993 to clamp down on illegal migration. A section of this bill, which would have required French citizens to 'inform' on foreign nationals, was dropped when the government was confronted by protests, which saw the bill as evoking the spirit of Vichy, when Catholic French were compelled to report when they lodged Jews.

Nonetheless, the hard line immigration bill received the support of 60 per cent of the French population. In national polls, in 1997 roughly 30 per cent of the French declared support for the National Front whose leadership promises to 'ethnically cleanse France' and deport foreigners.[111] In the first round of France's presidential elections in Spring 2002, the leading contender to the Gaullist incumbent, Jacques Chirac was Jean-Marie Le Pen, leader of the National Front, who received 17.2 per cent of all votes cast.[112] Both deteriorating economic conditions and cultivated concerns for 'cultural protection' figure in the hostility to migrants. Such animosity has especially targeted Muslim Algerians, and other Muslim Africans, who form almost half of France's legally resident foreign population. As Hollifield argues, until recently dissonance between the universalistic (human and civil rights) and particularist (religious, racial, linguistic, nationalist) aspects of French republicanism have been resolved in favour of the most expansive naturalization policies in western Europe.[113] The recent restrictionist immigration proposals and the worrying rise in electoral support for the National Front, however, suggest the continued instability in France's immigration and citizenship policies.[114]

Germany is an important test case for those who argue for the disappearance of distinctions between citizens and foreigners and 'the international standardisation of rights and status of non-citizens'.[115] With a large population of guest workers and their descendants from countries such as Turkey and the former Yugoslavia, and their acquisition of many significant social and civil rights, the German experience of incorporation of migrants without granting formal citizenship status would appear to bear out the 'post-national' basis of contemporary European rights. Moreover, the more inclusive citizenship law enacted in 2000, which replaced the framework for the ascription of citizenship dating back to the imperial period in Germany in 1913, has undermined the notion of citizenship defined in terms of 'German blood' and brought Germany's citizenship laws more in step with other European countries. As Lemke suggests, '[d]emographic trends and the need for qualified workers in the IT-sector were important aspects in the pro-immigration approach of the SPD/Green coalition' which made citizenship policy a priority area of reform upon their election in 1998.[116] Yet certain features of German naturalization and immigration policies clash with the post-national model. First, the process of naturalization is lengthy – a minimum of eight years – and is laden with other conditions such as residency entitlements for which only a fraction of non-German residents apply. For Lemke, 'the fact that dual citizenship remains formally excluded raises probably the strongest doubts over the capability of the new provisions to effectively depart from the ethno-cultural notion of citizenship'.[117] Non-citizens continue to be excluded from basic political rights such as voting. They are also subject to the responsibilities imposed by other states in which they have formal citizenship, such as military service for Turkish youth permanently residing in Germany, further suggesting the continuity of exclusion from full citizenship.[118] Second, the German government has enacted immigration policies for the new guest workers designed not to repeat the 'mistakes' of the earlier programmes by building in 'rotation' mechanisms, which actively discourage settlement of the new guest workers and their families. To deal with re-emergence of labour shortages in lower wage sectors, since 1989 'Germany has developed seasonal worker, work-and-learn, firm-to-firm subcontracting, and frontier work programmes'.[119] The complaints by labour migrants of abuses in these programmes indicate that 'migrant workers today have far fewer rights than did the guest workers of the 1960s'.[120]

In order to cope with the tremendous upsurge in asylum applications during the 1980s, encouraged by a liberal asylum policy, Germany introduced new provisions in 1993, which would permit German officials to turn back asylum applicants who arrived through 'safe third' countries.[121] Thus, Germany is in step with other countries such as the United States and Canada, which have adopted policies that increase the bars to access for refugees. These policies are designed to meet the letter of universal conventions on human rights and refugees but their intended effect has been to cut the numbers of asylum seekers granted access to refugee determination systems and permanent residence. The narrowing of rights for refugees, and the increased risk of refugees being sent back to face persecution and torture in the refugee reforms of states in the economic North dramatically contradicts the post-national conception of citizenship where universal rights of personhood are said to preempt nation-state rules of membership.

The question of the development of non-citizen rights in European countries is intimately tied with the ongoing efforts to define European or 'Union' citizenship and the European policy on migration. The development of a new, unmediated relationship between individual Europeans and a transnational body, holding out the promise of enforceable rights and duties, appears to 'exemplify and prefigure the detachment of citizenship from state territorial bodies'.[122] The European Union (EU) presents a unique case of regional and supranational citizenship that does not find a parallel in the North American context, for example under the North American Free Trade Agreement.[123] The move to formulate a common European citizenship, allowing only nationals of EU member states rights to move and reside freely within the territory of the European Economic Community, however, would seem to have rigidified rather than eliminated citizenship hierarchies.

The seeming instance of 'post-national' membership offered by European citizenship actually discriminates against the 10–13 million 'third country nationals', nationals of non-EU states who have acquired legal permanent resident status in an EU country. Far from exemplifying independent, de-territorialized criteria for membership, which rest on international human rights principles, European citizenship reinforces the equivalence between citizenship and state formulated and racialized concepts of nationality.[124] Jacqueline Bhabha contrasts the generous and swift family reunion provisions for EU nationals, with the 'Kafkaesque' restrictions facing non-Europeans seeking entry of their family members.[125] Thus, rather than citizenship rights and membership having become uncoupled from nationality and nation-states, or linked only to mere residence, formal nation-state citizenship continues to differentiate European citizens from non-European residents, thus contributing to an increasingly racialized definition of European citizenship identity.[126]

Conclusion: national citizenship and transnational communities

As Bridget Anderson has pointed out, current citizenship debates 'have rather taken for granted the right to citizenship in the formalized sense of what passport a person holds and an individual's right to be present and work in a particular nation state'.[127]Moreover, the history of national rights has never been universal in experience, despite claims to universality.[128] Citizenship debates that presume nation-state boundaries are limited in their consideration of the types of citizenship entitlements that are the focus of struggle and negotiation in an interdependent global economy, based on imperialist and neo-colonial relations between states. The classical tripartite scheme of civil, political and social rights suggested by T.H. Marshall[129] fails to capture *mobility rights*, or a set of rights to cross nation-state boundaries and access other fundamental rights in different states that are especially significant for migrants. Mobility rights, unlike the other conventionally named categories of rights, are cross-national; they serve to de-link other types of rights (social rights, voting rights, etc.) from specific territories and nation-states.

By disconnecting the provision of rights from the requirement of formal membership in the state, 'post-national' citizenship 'presents itself as a just and humane response to the problem of global migration and the internationalisation of the labour market'.[130] Post-national, global or transnational citizenship models contest the injustices and inequalities of a conception of citizenship that 'inflexibly persists in grounding membership in principles of nationality [that] leave many disadvantaged by denying them the most basic access to community and rights'.[131] The ideas of post-national, global or transnational citizenship thus have considerable appeal, yet such border-erasing postulates must deal with two major barriers: first, they must contend with the absence of democracy in international institutions and relations of governance; and second, they sidestep the crucial ontology and reality of state sovereignty.[132]

Many observers have noted that the constellation of political and economic forces falling under the rubric of corporate globalization has resulted in a large-scale transfer of political decision making to international institutions.[133] Yet a formidable obstacle to realizing a regime of human rights based on global citizenship is the near total absence of democracy at the international level, which fuels deep scepticism and fear about supporting a form of global government that would administer global citizenship rights.[134]

Ideas of post-national or global citizenship also remain 'trapped in the web of national sovereignty', that permits nation-states to regulate and deny mobility rights.[135] The international order is based on recognition of sovereign states, with sole rights to jurisdiction over their particular territory and peoples.[136] There is a virtually iron clad equation in international law between state sovereignty and immigration control that is continuously defended by politicians, and national courts of law.

It is an accepted maxim of international law that every sovereign nation has the power, as inherent in sovereignty, and essential to self preservation, to forbid the entrance of foreigners within its dominions, or to admit them, only in such cases and upon such conditions as it may see fit.[137]

Jacqueline Bhabha notes that curtailments of sovereignty cannot be wrenched from states; they must be ceded willingly.[138] This basic premise of national self-determination only applies, however, to states at the upper end of the imperialistic hierarchy. The inability of international human rights to trump sovereign state interests in the realm of refugee policy where there exists far greater international consensus than in immigration policy is noteworthy.

Through an internationally legitimated prerogative to guard their national borders, nation-states largely decide on whether to grant or withhold cross-national rights to migrants. Nation-states may also legally and systemically discriminate in their selection of candidates for mobility, and thus national citizenship rights, on grounds of national origin. Entire national immigration policies, or specific programmes, may reflect biases of race, ethnicity, gender, disability, sexual orientation and so on. Often, these discriminatory practices are explicitly prohibited in the constitutions, national laws and international human rights conventions nominally endorsed by the host states.

Those for whom global citizenship is a reality are those whose wealth and corporate ties allow them to pass quickly and expeditiously through the inconveniences of nation-state borders. In Aiwa Ong's terms, mobile capitalists, managers, technocrats and professionals who engage in capital/financial operations on a global level are practicing 'flexible citizenship'. They are able to bypass or exploit national citizenship rules to their advantage.

'Global citizens', such as the Chinese investor immigrants from Hong Kong, the subject of Ong's research, employ an array of strategies both to circumvent and to benefit from different nation-state regimes regarding the selection of multiple and shifting sites for investment, work and family relocation.[139] In contrast, there are heightened tendencies of states rigorously to monitor, restrict and criminalize the movements of 'undesirable' migrants and asylum seekers, reflecting the experience of citizenship for these border crossers to be markedly more inflexible. For poorer migrants, national citizenship in the state where they reside is fundamental in that only national citizenship guarantees the right of access to the territory of the state and protection from deportation.[140]

For poor migrants, transnational rights are thus less a reality than an ideal. They are nonetheless an important normative response to the reality of these migrants' own transnational existence and conscious-ness.[141] Temporary, circular, and what Rodriguez terms 'autonomous inter-national migration'[142] has become a prevalent and important means of survival for trans-border families, and has rendered transnational com-munities a growing reality. Employment and education strategies, pat-terns of family building, investment of savings and consumption patterns are transformed by binational and even multinational patterns of gender and familial roles, child-bearing and rearing and so on. These are significant trends affecting multiple and fractured ties of loyalty and affiliation to particular political communities. Even among disadvan-taged migrants, an effort to procure two or more citizenships, with at least one in an advanced industrialized state, is increasingly a strategy deployed to enhance family survival and opportunities.[143] Strong ties of migrants to the homeland, sometimes nurtured actively by homeland states,[144] have fostered forms of collective consciousness and solidarity that are certainly hybrid and mixed, but nonetheless signal enduring relationships to a specific nation-state.

Thus, the praxis of gaining citizenship rights and status for migrants is notably transnational in several important ways. Migrants struggle to retain the citizenship status of their home countries; many maintain transnational household structures; they are part of a transnational labour force and 'imagined global community' defined by their national origins, shared culture and exploited occupational and citizenship status across the globe.[145] Their diasporic politics are geared towards change in both host societies and homeland, and invoke international human rights conventions that transcend nation-state borders and restrictions. Thus, migrants negotiate national citizenship(s), but in the context and through a network of sustained linkages that evince their transnational existence.

3
Underdevelopment, Structural Adjustment and Gendered Migration from the West Indies and the Philippines[146]

Among critics of neo-liberal globalization policies, the recognition that structural adjustment programmes operate to the detriment of the majority of the residents of underdeveloped countries is widespread. The literature in this vein is extensive, documenting the alarming growth in unemployment, underemployment, consumer prices and disparities in wealth, and the nose dive taken in incomes, basic government services and the status of women and children.[147] In this chapter, we examine one aspect of the detrimental effects of structural adjustment programmes – the increasing pressure felt by women of Third World origin to emigrate abroad and take up positions as nannies, maids and caregivers in First World households.

A brief summary can identify the parameters of the conditions underlying and shaping this migration process. Within developing countries, dislocated rural labour is inadequately absorbed in the factories of the export processing zones. The World Bank and the IMF have insisted that in return for the service of debts, Third World governments pursue policies which induce their citizens to seek jobs and money elsewhere.[148] Foreign currency earnings are important means of procuring foreign exchange for labour-sending states.[149] Changes associated with structural adjustment have had a considerable impact on migratory flows, especially, though not exclusively, from less developed to more developed states. The governments of developed, or economically advanced, countries, in turn, have accepted the cheap and exploitable labour of these migrants, for both political and economic reasons.

The acceptance of migrants from the South, however, has occurred within strict terms. Third World migrants filled labour shortages during periods of expansion from the 1950s to 1970s, at times despite considerable opposition and anti-immigrant hostility from some sections of the more established populations of these countries. Even during periods of recession, however, which have become increasingly frequent since the mid-1970s, migrants and immigrants of colour have been recruited to fill occupations spurned for their degraded conditions by workers with other employment options.[150] In addition, labour-receiving states are increasingly recruiting temporary rather than permanent forms of migration to augment the flexibility of their labour markets and facilitate the process of migrant return during periods of retrenchment.

The global implications of structural adjustment have also influenced recent debates on the politics of citizenship. First World countries, drawing upon long historical practices of racial/ethnic exclusion, and since the mid-1970s experiencing growing deficits, have increased the policing of Third World migrants' access to the rights normally associated with First World citizenship. Referring to Europe, Balibar[151] points out how complex the mapping of citizenship and citizenship rights has become. Some 'fundamental social rights' have been extended to 'guest workers' and their families both through 'national law, and even Community law', yet national laws in most advanced societies are decidedly discriminatory against non-nationals. In First World states, citizenship, and access to rights traditionally associated with citizenship, are withheld even to long-term residents and their second-generation children of races and/or ethnicities viewed as alien, inassimilable and undesirable. While this is not a new phenomenon, since the return in the mid-1970s of an era of long-term economic crisis and instability, and especially since the post-September 11, 2001 'security' regimes, nationalist policies have reversed an earlier postwar trend of a relative relaxation of border controls.[152]

The implications of these recent shifts in global labour allocation and the politics of citizenship are also gendered. Despite considerable debate regarding the relative merits of the preferential employment or exploitation of women workers in global export processing zones, there is growing recognition that, on balance, structural adjustment policies have increased the burden of women's oppression in Third World states.[153] Diane Elson, for example, has identified the dependence of structural adjustment polices upon the increased provision of women's unpaid labour as a means to compensate for a decline in the level and quality of services, devaluation in local currency and the rise in prices of consumer goods. Women's increased and unpaid work operates as a shock absorber to promote the apparent 'efficiency' of market-oriented mechanisms.[154]

One major growth area of First World employment for impoverished Third World women that has resulted from this global pattern is domestic service, in particular the provision of childcare or nanny service, and increasingly elder care in the private homes of First World families. Despite the contraction in access to legal migration channels for poor Third World citizens to First World countries, available evidence suggests that employment demands for migrant women as domestic workers in Europe and North America are either remaining the same or increasing. The sheer volume of Third World migrants seeking domestic service jobs in First World countries, as well as in newly industrializing countries, have rendered contemporary domestic work 'an international business with political implications'.[155] The industry has been further augmented by the involvement of governments of both employers and domestic workers, the IMF, and a host of intermediaries such as recruiting and placement agencies. The increased 'supply' of women to work in this occupation has coincided with a socially and economically constructed 'demand' for in-home care, particularly the provision of childcare, in the core zones of the global system.

The demand side of the equation has also resulted from changes in the contemporary world system. The increased participation rate of married women with children in the waged workforce that began after the Second World War has tended to continue over the years of long-term global crisis. Provision for childcare in most advanced capitalist states, however, has not kept up with the increased demand. The prohibitive costs of public childcare ensure that there is an economic incentive to opt for live-in care rather than childcare organized in the public sphere.[156] The unabated demand for live-in childcare is a consequence of cuts in the provision of state regulated and/or subsidized childcare.

The following discussion focuses on the impact of poverty and underdevelopment in producing an increasingly large pool of women workers in search of First World citizenship rights. The migration of Third World women to Canada through the foreign domestic worker policy (currently the LCP) is taken as a clear instance of the link between the global debt crisis and international migration of Third World women. Our argument is twofold. First, we argue that structural forces, that is, generalized conditions of global unevenness exacerbated and amplified by imperialist structures and policies, tend to create conditions which force female citizens of poor states to seek citizenship on virtually any terms in richer states. Second, we maintain that First World states, such as Canada, are both able and willing to exploit this increased supply in order to advance their own policies of structural adjustment. The example of domestic worker policy illustrates how policies damaging to the interests of women in general, such as the cutting or elimination of public childcare, is rendered palatable, and even beneficial, to women of selectively high income and status within the boundaries defined by First World citizenship.

Central to this argument is the claim that the Canadian example is, in its general contours, typical of state policy internationally in the construction of the non-citizenship rights of foreign domestic workers. Such a claim could be contested insofar as Canada's foreign domestic worker policy is often regarded as the least abusive among the many countries across the globe employing foreign domestic workers. For example, in January 1988, the Aquino government in the Philippines responded to public protest of the abuse of overseas domestic workers by announcing a blanket ban on Filipina domestic workers going abroad. Within a few months of the announced ban, Canada was exempted from the Philippine government's restriction on the grounds that the domestic workers employed there were not subject to objectionable conditions.[157] Similarly, in Bridget Anderson's impressive comparative analysis of the conditions of domestic workers on an international scale, Canada's LCP is described as a policy that goes 'a long way to regulating the situation'[158] of abusive conditions for domestic workers.

The argument presented here takes exception to this pride of place for Canada's domestic worker policy. We contend that the LCP appears as a favourable policy only because the conditions of domestic workers on a world scale are so universally oppressive. Yet the measure of abuse considered to be 'acceptable' for domestic workers is itself subject to specialized criteria. These criteria are a feature of several factors: the generally degraded status of women's work in the home, the absence of comprehensive public support for childcare, the denial of citizenship rights to immigrant labour, racist assumptions about women of colour and the social construction of class divisions among women that are brought into focus with the private employment of domestic workers. Thus, we argue that Canada's foreign domestic policy is more typical than atypical on an international scale, and therefore offers lessons that have relevance well beyond Canadian borders.

Poverty, underdevelopment and migrant women

The process of recruitment of migrant women workers to perform paid domestic labour in developed capitalist states is structurally linked to the uneven process of international economic development, international migration patterns and regulations, as well as racially and ethnically specific ideologies. Despite the end of formal colonial dependence, the legacy of imperialism has combined with modern conditions of indebtedness to generate large pools of Third World migrant labour. Female migrant labour in most Third World states fills the demand in the domestic care industry of economically advanced states. Kathy McAfee summarizes succinctly a view now commonly identified in the critical literature:

> The historic policies and practices of First World countries, and the international organisations these countries dominate, have served to exacerbate the conditions of poverty from which migrant women hope to escape. Structural adjustment policies, readily advocated by the International Monetary Fund (IMF) and the World Bank in particular, entail government cuts in social service budgets and public sector employment, economic controls which favour the export of commodities over local market expansion, and tax incentives to transnational corporations. Adjustment programmes are designed to ensure that indebted countries earn more foreign exchange and that the money they earn is used to repay their loans and to promote private investment. But the actual effect of structural adjustment is to deepen the dependency, poverty and debt ... Structural adjustment programmes are tailor-made by the World Bank, USAID and other creditors for each country, but have a common thrust: to transfer more funds from impoverished debtor nations into the coffers of the Northern governments, commercial banks and multilateral lending agencies to which they are officially indebted.[159]

Extreme economic and political crises have arisen in Third World countries directly as a result of decades of the burden of international debt. One result of escalating poverty, income inequality and unemployment is increased pressure to migrate in search of employment. Migration often occurs first from rural to urban areas and to export processing zones, but much of it is directed to newly industrializing countries and developed economies of the North. While pressures to migrate from poor sending countries have increased, opportunities for legal immigration are directly tied to occupational demand in the receiving countries. Moreover, the gendered and racialized ghettoization of the labour markets of prospective countries of destination limits, conditions and moulds the character of prospective migration. Those who wish to migrate can do so legally only if they can prove that they are specifically suited to meet the employment profiles in demand: enter the female Third World immigrant domestic.

Before turning to the specific case of foreign domestic workers in Canada, and the conditions in the primary Third World source regions of the Caribbean and the Philippines from which they originate, a brief consideration of the more general place of paid domestic labour within conditions of modern capitalism is in order.

Domestic service and third world migrant women

Domestic service in the home long pre-dated contemporary capitalist global relations. In fact, pre-capitalist economies were largely based on the provision of family labour.[160] With the emergence of modern capitalism came a contraction in family size, and a reduction in the amount of labour performed in the private home relative to that performed in socialized industrial and service production units. Changes in this direction have been particularly rapid and pronounced since the large-scale participation of married women in the paid workforce, characteristic of the most advanced sections of the global economy. As Mary Romero summarizes:

> The transformation of homemaking activity from production to consumption became more complete and led to new developments for homemakers after World War II. ... Both working- and middle-class women's entrance into the work force contributed to the general upward trend of women's employment in the twentieth century. ... [However,] [t]he double-day syndrome originated from the social expectation that employed women would fulfill their families' needs through daily activity in the work force and in the home.[161]

As new employment opportunities for women workers have developed, those able to gain alternative employment to paid domestic work have continually elected to do so. In advanced Western countries in Europe and North America, women moved out of private domestic service and into the growing industries and services in ever increasing numbers. A situation of chronic labour shortage came to characterize domestic service under conditions of modern capitalism. The so-called 'servant problem' emerged as the number of women willing to work as the private servants of other women declined. By the 1950s, even the anthropologist Margaret Mead offered suggestions on 'how to survive' without a maid.[162]

Commercial enterprises also took advantage of the market opportunities that became available. As economic boom conditions continued in the 1950s and 1960s, household appliances were advertised in North America as a means of automating housework and technologically 'solving' the 'servant problem'. The single most demanding arena of private household labour, however, the provision of childcare particularly for children of pre-school age, is resistant to automation. Under conditions of a chronic labour shortage, classical economics would predict an increase in wages and an improvement in the quality of working conditions as a means to attract and retain labourers. Domestic labour, however, has proven to be remarkably 'immune to the regulatory infection'[163] of the market.

Generated by conditions of chronic poverty in the Third World, the large supply of workers who are collectively highly motivated to achieve secure employment for themselves and their families has been used to offset pressures for improvements in the conditions of domestic care. The existence of this labour pool has thus mitigated against the operation of a pure market model of supply and demand with reference to domestic labour. The denial of citizenship rights to immigrant workers and the racialized image of the Third World domestic worker, who is considered uniquely and 'naturally' suited to serve the needs of First World women and their families, has tended to ensure that what one author has called 'the despised calling' has become identified with the labour of women of colour.[164]

These restrictive conditions have ensured that domestic service in the context of global restructuring has taken on contradictory dimensions. At the same time as being the most spurned occupation for those who are entitled to the right of labour mobility, it is one of the most coveted for those with no other employment or migratory options. In the United States, for example, the notion of 'housekeeping for the Green Card',[165] is paralleled in the Canadian context by the practice of 'doing domestic to get landed'.[166] Moreover, racial and gendered barriers to labour mobility also restrict the alternative employment options for domestic workers, even once formal citizenship is obtained. Palmer points out, for example, that in the United States, Black southern women who had migrated north in the 1930s to work as domestics, found that unlike earlier generations of Euro-American immigrants, alternative sources of employment were not made available to them, even years after arrival in Northern cities.[167] In Canada, Brand notes that at least until the Second World War, 'at least 80 per cent of Black women in Canadian cities worked in domestic service. Industrialisation did not have the overwhelming impact on Black women wage earners that it did on white women'.[168]

Migration and paid domestic service are thus elements of a global process of linkages, in which gendered and racialized ideologies play a central part. The particular legislative restrictions and conditions governing foreign domestic labour vary from country to country. Nonetheless, there is clearly an overall pattern in which domestic labour is subject to greater and more exceptional levels of restriction relative to other forms of employment. In countries where labour rights in general are minimal, foreign domestic workers will be subject to the greatest level of oppression and abuse, when measured on an international scale; where labour rights in general are relatively greater, as in the Canadian context, the conditions of foreign domestic workers may indeed be relatively less abusive compared with those of domestics in other countries. The conditions for domestic workers are, however, in all countries, at a level considered unacceptable for virtually every other occupation within the norms of nation-specific labour force conditions.[169]

Canada's foreign domestic worker policy

It is in comparison with the experiences of domestics in countries such as Saudi Arabia, Bahrain and Hong Kong that Canada's foreign domestic worker policy appears to offer some protection and security for the employees involved. The argument presented here departs from this view of the Canadian policy. Rather than preventing or ameliorating the threat of abuse of workers, Canada's LCP actually only serves to institutionalize such a threat. Moreover, the LCP has been structured by various federal governments over decades with the full knowledge of a highly vulnerable pool of foreign worker applicants, upon whom exceptionally restrictive conditions are imposed.

In Canada, the federal legislation governing the recruitment of in-home domestic care, the LCP, was formulated to facilitate and regulate the recruitment of migrant workers. To be eligible by Canadian law to hire a domestic worker through the LCP, the prospective employing family must indicate ability to provide a room in the family home, for which rent would be deducted from wages earned, and to meet a minimum combined annual income.[170] The policy itself is constructed as a 'special', separate piece of immigration legislation, applying only to those foreign workers seeking work in Canada as live-in domestics as a temporary means to obtain permanent immigration status. This fact alone indicates the unique conditions to which foreign domestic workers are subject, separated out from the normal pool of immigrant applicants to Canada. This distinct immigration policy, administered at the federal level, also exempts foreign domestic workers from the generalized regulation of labour legislation, which is administered provincially. The employment standards for domestic workers vary from province to province. Moreover where foreign domestic workers are covered by specific provincial labour legislation, this has tended to be the result of domestic advocacy movements organizing to ensure coverage, not the largesse of any particular provincial government.[171]

From the mid-1950s, when legislation was enacted specifically to recruit Caribbean women workers to Canada as live-in domestics, to the present policy enacted in 1992, the federal government has insisted upon maintaining a distinct and exceptional institutional mechanism to govern the migration and work lives of foreign domestic workers. Another notable characteristic of the foreign domestic legislation is that there has been a secular trend towards increasing restrictions on the rights of the workers themselves, despite public lobbying and documented studies calling for equalizing the rights of foreign domestics with those of other workers.[172]

With the 1973 introduction by the Canadian federal government of the Temporary Employment Authorization Programme, for example, domestic workers received short-term work permits rather than the previous scheme's provision of permanent resident status upon arrival. These women were permitted to stay in Canada conditionally upon the performance of domestic work for a designated employer, thus transforming 'domestic workers into ... disposable migrant labourers, not unlike European "guest workers" '.[173] During the 1970s, the citizenship rights of foreign, and especially Caribbean, domestics thus deteriorated further. While many European domestics continued to enter Canada as landed immigrants, Caribbean domestics increasingly entered on temporary employment visas, which gave maximum control to the state and employers over the conditions of work and residence of women of colour domestics.[174] Migrant domestics were compelled to endure restrictions in freedoms generally considered unacceptable under liberal democracies, and rejected by other workers, including those performing the same type of work outside private households.[175]

The Canadian government's programme of recruiting foreign domestic workers under temporary work permits effectively created an indentured or captive labour force. Moreover, this was a source of cheap labour: the costs of original production (nurturance, education, etc.) had been borne elsewhere, and workers were often reluctant to quit regardless of how exploited or intolerable their work and living situations. The motivation for administering foreign domestics through the temporary employment visa system, with no recourse to the previous option of applying for landed immigrant status from within Canada, was clearly stated by the government in 1976: the aim was to impede the turnover of foreign workers out of compulsory live-in domestic service.[176]

In 1981, a revised policy, entitled the Foreign Domestic Movement (FDM), was introduced which further institutionalized this objective. Under this programme, a foreign domestic worker was eligible to apply for landed immigrant status after two years of live-in service with a designated employer. Employers could only be changed with the approval of a federal immigration officer. If the worker successfully achieved landed status, all of the restrictions associated with the FDM ceased to apply, providing access to all formal citizenship rights open to permanent residents.

The right to apply for permanent status after two years of residence from inside Canada was heralded as a victory by domestic worker advocates, and it was indeed a concession to the demands of domestic workers themselves. Nevertheless, the 1981 policy included a number of regulations that continued the pattern of exceptional, and discriminatory, treatment for foreign domestic workers. It institutionalized the potential for employer abuse, including the threat of deportation while the worker remained effectively imprisoned by temporary residence, and compulsory live-in, status. If after three assessments the domestic worker had not been accepted for permanent resident status, by law she would be required to return to her country of origin. The alternative would be to remain illegally in Canada and to work in the shadow economy.

Other criteria, such as the requirements of educational upgrading to prove 'self-sufficiency' as a condition of achieving landed immigrant status, were also imposed on those who entered Canada through the FDM. Domestic workers and their advocates challenged these restrictions and criticized the use of criteria not applied to assess the suitability for landing of any other group of immigrants whose occupations, like those of domestic workers, were in high demand in Canada. Notwithstanding these protests, the government's policy remained in place for a decade. Only when the government came under a legal challenge was the policy altered. The government's failure to withstand a 1990 legal challenge to the FDM policy was pivotal in prompting the raising of formal qualifications for entry into Canada of foreign domestic applicants.[177]

Once again, the specific reforms to the policy in 1992 did not decrease the considerable restrictions imposed on the rights of foreign domestic workers. Under the 1992 LCP guidelines, the upgrading requirements were eliminated in assessments for landed status for foreign domestics, who were now called 'caregivers'. To offset this apparent liberalization in the policy, however, eligibility criteria for entry into Canada by migrant caregivers became more restrictive. In other words, the exceptional criteria for eligibility for permanent residential status under the FDM were simply front-loaded to the point of application for admission into the LCP.

Criteria for entry into the LCP originally called for the equivalent of a Canadian grade 12 education, plus six months of full-time formal training in a field or occupation related to the caregiver job sought in Canada. Within months of the programme's inception, the latter training requirement was amended to allow for experience in lieu of training. Once again, however, this amendment resulted from the public outcry from domestic workers and worried potential employers.[178] The official reasons given by the Immigration Department for upgrading the admissions criteria for foreign domestics were, first, the perceived need to upgrade the quality of childcare, and second, to facilitate the entry into the larger labour market of those domestics who had attained landed status. According to the federal government, without adequate educational backgrounds, domestic workers who had obtained permanent resident status after completing the required two years of live-in service, continue to find employment in only the most poorly remunerated jobs.

The two most repressive aspects of the Foreign Domestic Movement were retained under the LCP. This in spite of the government's attempt to sell the new programme through the rhetoric of 'reform' resulting from 'widespread consultation'.[179] These features are: (i) the temporary migrant or 'visitor' status; and (ii) the compulsory live-in requirement for foreign domestic workers. Accordingly, it is recognized that this 'program is unique'[180] as it applies specific restrictions on the rights of foreign domestic workers that are relevant to no other category of workers, regardless of their immigration status. The two restrictions of compulsory living-in with the employer, and the temporary immigration status of the labourer, go hand-in-hand. According to the governmental reviews that led to the formulation of the LCP, Canada's shortage of waged domestic labour exists only within the live-in market. Were it not for this labour shortage, foreign labour would not be in demand.

While the most repressive features of earlier domestic worker policy were retained, a change was introduced in regard to the legal status of the programme. It became a regulatory programme, rather than one established by policy.[181] Several scholars had pointed out the tenuousness and ambiguous legal status of the FDM and previous domestic worker policies which had existed in a series of revised policy decisions,[182] and a 'myriad of little rules ... applied to monitor and control' foreign domestics.[183] While the impact of the FDM had been extremely coercive and punitive of the behaviour of foreign domestics, the rules and regulations of the FDM programme had no legal authority, forming part of the Immigration Manual only rather than part of the Immigration Act and the Immigration Regulations.[184] Despite original hopes on the part of some advocates that such a change in the legal status might benefit domestic workers seeking permanent residence, the evidence points to a continuation of harassment and bureaucratic challenges.

The features of compulsory living-in and enforced temporary residence are those most commonly identified to produce abusive and unsafe working conditions. These features also have been consistently opposed by leading domestic workers' rights advocates in Canada.[185] Studies of paid domestic service in the United States have repeatedly identified the single most effective change in domestic labour leading to improved working conditions as the move away from live-in to live-out service.[186] The continued imposition of the combined compulsory live-in requirement and temporary residential status is therefore notable for its exceptional treatment of an identifiable group of women workers, usually of Third World origin, recruited for the sole purpose of private domestic service. Effectively, the Canadian government's insistence on retaining these restrictive measures as a pre-condition for eligibility, 'established a class of people good enough to do their dirty work, but not good enough to be permanent residents'.[187]

While the percentage of entrants into the LCP from the Philippines has remained high (between 61 and 75 per cent of total entrants in the 1990s), the overall numbers of domestics entering under the LCP have been drastically reduced. Thus, the number of entrants into the LCP in 1997 (1606) was less than one-fifth of the number of entrants in 1991 (8630), the last year of the FDM, and only 15 per cent of the 1990 figure (10 739).[188] The precipitous drop in numbers of migrants entering through the LCP reflects a choking off of an important source for legal entry into Canada, and of the prospect for acquisition of Canadian residence and citizenship for Third World women.

The difficulties in gaining access in Canada to positions as a foreign domestic have forced many female migrant workers to work in undocumented statuses, for example, entering as visitors, asylum seekers or refugees or students, and remaining to work illegally. Although there are no accurate figures regarding undocumented foreign women working as private household workers, anecdotal sources suggest that the numbers are large and growing. The results of the questionnaire survey in our study of 50 domestic workers in Toronto conducted in 1994 and 1995 suggest that for national origin/regional groups facing barriers to legal entry as domestic workers, entry as visitors and unlawful work in a shadow economy are already well-established practices.[189] Workers' undocumented status further increases the power of employers within personal domestic service. Employers may utilize the threat of the employee's conviction under Canadian law or deportation to enforce arbitrary demands. They are particularly apt to do so in a context where the Canadian government is under no obligation to offer labour protection to undocumented workers.

Canada's foreign domestic worker policy thus shares in common with the policies of other countries the imposition of exceptionally harsh restrictions, considered unacceptable for workers in other industries, or for those, such as legal citizens, who have the option of seeking alternative sources of employment. In studies on domestic labour internationally, the terms used to describe situations normally considered to be illegal, archaic and barbaric include 'precapitalist' and 'premodern', with analogies made to 'slavery'.[190] Canada's institutionalization of compulsory live-in status, combined with the threat of denial of permanent residence, amounts to a condition of indentured labour. The fact that the condition of indenture is temporary does not in any way mitigate the susceptibility of the employee to abuse. The temporary condition is a standard feature of indenture, and is rendered effective in regulating domestic workers precisely because it holds the promise of increased citizenship rights at the end of the two-year term. In other words, the stick would not be effective without the promise of a carrot.

There is extensive documentation of conditions of abuse commonly experienced by foreign domestic workers in Canada. Since such abuse takes place within the confines of a private home, however, enforcement and regulation of procedures to correct such abuses are both rare and extremely difficult. The overriding threat of deportation to conditions of poverty and chronic unemployment in the Third World ensures a structural pattern of intimidation, where the citizen-employer and the non-citizen employee do not face each other on equal terms. Since the 1950s, Canada has drawn upon two major Third World source regions as recruitment areas for foreign domestic workers where the threat of deportation is sufficiently harsh that even the most oppressive employment options within Canada seem to offer a more secure alternative. It is to the conditions in these regions that we now turn our discussion.

Conditions in the Caribbean and Philippines fostering female migration

The conditions of underdevelopment within the English Caribbean and the Philippines are central to the historic role of these regions as the major Third World source areas for the recruitment of foreign domestics in Canada. How Canadian domestic worker policy has been constructed to take advantage of these conditions, and has adapted its regulations accordingly, is critical to situating Canada's foreign domestic policy in the context of global restructuring.

The English Caribbean region as a whole incorporates a wide variety of nations and is influenced by a complexity of economic, social and political factors. In general, however, until the nineteenth century internal migration was negligible and external migration involved only a fraction of the population. Those who did migrate were usually of middle- or upper-class background, hoping to advance their prospects by obtaining permanent residence in Europe or North America.[191]

During the 1960s and 1970s, this pattern started to change, with large numbers of residents from the Commonwealth Caribbean seeking migration abroad. Most of the major studies of Caribbean migration for this period maintain that the increase was not necessarily a response to unemployment, but of increased opportunities elsewhere for well-educated, relatively high status professionals.[192] This is not to suggest that unemployment did not exist. On the contrary, the British West Indies has seen chronic rates of unemployment ranging between 20 and 30 per cent of the workforce. Instead, it was the effect of restrictive immigration laws in some of the most favoured destination countries that ensured only the most skilled workers were permitted to enter.[193]

The period of the 1960s and 1970s saw an increase in emigration outlets for Caribbean workers at the same time as political independence was negotiated with the British imperial state.[194] Newly independent Caribbean governments hoped to offset chronic unemployment and secure sources of foreign currency in the form of remittances by encouraging migration abroad. Studies of trends in West Indian out-migration indicate that there have been two major post-Second World War waves, one from 1955–61, with destinations mainly to the United Kingdom; and a second from 1979–85, matching the previous wave in terms of both volume and rate of departure, but destined primarily to North America. By 1980, it was estimated that 20–30 per cent of the Caribbean region's total population was residing outside the region, largely in Europe and North America.[195] This diaspora was not evenly experienced among the island nations of the Caribbean. By 1973, Jamaica, the largest of the British Caribbean nations with a population of about 2 million, registered more than half a million citizens living off the island.[196] Remittances have therefore developed into a critical component for family survival in the region. Estimates of the value of remittances to the British West Indies are difficult to verify, given the variations among the islands and poor statistical records. One study provides a 1978 estimate of US$23 billion, roughly equivalent to 10 per cent of the region's merchandise exports; a 1982 study suggests that remittances were the principal source of hard currency in several of the small islands in the region.[197] Though there is only 'fragmentary evidence', over long historic trends, available data indicates that 'remittance flows are significant'.[198] Remittances from Latin America and the Caribbean taken as an aggregate indicate a significant increase in family dependence on overseas remittances, particularly since 1990.[199] Jamaica has seen the level of remittances exceed 10 per cent of the country's GDP.[200] In many rural districts in Jamaica, remittances have surpassed farm income as the main source of revenue.[201]

Evidence suggests that the early years of this emigration wave favoured the exodus of male workers. This coincided with the internal migration of female workers from the rural areas into the cities, particularly to work as domestic servants for private homes and in the burgeoning tourist and hotel industries.[202] This pattern reinforced another: the historically large proportion of households headed by sole-support mothers. According to Momsen, though the proportion of female household heads varies greatly across the region, in general '[w]omen have had to accept responsibility for the financial support of their children since emancipation because of both male migration and male economic marginality'.[203] In 1970, the Commonwealth Caribbean recorded 35 per cent of all households headed by women; a 1986 study confirmed this figure, finding a ratio of one in three households to be under female headship.[204] This factor, and the decline of agriculture as a source of profitable employment, compelled women to seek new sectors of work.[205] Domestic labour in Canada was one such avenue.

Prior to 1962, Canada had an explicitly racist governmental policy restricting West Indian immigration to Canada. According to the 1958 Director of the Immigration Branch of the Department of Citizenship,

> [I]t is not by accident that coloured British subjects other than negligible numbers from the United Kingdom are excluded from Canada ... They do not assimilate readily and pretty much vegetate to a low

standard of living. Despite what has been said to the contrary, many cannot adapt themselves to our climatic conditions.[206]

In 1955, this policy was amended to permit a limited number of West Indian women workers to enter Canada on condition that they remain in domestic service with a contractually designated employer for one year; after this time they were permitted to obtain other employment. This policy, like those that were to follow, was distinctly discriminatory. Unlike domestic workers from Europe, the West Indian workers received no government assistance in the cost of passage. Moreover, although permanent resident status was obtained upon arrival, Caribbean domestics were subject to special conditions of compulsory live-in domestic labour and the threat of deportation. Such restrictions did not apply to domestics from European source countries.[207]

Between 1973 and 1981, West Indian women workers were admitted as domestic workers on temporary employment visas. Others entered as skilled workers, particularly in nursing when there were periodic labour shortages, or as sponsored relatives. The numbers as a whole, however, were relatively small and since that period have been declining relative to other source countries. Canada's labour policy favoured female over male West Indian migrants. In 1967, the ratio was 43 males to 57 females; by 1980 the ratio had narrowed slightly but remained skewed, with 46 males to 54 females. By 1987, the ratio had stabilized at approximately 45 males to 54 females.[208] Regardless of the ratio however, total numbers of West Indian migrants declined. Between 1973 and 1978, of all those who obtained landed immigrant status in Canada, those from all Caribbean source countries totalled only 10 per cent; by 1980, that figure was 6 per cent.[209] Conversely, one of the most rapidly increasing alternative source regions of immigration to Canada overall, as well as in the migration of foreign domestics, was the Philippines.

In the year from July 1975 to June 1976, 44.8 per cent of all entrants to Canada on temporary employment visas assigned to in-home domestic work were from the Caribbean, and only 0.3 per cent were from all countries in Asia; by 1990, only 5 per cent of entrants on the Foreign Domestic Movement programme were from the Caribbean, while over 58 per cent were from the Philippines.[210] Canada, however, is only one destination country for Filipino migrants. While Filipino workers are scattered in almost all regions of the world, the vast majority of Filipino migrant household workers abroad work in Asia (particularly Hong Kong and Singapore) and the Gulf Region (Saudi Arabia, United Arab Emirates). Between 1982 and 1990, the total number of Filipino processed contract workers had almost doubled.[211] Throughout the 1990s, the numbers of migrants deployed abroad continued to climb, increasing from 660 122 in 1996 to 841 628 in 2000.[212] Only immigration that passes through official channels, however, is counted in reported statistics. According to the International Labour Organisation, among Asian women in general, the 1990s have also witnessed considerable increases in illegal migration, when workers are considered to be the most vulnerable to abuse.[213] This trend is known to be widespread in the Philippines. Even if we only consider the official statistics for labour migration, however, by 1995 the estimated size of the total Filipino workforce abroad, comprising both temporary contract migrants and those who have settled permanently abroad, was about 4.2 million.[214]

The period since the 1980s has also witnessed an increasing proportional exodus of female migrant labour. By the end of the 1980s, women comprised between 40 and 50 per cent of all Filipino migrants.[215] The proportion of female Filipino migrants has increased rapidly as their share has grown from 61 per cent in 1998 to 70 per cent in 2000.[216] This has in part been a response to high levels of demand for nurses, office workers, domestic workers and other types of service worker, as well as entertainers, sex trade workers and mail order brides in Asia, the Middle East, Europe and North America.[217] By 1991, domestic workers comprised the majority of Filipino women workers registered with the central government's Philippine Overseas Employment Administration (POEA).[218] By the mid-1990s, domestic workers counted for nearly 45 per cent of the overall number of newly hired overseas female contract workers registered with the Philippines government.[219]

The unprecedented rise of Filipino emigration reflects both the growing internationalization of labour markets and the persistence of underdevelopment in the Philippine economy.[220] Development in the Philippines has been hampered by colonization by the Spanish, and since the turn of the century, by colonial and neo-colonial policies of the United States. A pervasive legacy of the Philippine neo-colonial status vis à vis the United States has been the latter's right to maintain over 20 bases and military installations in the country. The withdrawal of the US military in 1992, though a symbolic recognition of greater Philippine autonomy, proved only a token concession. The Philippines' development problems were exacerbated in the 1990s not least through a significant reduction in American aid.[221]

A number of structural factors linked to underdevelopment have triggered the large volume of labour flows from the country. These include the increasing scarcity of land, urban growth without sufficient expansion in urban employment to meet the supply of dislocated and landless agricultural workers, massive overseas indebtedness and the general poor performance of a predominantly foreign-owned economy.[222] The Philippines achieved formal independence from the United States in 1946. Prior to this, the semi-feudal landlord–tenant system was heavily promoted by the ruling elite at the expense of the freeholding sectors of the peasantry.[223] Critical development problems in the Philippines are, however, not only economic; they have been exacerbated by political instability. Between 1972 and 1981, Philippines President, Ferdinand Marcos, sought to suppress civil unrest in the form of peasant, worker and student militancy, through the imposition of martial law.[224] Marcos's economic policies provided an open invitation for foreign investors to control any area of the economy through 'service contracts' entered into with Filipino citizens and domestic corporations.[225]

In 1984, following the assassination of Senator Benigno Aquino, leader of the opposition to the Marcos regime, some 86 000 workers were laid off by various corporations. More than 50 per cent of families were living below the officially defined poverty threshold. The removal of Marcos and the installation of the Aquino government in 1986 through a popularly supported military revolt, while increasing popular hope for change, did not in fact lead to further economic development. The government of Aquino, and since 1992, those of Ramos, Estrada and Macapagal-Arroyo have not significantly alleviated the economic distress felt by almost all Filipinos. The exception is only of an elite section of Philippine society, fully committed to intensifying domestic and international links to free market policies. Official unemployment in the Philippines is among the highest in the Asia Pacific region, at 10.5 per cent in 2001, with an additional official rate of underemployment at 17.5 per cent.[226] Out-migration has become a structural feature of the Philippine capitalism. The export of labour offsets domestic unemployment rates. In addition, remittances support the domestic economy and help to service the government's huge foreign debt. According to the POEA, the government agency tasked to oversee the systematic export of labour,

> about US$2.17 billion was generated by the government on remittance of migrant workers from 1982–85 alone. Under Aquino, US$5.98 billion were remitted through legal banking channels from 1986–91. Under Ramos, a total of US$16.68 billion was generated from remittances of migrant workers in a period of 4 years (1992–95). ... For the year 2000, total remittances recorded by the [Central Bank of the Philippines] is US$6.05.[227]

Key to understanding the unstable nature of the Philippine economy is the debt crisis and the impact of structural adjustment policies. The effects of the chronic debt crisis is summed up by Pomeroy: 'A relentless chaining of the Filipino people into a helpless debt situation constituted part of the coldly planned process of reorganizing and reorienting the Philippine economy to suit the needs and operations of U.S. big corporations.'[228] The Philippine experience with IMF–World Bank lending policies began in 1958, and has resulted in enormous and escalating international financial debt, amounting to $28.6 billion by 1986; by 1999 the official debt figure had risen to $52.2 billion. Augmenting the size of international debt for the non-oil-producing country were the 1973–74 and 1979–80 increases in world prices of oil, which plunged the trade balance of the Philippines into ever-steeper deficit.[229] The significance of these remittances to servicing the foreign debt are illustrated by the fact that '87% (US$5.9 billion) of the US$6.79 billion remittances in 1999 went to debt servicing ... [Moreover,] given the fact that as of June 2000 Philippine debt ... reached US$52.2 billion, labor export is likely to continue to be tied to the politics of foreign debt ...'[230]

US-dictated demands by the World Bank for 'structural adjustment' of the Philippine economy included several policies: a devaluation of the peso, import liberalization, export-oriented development, wage restraints, no-strike measures, cuts in social services and further concessions for foreign investors.[231] Export-oriented development led to land conversions that displaced peasants from their livelihood, and thus contributed to unemployment in the rural areas.[232] '[U]nofficial figures suggest that combined under and unemployment run as high as 40–50%.'[233]

Women have suffered disproportionately from job loss in the Philippines' service industries, and through the retrenchments and shutdowns in manufacturing that have formed part of the structural adjustment process. The bulk of private sector service workers in the Philippines are found in retail trading, and composed of street vendors, hawkers and operators of five-and-dime stores, beauty parlours and repair shops. These are enterprises based on minimal capital and technology, offer little potential for improving productivity, and reflect unstable wage relations or ownership only of the most minor means of production.[234] However, women workers are often favoured as employees in the large export processing zones. Even these conditions, however, where there is employment but also extreme exploitation, have not produced any generalized decline in emigration.[235] CALABARZON, one of the largest export processing zones and a model of future Philippine development, is a case in point. CALABARZON is a massive industrial development complex named after the five provinces which intersect in the 16 229 square kilometre zone with a population of 8.3 million – Cavite, Laguna, Batangas, Rizal and Quezon. Billed in the region's promotional literature as 'CALABARZON – Where doing business is a pleasure', the investment haven is described as 'The most dynamic region in the country', one which 'also enjoys social and political stability'.[236] The CALABARZON project is a 20-year model project in the government's Medium-Term Philippine Development Plan. Under the official development assistance package from Japan, US$3.126 billion was expected for the first five years. Of 441 factories operating in the CALABARZON industrial area, 195 of them employ predominantly women workers. The plants are mostly assembly type factories – in electronics, automobile assembly, garments and textiles, food and beverages and ceramics. According to one study:

> Some companies have a policy of hiring only young, single women. Applicants are required to undergo pregnancy tests, even if they are single. There is no consideration for the conditions of pregnant workers nor for mothers with young children – pregnant workers also work the night shift, and those whose children are sick are forced to resign.[237]

Thus in spite of high and rising levels of education, working women in the Philippines continue to experience gender discrimination and stereotyping at all levels of the occupational structure.[238] The consistent decline in the value of the peso that has accompanied structural adjustment has made it difficult for Filipinas to meet the daily basic needs of their families as real incomes have decreased while prices of goods and services have increased.

Since 1974, with the formulation of the Philippine Labour Code,[239] the Philippines government has vigorously pursued overseas employment as a means of alleviating chronic unemployment and balance of payments problems.[240] Individuals and households have also pursued overseas employment as a means of survival, and of improving economic opportunities for Filipino families.[241] A 1988 household income and expenditures survey revealed that 15.5 per cent of families in the Philippines receive income from abroad contributing about 30 per cent of their total incomes.[242] By 1998, one-third of the Filipino population, or approximately 20 million people, were estimated to be directly supported through remittances of overseas workers, a majority of whom are women.[243] One common family strategy is to subsidize the higher

education of one family member who is then sent abroad to earn wages
that are comparatively much higher than potential earnings in the
Philippines. However, the structural pressures towards overseas migration are demonstrably greater than individual family strategies. As
Mitter summarizes:

> By 1979, the Philippine government was earning $1 billion from
> foreign remittances, nearly 15 per cent of its total export earnings.
> Recruitment and the sending of remittances were not left to the per-
> sonal choice of the workers either. ... In 1983, to increase the amount
> of currency coming back to the Philippines, the government passed
> a decree which compelled a large number of Filipino workers abroad
> to remit between 50 and 80 per cent of their wages. The penalty for
> non-compliance would be refusal to renew or extend passports,
> non-renewal of employment contracts, and in cases of subsequent
> violations, repatriation to the Philippines.[244]

Filipino migrant workers tend to have higher than average education.
According to a 1980 study, over 50 per cent of Filipino migrant workers
surveyed had completed some college education, in comparison with
only 12.5 per cent of the Philippine labour force.[245] In the context of a
40 per cent unemployment rate among nurses in the Philippines, nursing degrees are deliberately acquired as passports to work abroad, and
thereby increase family living standards. What is calculated less frequently than the economic impact of overseas employment, both for
the individual migrant worker and for the Philippine economy, are the
dire social consequences of long-term separation of family members
entailed in contract migration, as well as widespread abuse and exploitation of migrant workers abroad.[246]

Implications for citizenship

Poverty and underdevelopment, exacerbated by structural adjustment
policies, serving the interests of foreign commercial banks and corporations, are responsible for producing the pool of migrant female labour
available to work as maids and nannies abroad. Nonetheless, foreign
domestic worker policies of states such as Canada, and the gatekeeping
mechanisms that serve to enforce such policies, fashion the specific
terms and conditions of access for Third World migrant women into
developed states as a means of escaping such extreme poverty.
Regulation of citizenship rights is thus central to the process that
compels – to put the case crudely – poor women from Third World

countries to work as domestic employees for rich women and families in First World countries.

A common analytical expression used to explain the increasing role of poor women in the international migration matrix is the trend towards 'the feminisation of (im)migrant labour'. This phrase summarizes the increasing proportion of female migrant labour relative to male. This gendered transition is fairly recent, but it has taken place in some countries at a very rapid rate. The Philippines is particularly notable. Since the mid-1980s, the migration trend has tended to shift from one consisting largely of single males, or male workers with dependent family members, to one in which women are now, at 60 to 70 per cent of the total migrant population, far exceeding men.

However, the phrase 'feminisation of (im)migrant labour' risks distorting the actual implications of this trend. Rather than seeing increasing opportunities for migrant women workers relative to male workers, in fact tightening controls on poor, Third World immigrant labour, both male and female, have created a decline in opportunities. It is in the most oppressive employment niches that women have tended to be 'favoured' as migrant workers. Secure industrial opportunities for male immigrant workers have tended to decrease. Women workers with no other source of employment at home or abroad are forced to accept highly exploited working conditions where sex stereotyping and abuse are virtually endemic. Domestic and personal service labour, which in the receiving countries is overwhelmingly stereotyped as female labour, has grown proportionally as an international employment outlet for Philippine and other Asian migrant women as the gender ratio has shifted.[247] Moreover, in receiving nations, including Canada, Europe and the more developed nations of Asia such as Hong Kong and Singapore, foreign domestic workers are overwhelmingly employed in households where they are under the managerial direction of other, wealthy, women. As Heyzer and Wee note, an 'ironic consequence of these class implications is that the employment of a foreign domestic worker has become a status symbol of the newly prosperous in the richer countries'.[248] Class issues regarding immigration patterns, and the presence or absence of immigrants' rights, reinforce gender-based discrimination in specific and selected ways, which the term 'feminization' tends to falsely universalize and obfuscate.

An alternative approach, suggested here, includes a consideration of rights constituted and denied through citizenship policies of nation-states. While migrant domestic workers lack many basic citizenship rights, including the choice of employer and domicile, their employers, in contrast, generally enjoy full citizenship rights. For citizen-women with economic and social means, the in-home employment of migrant domestic workers provides an outlet to partially alleviate the conditions of their female oppression. However, this happens on an individual basis, paid for on the market, leaving the systemic conditions of women's oppression intact and in some ways reinforced. Despite individual relief of the burdens of private home care, the generalized condition of women's oppression is perpetuated. Rather than female employer and employee experiencing a commonality of oppression based on gender, the result is a division of interests, where class, racial and citizenship distinctions become paramount.

The international circulation of Third World female domestics is but one of several major flows in contemporary global migration. The systematic reproduction of foreign domestic workers is legally separate from, and structurally subordinate to, 'normal' immigration flows internationally. Despite Canada's less abusive foreign domestic worker policy relative to those of some other countries, Canada is inextricably linked to this global pattern, both benefiting from and contributing to the structural exploitation of Third World women. This global pattern of structural exploitation suggests the need for a critique of contemporary policies of structural adjustment in both national and global state contexts. In the following chapters, a specific focus on the experience of Filipina and West Indian women workers in Canada will serve as a case study to illustrate the impact of such trends.

4
Gatekeepers in the Domestic Service Industry in Canada[249]

The previous chapter considered the global conditions under which migration from the Third World to the First World, and the migration of female domestic workers in particular, occurs. These broad parameters, however, are not predetermined forces operating in the absence of human agency. Citizenship rights, and the denial of those rights, are negotiated in a global nexus of human relations where various interests, ideas and practices are enacted, and come into conflict in contested arenas. These negotiations arise within and challenge a variety of structural and legislative restrictions, each with distinct but parallel processes of individual and collective strategies.

The interaction of these processes involves a range of 'gatekeepers' who serve to select, reject and/or restrict the conditions of entry of migrant workers in general into developed states, and of migrant women domestic workers in particular. These gatekeepers include state policy-makers and legislators in both sending and destination countries, government visa officers and other immigration personnel, the officers of various professional accreditation bodies and educational institutions, and the personnel of recruitment and placement agencies. These actors – individually and in interaction with one another – also help structure the opportunities for future occupational trajectories and subsequent options for access to, and fulfilment of, citizenship rights in the receiving countries. In addition, the gatekeepers interpret information and influence future policy changes that have a direct impact on the socially and politically constructed 'needs' and citizenship rights available to families in the advanced states.

In Canada, there are two central gatekeeping mechanisms that impact specifically on migrant domestic workers. These are first, the specific legislation that governs the recruitment and residence restrictions on foreign domestic workers, currently the Live-in Caregiver Programme (LCP), discussed in the previous chapter; and second, private domestic placement agencies. The focus of this chapter is on the role and impact of these agencies.

Private domestic placement agencies are one of the most important enforcers of the government's domestic worker policy in the receiving country. This chapter illuminates the influential role of these gatekeepers in reproducing a highly racialized set of practices and criteria in the recruitment and placement of female migrant domestic workers to live and work in upper-income Canadian households. Before focusing on the activities of the placement agencies and the views of those who operate them specifically, two elements that shape the context in which they function, and through which they serve as mediators between the federal state and the private household unit, will be considered. First, we examine the implicit mandate that is provided to private domestic placement agencies by the LCP to allow and encourage unequal citizenship rights between the employing family and the foreign domestic worker; second we consider the 'demand' side of the private home, the crisis of public childcare.

Context: gatekeepers and the LCP

The specific context in which these gatekeeping mechanisms operate is mediated by the more general legislative context. The LCP, regulated at the federal governmental level, acts as a mediating instrument linking the interests of the Canadian state and the private domestic placement agencies. The agencies can operate in a formally legal manner, within the confines of the legislation, and at the same time enforce overtly discriminatory practices that violate the norms of liberal democracy. The compulsory live-in requirement and the enforced temporary residential status of the domestic worker, embedded in the programme, create an unequal relationship of citizen-employer/non-citizen employee at the outset. The employment 'contract' between the foreign worker and the Canadian employer under the LCP (and formerly under the Foreign Domestic Movement (FDM)) reveals the unequal rights of the two parties.

Under the FDM (1981–92), the domestic worker and her employer signed a 'Domestic Worker/Employer Agreement' witnessed by Canada Employment and Immigration. This Agreement stipulated wages, working and living conditions of the employee.[250] Although the Agreement was signed by both the employer and the employee, the employee agreed to 'accept the terms and conditions as outlined', whereas the employer signed a statement that merely 'certifie[d] that the information is accurate'.[251]

As stated in an article in the West Coast Domestic Worker Association (WCDWA) newsletter from 1987, when the FDM was still in operation,

> If an employer refuses to live up to the terms of the employment contract, there is nothing she can do to make her employer change. Employment and Immigration will not investigate a complaint and make the employer behave properly. The contract is not binding on the employer. The Immigration Department pretends that employment contracts are serious documents but only takes action if domestics are at fault.[252]

Though the agreement stated that employers failing to abide by the terms of the contract would be denied further requests for domestic workers, there was no method of enforcement of this provision.[253] The enforceability of the contract/agreement had not, and still has not, been tested in the courts. The WCDWA therefore recommended that domestic workers 'treat the agreement as a contract ... Since the employers themselves do not know whether the agreement is a contract or not, do not tell them it isn't. Instead try to convince them that it is a contract to which they are legally bound.'[254]

In the current programme, the LCP, the legal ambiguity in this regard has remained. However, the information distributed to employers and domestics by Citizenship and Immigration Canada regarding the role of contracts under the LCP alerts employers to the fact that, 'Citizenship and Immigration Canada is not a party to, nor does it bear responsibility for the enforcement of, this contract.'[255] In the guise of a neutral party, the federal government reinforces the unequal power relationship employers wield over domestic employees by giving them implicit permission to violate contractual provisions. It is a fundamental principle of contract law that both parties are bound. Hence these 'contracts' cannot actually be defined as such. Nonetheless, the foreign domestic worker is bound on pain of deportation by the federal department of Citizenship and Immigration Canada.

The non-enforcement of the agreement in investigating complaints against employers is one aspect of the domestic worker policy that highlights the 'employer's almost complete immunity from government regulation, monitoring and enforcement'.[256] There are no sanctions mandated by Citizenship and Immigration against abusive employers, and immigration authorities do not keep statistics on complaints they have received from workers.[257] The *Immigration Manual* does, however, instruct immigration officers to investigate domestic workers dismissed for serious cause – such as child abuse, theft and gross neglect.[258]

The one-sided nature of the employer and foreign worker contractual agreement under existing legislation reinforces the propensity of domestic employees to refrain from reporting breaches of employer obligations, including gross abuse, to immigration authorities or to provincial authorities. This reluctance stems from fear induced by a perpetual threat of deportation through employer-initiated reprisals. Live-in foreign domestic workers in Canada depend upon the goodwill of their employers to enable them to apply for and obtain permanent residence and landed immigrant status. They are also dependent upon the employer's graces simply for a roof over their heads. There is ample evidence to show that employers are ready to take advantage of the state-imposed constraints on their domestic employees to disregard the rights to which foreign domestic workers are legally entitled.

However, even before arriving in the employer's home as a workplace, the gatekeeping mechanisms behind this legislation impose a series of highly racialized and gendered criteria that presume a divide between the citizenship rights of employers and their employees. The role of private domestic service placement agencies, operating as private institutional gatekeepers shaping the conditions of foreign domestic service work in Canada, is pivotal in this process.

Context: the employers and the crisis of childcare

Another element in the background to the particular role played by these agencies and their personnel is the nature of private labour in the home as a unique and distinct employment context. Domestic labour as an abstract category appears to be universal. In advanced western states, the increasing employment of women outside the home, and the growing dependence of family earnings upon two adult incomes, has been expressed in what has been described as an increasing 'crisis in the domestic sphere'.[259] In Canada, the labour force participation rate of Canadian women with children aged zero to six has been above 65 per cent for several years, and is higher than in many other industrialized nations.[260] While women today wait longer to have children and have smaller families than previous generations, the demand for publicly supported and fully funded quality childcare has increased. A number of factors have combined to create this situation. The increase in the number of women with children entering the paid labour force, the trend towards irregular hours of work, the high cost of regulated care and the difficulty in obtaining public childcare, and especially subsidized care, are factors that have combined to create a pressing need for affordable and flexible childcare arrangements.[261] Despite these trends, successive federal governments in Canada have refused to honour a long-standing policy commitment to implement a national childcare programme.[262] Canada lacks a comprehensive and equitable federal childcare policy to ensure reasonable access to regulated childcare. This is despite the fact that there is a growing consensus that quality childcare is an essential feature of a healthy, equitable and productive society. Martha Friendly summarizes:

> Research and policy analysts in diverse fields – economics, health and medicine, education, and human rights – have come to support traditional advocates in feminist, social justice, and trade union circles that action on child care is imperative. There is broad recognition that a strategy for developing early childhood services that offer both early childhood education to strengthen healthy development for all children and child care to support the participation of mothers in the labour force is in the public interest.[263]

By the early 1990s the vast majority of children in public arrangements were cared for in the unregulated sector. Of these, approximately half were cared for by relatives, and the rest by other babysitters and nannies. The latter form of care takes place either in the child's own home, the home of another child or the home of the provider. Thus, while the number of regulated childcare spaces in Canada jumped 600 per cent between 1974 and 1991, from 55 181 to 333 082, there were still 800 000 more children in 1991 who were not in regulated care than there had been 18 years previously.[264] Throughout the 1990s, demand continued to increase faster than the provision of quality accessible childcare spaces. According to Friendly,

> That Canada does not provide adequate early childhood care and education has been well documented and is not in dispute. … Child 'care' services to permit parents' workforce participation are in short supply, meeting only about 12 per cent of the need, and inadequately funded so that they are often too expensive for ordinary parents. Early childcare educators and other caregivers earn poor wages and believe that their work is not valued by the public.[265]

A variety of factors contribute to the decision of parents to seek live-in care for their pre-school children. These include the high fees of regulated care – commonly around $1000 per month for infants in Toronto, Ontario, for example – the difficulty in obtaining subsidized daycare spaces, and the limited access to subsidies of middle-income families. Spaces are limited, however, even for parents paying full fees for day care.[266] An additional factor in determining the option to hire a live-in nanny is the irregular working hours of many working parents. Public childcare is commonly available only to parents who work a five-day week, Monday to Friday, from nine to five. Parents who work in the evenings or weekends, or whose working hours vary from week to week or day to day, find little support in the limited services available through public childcare.

Further, over recent years an ideological argument, characteristic of a general backlash against feminism and women's rights, has tended to discredit public childcare. There is no basis in fact to the claim that public childcare risks the emotional or physical development of healthy children. On the contrary, the most rigorous studies conducted to date have indicated quite the opposite.[267] However, the growth of demand for in-home childcare in advanced western societies is fuelled by the popular purchase of the idea that private in-home childcare is the best quality care.[268] Private domestic placement agencies have both promoted and benefited from the results of the backlash against public childcare and the rise of parental fears. The private domestic placement agency is fundamentally a 'middle-man' between parent-employers and caregivers, or more precisely, a 'middle-woman', since the majority of these businesses are owned and managed by women.

Public childcare, where it is available, is regulated and governed by certain expectations of performance, scheduling, supervision and quality of care. Privately based home childcare is almost entirely unregulated. When childcare takes place in the home of the family, and the family hires the employee, it is normally under the direction of the female head of the household. Though there is little comprehensive information on the employers of foreign domestic workers in Canada, Langevin and Belleau offer a useful general profile:

> Today's typical employers are a couple who are working, 35 years of age on the average, with two children, involved in the business sector, with a gross annual income of at least $100 000. The employers wish to hire a live-in caregiver to look after their household chores and children, so as to enable them to devote themselves to their paid employment.[269]

The assumption that there is a universal character to private domestic labour in the home, that it is 'natural' and 'women's work', serves to limit the expectation of managerial direction, training or definition of job description considered standard for most employment contexts in advanced western societies. A false universalization of domestic labour patterns suggests that certain gendered, class and racial attributes are neutral, or even natural, characteristics, when they are in reality charged with hierarchical and oppressive assumptions.[270] The homes and family environments with which West Indian and Filipino women are familiar are very different from the homes that become their workplaces, in upper-income, usually white, Canadian family homes. The inevitable conflicts of expectations between the employers and the employees are anticipated, interpreted and encapsulated into highly racialized and gendered stereotypes, largely championed by the domestic place-ment agencies. These ideological constructions, enforcing the lived constraints of temporary employees from the Third World seeking citizenship status while living in their citizen-employer's homes, overwhelmingly favour the employer and work to the detriment of the employee. The domestic placement agencies operate within this space, ostensibly neutral, but in reality serving the needs of the employers and attempting to ensure employee accommodation in highly unequal circumstances.

A note about the emphasis on 'the female employer' in this chapter and elsewhere in the book is in order. While the 'employer' might be an adult heterosexual couple, a single-parent male adult, or two male or female adults in a same-sex couple, typically it is mainly or only the female adult who is 'in charge' of the domestic worker or interfacing with a placement agency. This does not mean that live-in domestic workers serve only the interests of women working outside the home, although the labour of the former facilitates that process by relieving women of some of their childcare and housework tasks. The fact that it is commonly the female adult in a heterosexual couple who hires and manages live-in workers is a continuation of the responsibility women have traditionally held for the organization of domestic labour. The employment of domestic workers is a means of alleviating the gendered conflict over division of household labour, and serves the interests of male employers who reap benefits such as cared-for children, prepared meals, ironed shirts, increased leisure or work time and as importantly the ideological assurance that childcare and domestic labour remain 'women's work'.

The placement agencies: 'making the match'

We now turn to consider the ideological and placement activities of agencies that specialize in the recruitment of migrant domestic workers and their placement into private family households. This analysis is based largely on intensive qualitative interviews with ten of the leading and most established domestic placement agencies in Toronto, Ontario.[271] The analysis illuminates the influential role of these gatekeepers in reproducing a highly racialized set of practices and criteria in the recruitment and placement of female migrant domestic workers in upper-income Canadian households, specifically to work as nannies responsible for the care of small children. The method of elaboration relies extensively on direct quotation, analytically contextualized to reveal the central gatekeeping role of the domestic placement industry in regulating citizenship practices and ideologies. While the sample presented here is not statistically representative, the relations that are brought to light are analytically reflective of wider and systemic processes.[272]

Domestic placement agencies serve to 'match' employers' demands for private in-home care from among the available applicants of nannies, domestics and/or housekeepers. As one agency owner put it, 'Making a placement in a client's home is almost like a marriage. It has to fit.'[273] An arranged marriage is a suitable analogy; the oppressive conditions of such marriage also imply the 'need' for a masterful matchmaker. Another agency owner used a different analogy to make the same point, stating that, 'Getting a nanny is like getting a custom-made dress. You don't just take it off the rack.'[274]

One of the critical tasks undertaken by the domestic placement agency is the screening of potential employees to ensure the most appropriate match for the employer. Should the employer feel sufficiently confident and capable of performing such a selection process independently, the need for the agency's services disappears. One role of the agency is therefore to manufacture greater demand, impressing upon potential clients the need for professional screening.[275] Because of the requirement of the FDM/LCP that household workers secure employment prior to migration to Canada, domestic placement agencies also serve to access the Canadian labour market for migrant workers. The gatekeeping role involves not only determining who comes up to the gates, and who passes through, but also under what conditions those who pass may stay on the other side.

One highly reputed agency owner summarized her company's success as follows:

> Our philosophy is 'quality childcare'. The average Canadian child is poorly mannered and poorly brought up. Unless the parents are lucky enough to have had European parents who are more strict. ... And the school system isn't helping here either. They have these routines in Europe, but here it's one big Montessori school. You take a spoiled Canadian child, a stressed-out family, and a Third World woman from a laid-back culture. That's a recipe for trouble.[276]

Another agency owner arrived at the same conclusion about the desirability of European caregivers:

> A lot of families would like a European, with a culture and standard of living similar to their own. They don't want someone who wants to be a nanny all her life. It's a good way for other cultures to learn to speak the language. ... I don't want to sound prejudiced, because I'm not. But Canadians are – well, culturally – more educated, different.[277]

Assessing the quality of childcare in terms of the nationality or 'race' of the childcare giver is a standard feature of the matching process. The racialization is enforced by gendered stereotypes. Because childcare is considered to be 'woman's work' in Canada as well as internationally, the assumption is that it is a skill that requires little formal training. Rather, a 'very special' combination of 'natural' characteristics is usually called for. Racialized stereotypes prevail, both in terms of interpreting the 'needs' of the employers and in shaping the projected characteristics of the prospective employees. The normal procedure is for agencies to be paid by the employer on the completion of a successful placement, usually at the rate of one month's salary, and backed by a three to six month guarantee to replace the domestic if the employer is not fully satisfied. It is therefore not surprising that the agencies tend to indicate that their economic success is based on carefully meeting a highly racially and ethnically sensitive, and stereotyped, client market. A few examples illustrate the allocative role of racial and ethnic stereotypes in the selection process.

> I'm not prejudiced at all, but if a family says they don't want someone who speaks Chinese, I can't place someone in their home who is

Chinese. We are different as domestic placement agencies from other types of employment agencies. We are dealing with the right of families to have someone live-in, and to raise their children.[278]

Another agency owner put it this way:

I cannot say this, I know, because I could be charged for this under the Human Rights Code. But let me give you an example of this business. I have a client, a man, who said that he couldn't stand the hairdo of a girl I sent to him for an interview. He couldn't stand to look at her on a daily basis with that hairdo. He had nothing against Blacks, but it was all in little braids, and he hates that. His wife wanted to hire her. He and his wife had a terrible fight over it. ... The couple called me up because they were arguing. I said, 'I know you want her, but I won't recommend her. Because it's not fair to you, and it's not fair to the girl'. His wife was angry with me for taking his side, but that's how I see it.[279]

The most commercially successful agencies also screen prospective clients. The premise is that the most suitable employers for live-in domestic workers will likely return to them for replacement positions, refer the agency to their friends and be the least likely to complain about the selection they have received. Who is considered a 'good employer' is also determined by preconceived notions of 'good childcare' within the private family. Some statements of agency owners illustrate this point:

I am stunned by what Canadian women are willing to settle for in childcare. They don't check references. They worry that girls may be stealing or whatever, and I say, 'Well aren't you worried about the quality of childcare?' People are more worried about whether their property is being stolen than about how their kids are being cared for. If you are looking for a slave, you are not an ideal employer. A nanny is a human being, and she is looking after your most precious possession, your children. I ask the employers, 'What is going to suffer? Will it be the childcare or the housework?'[280]

And:

We spend a lot of time talking to the families. ... We screen the families as well as the girls. Lots of times we turn down families as placements. The families that appeal to us are usually ones with shared responsibilities. We meet with all the families before we place. ... We do a lot of work with new parents. If we can get them, we have them for several years while the child is young, and they may have more children. Also, they're fresh. We can educate them.[281]

The criteria of selection of suitable employers are often entirely subjectively determined, without even the pretence of a formal procedure. Some agencies screen simply on the basis of an initial telephone inquiry, or even a message left on an answering machine.

The employers do not have a clue about how to supervise a nanny, as you would for example a clerk or a secretary. I can usually tell which clients I should concentrate on. If I am extremely busy, I may not even have the time to phone back and say that I can't help you.[282]

Moreover, the time spent screening potential employers is considerably shorter, and the quality of the perusal more superficial, than that spent selecting employees. The scrutiny of the gatekeepers is therefore not a balanced or neutral process, despite the claim advertised to the contrary throughout the industry. The imperative of the agencies is to find a placement suitable to a preconceived, ideologically constructed ideal 'Canadian' family, from among a pool of applicants, similarly preconceived and treated with suspicion as unlikely candidates. To the extent that clients are screened by the agencies, the emphasis is on the approach and attitudes regarding childcare and 'family values'. Attention is also paid to economic issues, such as the capacity to pay the minimum expected wages and the provision of a private room required in the Canadian legislation.

Not only are the parties subject to differential scrutiny by the placement agencies; they are also entitled to differential rights of scrutiny of their prospective matches. Here, again the analogy with an arranged marriage, specifically 'mail order brides',[283] is relevant. In both types of arranged 'match', the scrutiny offered to the resident citizen is at a premium, whereas the non-citizen female applicant, is entitled to no such selection procedure regarding her future. The opportunity to scrutinize the application of the prospective live-in domestic, like the prospective 'bride', is virtually unlimited; in contrast, the opportunity of the applicant to obtain information regarding a future employer or 'husband' is basically non-existent.

Unlike an actual arranged marriage, however, the live-in domestic is usually expected to work as a professional caregiver for young children. A host of contradictory pressures combine in the matching process that relate to the genuine need for trained professional childcare on the one hand, and the low status of live-in care on the other. The work involves long hours, low remuneration, little job control or employee protection.

Agencies respond in two diametrically opposed ways to the predominance of Third World migrant women among foreign domestic workers. The first is that paid domestic work is not suitable for 'Canadian' women.

> If there is a Canadian applicant for a domestic job, then you are doing something wrong. Canadian applicants are non-existent. Maybe one in five months will be a Canadian, usually a mature woman.[284]

This perspective also presumes that non-Canadians, specifically migrant women of colour, are inherently suitable to perform domestic service. A second and contrasting response from the domestic placement agencies views the current predominance of migrant, and especially Third World, women in live-in care as unacceptable. These agencies perceive a need to improve the status and reputation of in-home care so that nannying will become a credible and respected profession for Canadian women.

> I feel we have to increase the status of nannying in Canada. You don't just need a physical body in the house if you need a nanny. A child orientation has to be a major concern.[285]

The racialized criteria therefore apply not only to the screening process of prospective in-home caregivers, but also to an ascriptive set of criteria regarding 'Canadian' family needs. The assumption of universality of a white middle-class, English-speaking nuclear family precludes, for example, the large percentage of families in North America for whom English is not a first language, and whose children may not normally speak English at home, as well as immigrant families of Third World origin, who predominate in current immigration to Canada. The overtly racialized discourse and practices, however, enter more directly in the recruitment and screening process assigned to the applicants. This brings us to a consideration of the construction of stereotypes, which is central to the matchmaking process.

Gatekeepers to citizenship serve to regulate the entry into and exit from nation-states and labour markets, as well as access to citizenship rights. All gatekeepers accomplish this work in part through the construction, articulation and reproduction of stereotypes about who is, or is not, an appropriate candidate for citizenship within a given nation-state.

Such stereotypes are most often inscribed with discourses and somatic images that simultaneously assume certain types of racial, ethnic, gender, class and sexual appropriateness. As defined by Barbara Bush, 'A stereotype is a composite picture of an individual which, while reflecting an element of reality, distorts it. ... It is flexible and [yet] can exhibit a massive durability, even in the face of historical change.'[286]

Racial stereotyping is endemic to the matching process that defines the parameters of the domestic placement industry. Successful domestic placement agencies pride themselves in their ability to render a perfect 'match' between client and applicant. In practice, this frequently means the ability to stereotype 'appropriately'. This is not, however, only a recent characteristic of in-home care, nor is racial stereotyping unique to this particular form of gatekeeper. From the early 1900s to the 1960s, white European domestics were favoured in Canadian policy, and were provided with less restrictive conditions for permanently residing in the country. These young women, primarily from England and Scotland, were recruited with an eye to a racially identified 'nation-building' project. The anticipation was that these women of 'good stock' would become the wives of white Canadian men and the future mothers of white Canadian children.[287]

In the early part of this period, the racially specific gender ideologies associated with the recruitment of white female domestic labour were supported by the historically dominant role of British imperialism in the western world. Similar domestic norms were characteristic in other parts of the empire. The availability of white European women for this type of work declined, however, as industrial expansion opened up other options for them. Moreover, as colonial policies dislocated millions of non-white women from agricultural subsistence production, another source of servant labour was brought in to replace European women. Male workers in the colonies were no less forced into poverty and unemployment, but with few exceptions (such as Japanese male domestics on the US west coast), domestic labour remained the domain of women workers.[288]

British imperialism was not, however, the only global force behind the racialized and gendered processes of allocation into domestic work. Other colonial powers have continually reproduced ideological models to support the exploitation of colonized women as paid domestic servants. For example, Belgian colonial policy in Africa after the Second World War included the opening of *foyers sociaux*, training centres to teach African women the proper gender norms of the European nuclear family.[289] Throughout colonial Africa, British, Dutch and French imperial policy included homecraft classes for women and young girls. In Latin America, Asia and the Caribbean, the legacy of centuries of imperialism has led to the unremitting creation of unemployed female workers who are recruited to perform domestic duties for the families of colonial settlers or the families of the indigenous urban elites.[290]

The African slave trade, and the expansion of plantation societies in the Caribbean and the southern United States, were similarly central to this global process and were pivotal linkages between racism and the exploitation of female domestic labour. Black women, as slaves and servants, were commoditized as both the labourers and sexual objects of their white masters. Out of these conditions flourished the image of 'Aunt Jemima', the Black 'mammy' who was expected to care for the children of white 'ladies' in the slave conditions of plantation America.[291] Slavery in the colonies coincided with slavery and domestic service in Britain. During the rule of Queen Anne, one advertisement is indicative of the conditions faced in the slave ports of Bristol. It offered a reward of a guinea for the return of 'a Negro Maid, aged about 16 Years, much pitted with the Small Pox, speaks English well, having a piece of her left Ear bit off by a Dog; She hath on a strip'd Stuff waistcoat and Petticoat.'[292]

This debased image of the Black domestic slave contrasts sharply with that of 'Mary Poppins' – the firm but loving white governess for white upper-class children. Even during *fin de siecle* Britain, however, Mary Poppins was a caricature of only one segment of British nannies. College nanny training in Britain began in 1892 with the opening of the private Norland Institute at Notting Hill in London. The purpose of the Institute was 'to supply the public with ladies as nurses for young children'. The Norland Nursery Training College, now near Hungerford, is today only one of a small number of private colleges among some 200 mostly public college programmes that offer the National Nursery Examination Board (NNEB) certificate in Britain.[293] Of the approximately 10 200 post-secondary students enrolled in the programme, the majority are 'upper working class or lower middle class', and are unable to pay the high fees required by the private institutions. A considerable portion of NNEB students are also of racial and ethnic minorities.[294] All of these students must follow the same basic curriculum of work and satisfy the same conditions to earn an NNEB diploma.[295]

In the nineteenth and twentieth centuries, various racialized and gendered images of domestic workers and caregivers resulted from efforts to supply white, affluent families with domestics out of conditions of slavery, colonialism and an increasingly international market. One purpose of the ideological stereotyping has been to portray a fictive universality of the non-white, female 'other' whose biological and 'natural' make up ascribes her to be inherently appropriate for private domestic service.

In Canada, the LCP and its antecedent, the FDM, link the tasks of the domestic placement agency with both external and internal stereotypical images. That is, the foreign domestic worker both in her home country and within Canada is subject to a specific series of ascriptive characteristics within a totalizing stereotype. Since the mid-1970s the largest single source region for live-in care in Canada through the LCP/FDM has been the Philippines. Among Third World source countries there has been a precipitous drop in the number of new entrants from the Caribbean and an inverse increase in those from the Philippines.

The reasons for the shift are difficult to determine, but it is clear that unemployment, poverty and pressure to emigrate abroad from the Caribbean source countries have not declined. There is evidence to suggest that the shift was not entirely accidental, and that gatekeepers in Canada played a significant role in nudging along this shift. A memorandum from Ranjit S. Hall, the 1974 Chief of Immigrant and Migrant Services, addresses the processing of temporary employment visas for domestics destined to arrive in Canada from Jamaica. It describes a situation whereby counsellors from Canada Manpower government employment centres were refraining 'from forwarding orders to Jamaica' and 'this has caused a build up there'.[296] Moreover, the shift in primary Third World source countries from the Caribbean to the Philippines coincided with a decline in the role of government counsellors in arranging the 'match' with prospective employers in Canada, and the emergent and stepped-up intervention of private employment agencies in recruitment and selection.[297]

Interviews with owners of placement agencies in Toronto, the major host city in Canada for foreign domestics, reveal a definite pattern of racial and ethnic stereotyping of domestic workers. Such stereotyping delineates sharply between domestics of Caribbean and Filipino origin. Regarding the image of the former, the passive and loving 'mammy' has been replaced by an apparently widely accepted image that is variously aggressive, incompetent and cunningly criminal. Shifts such as these are difficult to measure. But the favour towards West Indian nannies seemed to have slipped in inverse proportion to a rise in militancy and organized resistance among live-in domestics to abusive conditions in Canadian employment and immigration practices. This militancy arose at a time when Caribbean women predominated among Third World foreign domestic workers in Canada.

Symptomatic of this trend was the establishment in 1979 of one of the first and most effective domestic workers' advocacy organizations in

Canada, INTERCEDE, based in Toronto. This organization was ultimately successful in winning the right to earn overtime pay, or time off in lieu of overtime pay, and also participated in a high profile campaign to reverse the deportation of 'The Seven Jamaican Mothers'.[298] Militant organizing for domestic workers' rights was not consistent with the historic 'mammy' stereotype. Domestic placement agencies are not necessarily aware of this history. However, as mediators of federal immigration policy at the level of the private Canadian home, they play a central role in transmitting and reproducing stereotyped images that accord, in distorted form, with such a history. Here is how one agency owner put the case:

> I'm at the point now, where if I hear it's an island girl on my answering machine, I won't even interview. If you're from Jamaica, I won't interview you. I know this is discrimination, but I don't have time for this. Often at the end of a day, out of 20 messages on my answering machine, I'd say 18 are from the islands. I don't want them. ... Jamaican girls are just dumb. They are not qualified to be childcare workers. It's not their fault; they just don't have the education. They can take two hours to fill out a nanny application form. I'd love to get called up by Human Rights. If I were called in, I'd say to them: 'Do you have children? Do you care about them? Would you leave your child with someone who was incapable of dialing 911?'[299]

As 'middle-women', the agencies also reflect the stereotyped images held by their clients. If an employer has had what she perceives to be a bad experience with a live-in foreign domestic, a common tendency is to avoid repeating the problem by avoiding the racial or ethnic population of which the employee was a member. Because childcare and housework are expected to be natural and not learned or taught, drawing upon an alternative gene pool, rather than providing different instructions or seeking a different combination of acquired credentials, is seen as the best remedial approach. Moreover, racist stereotyping from the employers determines the employment position which the placement agent is hired to fill. As stated bluntly by one agency owner:

> The employers are very prejudiced against the West Indian girls.[300]

According to another agency owner:

> It is much harder to place a West Indian than a Filipino. We say to our clients that you can't stereotype, that there are good and bad candidates

in every race. We tell our employers, 'Leave it up to us. Let us present you with the best candidate for the job'. But we have a hard time placing West Indians in jobs. I know that that is discrimination, but they are looking for people to do jobs and to live as tenants. Sometimes the husband is really racist. Or the employers will say that their children are afraid of someone who is of a different colour.[301]

Because the law regulating the recruitment of foreign domestics requires an offer of employment before entering the country, this pattern of discrimination becomes supported by restricted access to the Canadian labour market. This means that more prospective domestic workers from the Caribbean are being forced to enter Canada on visitors' permits, refugee papers or as illegal immigrants, creating a vicious cycle in the stereotyped image. Unless a work permit is granted, placing domestics with these immigration statuses is illegal, and the employee, employer and the placement agent could all be charged under current Canadian immigration law with having committed criminal offences. The myth of the 'Jamaican criminal' has been cultivated in a series of major news stories and sensationalized crimes in the Canadian press, which reinforce the image of the illegal domestic trying to 'scam' a job.[302]

There are not too many West Indian nannies these days. A lot of girls from St. Lucia, Barbados, and so forth, a lot of them are illegal. Chances are if she's from there, she's illegal, on a visitor's permit and not allowed to work. I can't deal with her then.[303]

The negative stereotyping of West Indian 'island girls' has not, however, generated a more realistic image of foreign domestic workers from the other major Third World source region, the Philippines. Agency owners tend to present a composite stereotype of passive and active traits among 'your Filipinos'.[304] This image is notable for the contradictory manner in which passivity with the children is seen as a negative attribute, but a proactive relationship with the employer is not seen as a positive one. One agent's perspective in this connection is worth quoting at some length:

Most of my placements are from the Philippines, more than 50 per cent, by far the highest percentage. Filipino nannies are very soft, they don't stimulate the children. They cannot control the children, it doesn't come naturally to them. Socially, the Filipino nanny comes from a culture where they are extremely respectful of elders, of authority, and they are trained not to offer their views too aggressively. ... Filipino nannies were always more giving, very professional in a sense. But now the shine is coming off the Filipino nanny. ... I know this, because some clients have told me this. It doesn't apply to all the Filipinos. Generally, Filipinos are good with housework, but not always. You could always get a dud.[305] *? A dud >!*

As Filipino domestics increasingly look to collective strategies to challenge exploitative conditions, domestic placement agencies are similarly altering their formerly positive perspectives.

A group that you can say come to work here just to get landed are the Filipinos. For them, what they are after is money, money, money. With other groups, some stay and some don't. ... There is a surplus of Filipinos here who are being sponsored by legitimate offers. There is a surplus of bodies in this country.[306]

In response to a question regarding the relative number of Filipino domestics her business places, another agency responded, 'Too many ... But the Filipinos are smarter than the island girls.'[307]

Regardless of the personal views of the domestic placement agency owners, as small business managers operating in a highly competitive market, the structural pressures to accommodate racially and sexually oppressive ideologies are compelling. When the private household is transformed into a waged workplace, a class division takes place inside its walls. If the transaction is legal, the home literally becomes registered with the government as a small business, and the interests of the employee and the employer are delineated along class differentiated lines.

Despite the mediating and matching role of the private domestic placement agent, the agency's interests in the match are not those of a neutral arbiter. Rather, the profound structural pressures point to an identification with the employer over the interests of the employed domestic worker. The class interests of the agency as a small business supported by a clientele of employing families tend to mould and alter any countervailing forces that compel identification with the domestic employee.

Even though placement agents are commonly of the same gender as the domestic workers they place, and occasionally of the same race, the class dynamic separating their interests has a more profound and determining impact. Agency owners are also commonly of the same gender as the women employers who generally manage the working environment of the hired domestics, and more often than not are likely to be white and professional. Many placement agency owners are sympathetic to some notion of feminism, broadly defined as a commitment to the advancement of women's rights and opportunities. They define their work in terms of enabling working women with professional careers to advance unhindered by the burden of housework and childcare.

The options for the future that may be available for white professional women enjoying full citizenship rights in a developed capitalist state, however, are not the same as the options available to poor and unemployed migrant women of colour whose citizenship rights are severely limited and restricted. Moreover, the employment of the latter as a domestic servant can and does operate as a privatized means to advance the social citizenship rights of her employer. An identification with 'women's rights' in an abstract sense does not necessarily entail a challenge to the traditional sexual division of labour, with women responsible for the performance of domestic duties and private childcare in the home. In fact, in the example of the domestic placement industry, there is a decided ideological enforcement of that division of labour.

Regardless of the personal preferences of the agency owners, the market in which the industry operates is dependent upon the privatization of household work. Not all domestic care workers are women. As more domestic workers have become employed in elder care, the proportion of male domestic workers has risen to approximately 15 per cent of the total according to official government figures.[308] Many of these men are trained nurses from countries such as the Philippines. This is a significant increase over the course of the last decade, from a period when only approximately 2 per cent were male.[309] However, for live-in care in general, and especially for live-in childcare, there is a definite market bias towards the placement of women in these jobs. This is not the result of a lack of male applicants to these positions. The same conditions of poverty and unemployment that drive Third World women to leave everything behind and accept the most undesirable working conditions and wages available in North America also compel Third World men to seek the same means of escaping extreme poverty. Agencies indicate, however, that the job market in private childcare is not considered suitable for men. This affects the screening process of applicants from the outset. One agency put bluntly a case that is widely echoed, 'I don't interview males, though I get a lot of calls. I can't place males.'[310]

There are two explanations offered for the inability to place males in in-home childcare positions. The first is that North American families are particularly nervous about the threat of male nanny abuse of children. One placement agent offered a second explanation: that women were simply naturally better suited than men for childcare work. This view reflects and perpetuates the broader gender stereotyping in the business itself.

> I've placed two men since I've been in the business, one from Ireland, the other from Hong Kong. The Hong Kong boy was good, but one of the children, a baby he was looking after, got very ill, a brain tumor at six months. He couldn't cope with it. It's hard for the men if there's a sickness in the family. For women, females, normally their maternal instincts will kick in. Those instincts will get them through that. Men don't have these.[311]

The sexist stereotyping of domestic labour extends beyond the specific task of childcare, however. Because the placement agents depend upon 'selling their product' to the employer, they present a class-specific view of freeing women from the burden of domestic responsibilities. One agent developed the image of what making a successful placement could mean for the prospective woman client in detail:

> You have something more than money, you have your peace of mind. You have a wife at home. I have many, many employers who say to me, 'what I need is a wife'. Imagine coming home at the end of a workday, and all the stress is off. The kids are happy, the laundry is washed and folded, you can smell the chicken cooking in the oven. The girls don't want to stick around with you and your husband at the end of their work day, so you have all the time alone you want. They stay for half an hour, or an hour, and they communicate about the kids, and then they leave to their room and you are home with your kids. It gives you peace of mind and it gives you your equilibrium. There is no such thing as a superwoman.[312]

Because the industry is largely comprised of small businesses that require minimal capital investment or overhead, it is not uncommon for domestic placement agencies to have been started by former or current employers of in-home caregivers. The class identification between the agency and the employer, as professional working women who hire domestics, therefore has an instrumental component. One agent prided herself in helping to improve the reputation of the industry by helping former clients to establish their own agencies. Another agent decided to start a business of her own after having been 'caught in a scam with an unscrupulous agency'.

> I knew what I wanted. I said, 'I want a wife'. I was often away on business. And I thought, I can do this, and I can do it clean, I can do it right. So I started the agency. I don't have any nannies any more, because I don't want to deal with the garbage. And I was actually a terrible employer.[313]

Just as being of the same gender as the vast majority of in-home domestic workers does not mitigate against the gender bias of the placement agency industry, neither does it appear that ethnic and racial identification among women of colour agency owners with domestic workers offsets the tendency towards racial stereotyping. While it is difficult to know what percentage of placement agency owners in Canada are people of colour, among the high-profile public representatives of the business, the number is very small. However, maintaining a successful business that caters to employers tends to compel a racially biased business orientation, regardless of the colour of the agency owner. The low status of paid domestic work, and the structural inequities and systemic racism that drive immigrant and visible minority women to accept such work, colour codes, as it were, the market of the industry. One agency owner who was herself an immigrant indicated some identification with the experiences of foreign domestics.

> I understand what it's like living in one room with your whole family. It takes a lot of time to get established.[314]

Nonetheless, the general perception of this same agency owner was that those foreign nannies who seek good quality working and living conditions, or wages above the legal minimum, hold unrealistic expectations.

> I advise my nannies that they can get a good job these days, but they may have to compromise on the salary or the location. For example, they may have to take a job in the suburbs for minimum wage … For some of these girls, I think their expectations are much too high. The girls milk the system here for all it's worth. They are employed in nice homes, sometimes families that are very well to do. The girls want to have a really nice place to live in.[315]

Another agency owner whose business only places Filipino domestics, and who is of Filipino origin, was indistinguishable from other agencies in the racialized attitude displayed towards her applicants.

> We don't like to bring them directly from the Philippines. If they come directly here, you have to, well, baby-sit them. Even though they are the same merchandise, so to speak, they haven't blended yet. It's better if they have worked in Europe or Hong Kong or Singapore.[316]

Though the placements of this business are all Filipino, the clients are overwhelmingly white Canadians. The agency has developed a loyal clientele by providing Filipino domestics for white families who request them.

> We ask our clients, what is their preference. There is no point in giving a Filipino unless they want one. We get no requests for West Indians. My clients will say, 'Please, don't send me someone from the islands. Please give me a Filipino'. And I say, 'We have thick accents, you know'. Although they may be comfortable in English, I don't think the English training in the Philippines is enough.[317]

The class perspective of the agency owners is also reflected in their apparent widespread suspicion of domestic workers' advocacy organizations. In Toronto, INTERCEDE has aroused considerable concern among domestic placement agencies.

> INTERCEDE is basically like a union, and they want to protect domestic workers' rights ... What they want to do is fine, but they don't do it the right way ... They'll tell you all kinds of horror stories, and you don't get the other side of the story. There have been employers' agencies and employers who want to help, but they'll shun them. INTERCEDE is mostly Filipino girls. But it's just the radicals who are behind it. They have workshops that are completely negative. They'll do chants and things they make up. It's really just like a union.[318]

Another agency shared this view, as follows:

> INTERCEDE is almost like a union. It's very militant, and is giving the Filipino nannies a bad name. ... INTERCEDE will tell them: 'Don't work for one minute after 6:00 PM. If you work one minute more you are being abused'.[319]

Conclusion

Racial and gendered ideological stereotypes are necessary criteria to the effective gatekeeping process in implementing Canada's foreign domestic worker policy. The state and the private domestic placement agencies work in a parallel process of enforcing the scrutiny, restriction, selection and regulation of foreign domestic workers to ensure the maintenance of the citizenship divide. Moreover, there is an historic, and recurrent, hegemonic ideology that reinforces these processes through the production of specifically racialized, gendered stereotypes. Insofar as foreign domestic workers embody the cross-border dynamics of a globalized economy, they throw a searchlight on this divide that exists between certain populations of the North and the South.

The LCP and past domestic worker immigration policies in Canada play upon and reproduce this global disparity. At the same time, the programmes offer a means for individual Third World migrant women to scale the border's gates, on certain conditions and under considerable risk, in order to attain some of the rights associated with First World citizenship. The gatekeeping structures, processes and ideologies have served to affirm a hegemonic belief in the uncontested control of Canada's borders by the state, assisted and supported through various agencies in civil society. The discretionary power vested in the officers associated with the Canadian government and the attendant discriminatory uses of that power, offer potent means for maintaining the 'integrity' of Canadian citizenship, and limiting access only to those deemed to be 'deserving' citizen-recipients of a diminished pool of social rights.

5
Marginalized and Dissident Non-Citizens: Foreign Domestic Workers[320]

The systemic reproduction of migrant domestics as non-citizens within the countries where they work and reside renders them in a meaningful sense stateless, as far as access to state protection of their rights is concerned. This is despite the formal retention of legal citizenship status accorded by their home country, and, often, the legal entry as non-citizen migrant workers in the host country. In previous chapters, we have identified how the construction of non-citizenship is central to maintaining the vulnerability of foreign domestic workers in Canada. In this chapter, we consider the lived experiences of domestic workers themselves, based largely on a survey of foreign domestic workers living in Toronto. This chapter offers a comparative analysis of the experiences of two groups of women of colour, those of West Indian and Filipino origin, working in the homes of upper-middle- and upper-class Canadian families resident in Toronto, Ontario in the mid-1990s.

The limited literature on foreign domestic workers in Canada indicates patterns of structural discrimination, ranging from overt physical abuse, to denial of privacy rights, to denial of fair wages and adequate benefits. Our study attempts to identify both common and differential patterns of discrimination among foreign domestic workers originating from the two main regions of the English speaking Caribbean and the Philippines.

Our findings suggest that there are notable differences between West Indian and Filipino domestic workers in terms of immigration status, with a higher concentration of illegal migrants among the former than the latter. The recent pattern of discrimination against the legal entry to Canada of West Indian domestic workers, indicated in the previous chapter, is expressed in this finding. Illegal immigration status among a notable portion of West Indian domestic workers interviewed was indicated in the survey not only in response to directed questions, but also in terms of the impact of such status on working conditions and access to benefits that would otherwise accrue to workers who have legal means of access. Our survey findings suggest further, that upon securing live-in, domestic work with a Canadian family in Toronto, Ontario, there are great discrepancies between employment situations regarding wages, general working conditions, and parameters of employee bargaining rights. However, while certain discrepancies based on immigration status were clear, the findings suggest that other aspects of domestic work bear greater commonality based on similar workplace conditions and systemic structures that favour Canadian citizen employers over their non-citizen employees. The variability of conditions that was discernible in the survey results is reflective of the absence of standards of employment and mechanisms to enforce the labour rights of foreign domestic workers upon their arrival in Canada. The capricious control of private employers explains many aspects of the work experiences of foreign domestic workers, rather than the place of origin of the domestic workers. The commonalities in the overall experiences of these two groups of domestic workers from the West Indies and the Philippines are greater than the differences: both groups are seriously underpaid, overworked and treated with minimal trust or respect for privacy by their employers.

In sum, we were able to identify two main lines of demarcation revealed in the study. The first is determined by the gatekeeping mechanisms discussed in the previous chapter. The changes in immigration policy since the 1980s have tended to disfavour West Indian domestic workers and promote a patronizing racialized favour towards Filipinas that has directly impacted on the workplace experiences of these two groups of workers. However, the more profound line of demarcation appears to be not between the conditions and experiences of West Indian versus Filipino domestic workers, but between the employers on one side, and West Indian and Filipino workers collectively on the other. Racialized relations of exploitation within the private home are expressed in a hierarchy of class and citizenship, reinforced by the gatekeeping structures which overwhelmingly favour citizen/employers over non-citizen/employees. Even in a province such as Ontario, where certain legal rights have been won by domestic workers, the lack of enforcement mechanisms ensures relations of continued discrimination. The exercise of legal rights for domestic workers is dependent upon the registration of a formal complaint; such complaints, raised individually, are assessed by the domestic worker as a calculated risk. Any given complaint may lead to an improvement in the working conditions of the live-in, temporary status, female foreign domestic worker, but it alternatively may lead to a decline in conditions, as in the event of the complaint resulting in the dismissal and loss of job and domicile for the worker. Moreover, the restrictions associated with the FDM and the LCP, federal immigration policies, are not mitigated by labour legislation that resides in the jurisdiction of the provincial state.

Our findings suggest that various negotiating strategies among immigrant women seeking employment in Canada lead them to adopt various paths that culminate in live-in employment in private domestic service. Upon taking up residence and work in the homes of wealthy Canadian citizen employers, common structural conditions that promote systemic exploitation and racialization come into play. Here class exploitation is amplified by racial discrimination, and both of these hierarchical relationships are enforced by systemic patterns across the citizenship/ non-citizenship divide.

A note on the survey methodology is in order. The data is drawn from 50 questionnaires, 25 from interviews conducted with live-in domestics from the West Indies, and 25 from those originating from the Philippines.[321] Country of origin was determined by birthplace. The interviews were conducted by female research assistants of the same regional or national origins as the interviewees. They were conducted face-to-face, or in the rare cases when respondents were unable to meet, by telephone. In all cases, individual interviews were about 90 minutes long, and followed a questionnaire guideline. The sample was selected through a snowball approach of community contacts. No more than three names were suggested from each interviewee, among whom no more than one name was subsequently interviewed. Interviewees were asked to respond to all questions, though it was not uncommon for some questions to be declined a response.[322]

Because the study is numerically small, it is of qualitative rather than quantitative significance. However, as the previous chapters indicate, the Caribbean and the Philippines are not arbitrary reference points in terms of the general experience of Third World migration.[323] Data of this nature is based on generalizing collective patterns of work and living experiences and upon the assumption of social patterns of negotiation. While the size of the sample is small in regard to statistical trends, it is substantially larger than an approach based on individual life histories. The study effectively highlights the working and living conditions of women workers treated as temporary visitors who are compelled to live with their employers and who perform duties of private domestic service. Though they provide labour in serious demand, employers and the Canadian state designate them as menial servants. These findings are explored in more detail below, according to a series of specific topics, notably: immigration status; the live-in requirement and accommodation; working conditions, wages and benefits; and remittances and family support.

Immigration status

Faced with the threat of deportation for non-fulfillment of duties, domestic workers who live with their employers work long hours for low pay in very isolated and highly regulated conditions. Regarding their immigration experience and status, however, there was a divergence of experience between the two groups of women interviewed in this study. Among the West Indian women, 20 out of 25 responded to a question about place of work immediately prior to working as a domestic in Canada (Q7).[324] Of these, all but two (who had worked in Europe) had worked in the West Indies immediately before coming to Canada. Among the Filipinas, 23 responded to this question; only 11 of these came directly from the Philippines. Others had worked in the Middle East, Asia and Europe, immediately prior to coming to Canada to work.

This finding reflects divergent patterns of migration for the two groups of women, and distinct strategies for negotiating the global restrictions they face. The migration of West Indian domestics to Canada reflects historical and imperial country/region to country ties. In contrast, Philippine migration indicates the aggressive marketing of labour for export on the part of various Philippine governments. The latter process has had the unintentional effect of rendering unskilled or deskilled Filipino women experienced international migrants.[325]

We have demonstrated that negotiating citizenship involves navigating the selection processes of various gatekeepers. There is a preference among domestic placement agencies in Canada to recruit Filipinas from outside Manila; moreover, the experience requirement of the LCP in Canada has tended to favour those who had previously served as household workers in other countries. This trend is reflected in the survey findings, especially notable given the small size of the sample. In contrast, West Indian women in search of domestic service as a means of emigrating are no longer readily welcomed in Canada. Among the West Indian domestics in our study, ten entered Canada as domestic workers on either the FDM or the LCP, and therefore were legally admitted as foreign live-in domestic workers; 14 entered Canada as visitors, and one claimed asylum as a refugee (Q15). It is illegal to work in Canada while on a visitor visa, and refugee status is almost never granted to those who claim the need for asylum from the West Indies. Refugee claimants can only work with a separately issued work permit. Therefore, the majority of the West Indian respondents entered domestic service in Canada as undocumented migrant workers. Among the Filipinas, 23 had entered Canada on the FDM or LCP programme as foreign domestic workers, while only two entered as visitors.

The divergent patterns of entry into Canada and the subsequent differences in migration status for the two groups indicate the relatively more restrictive access for West Indian women compared with Filipinas. The relatively high proportion of undocumented workers among West Indian women reflects the effectiveness of gatekeepers in Canada in limiting the legal access of these applicants. However, evidence suggests that neither the numbers seeking work as domestics in Canada, nor the demand for live-in domestic service, have declined. Such racialized bias compels more and more West Indian women to enter the country as visitors and work without any formal status in the country. This pattern of increasing numbers in undocumented personal service is widespread in other countries such as the United States and Italy.[326] Despite a general trend towards increasing restrictions regarding the numbers of domestic workers admitted on the LCP, Filipino applicants are currently considered in a racist stereotype to be 'good servants', and therefore some continue to find it possible to pass through Canada's closely guarded gates. This legal passage is conditional, however, on their willingness to work as maids and nannies, to arrive on temporary visas and to live with their employers.

In response to another question regarding current immigration status within Canada, the picture changed somewhat (Q16). Among both groups of women workers, several had obtained landed, or permanent resident status, yet continued to work as live-in domestic workers. Among the West Indian domestic workers, 16 had temporary or unidentified status within Canada at the time of the interview, whereas nine had obtained landed immigrant status or actual legal citizenship. Among the Filipino domestic workers, 19 were legal temporary workers, whereas six had obtained landed immigrant status.

The notable feature here is that historically it has been unusual for any worker to accept live-in domestic service in Canada unless they are temporary workers. The implication is that the economy in Canada today is so restrictive for 'unskilled' immigrant workers of colour, that even those who are legally eligible to leave live-in domestic service are faced with few or no other options. At least some West Indian workers, and the more recently arrived Filipino workers, continued to work at least partially as live-in domestic servants despite having obtained landed immigrant or citizenship status. This is an unusual phenomenon within the postwar Canadian workforce, and one that has not been formally recognized by the Canadian government.

Regarding immigration status, then, our findings reveal two patterns. First, there are apparently more illegal or undocumented domestic workers among the West Indian sample. Second, the findings suggest that both West Indian women and Filipinas who have the right to work legally in occupations other than domestic service are compelled to remain working as domestics. This second pattern runs counter to the thesis of 'ethnic succession' whereby only the most recent of immigrant groups are to be found in the most exploited ('dirty, dangerous and difficult') jobs.

Live-in requirement and accommodation

These findings have implications for the live-in requirement of the LCP. The LCP obliges foreign domestics to work and live in their employers' home for two years within a three-year period if they are to be eligible to apply for permanent residence in Canada. Domestic workers will commonly share an apartment for weekend use in order to obtain some privacy and time away from what are often 24 hour on-call obligations. Such arrangements are not incorporated into the LCP, and employers and immigration authorities can challenge caregivers for doing so without their permission.[327]

Those who are illegal, however, and have no hopes of obtaining permanent legal status, would feel no obligation to live in their employers' homes to meet the FDM/LCP regulation. Yet workers with undocumented status are also at greater risk of deportation as they have no legal claim to residence within Canada. Therefore, there is likely more, rather than less, obligation among undocumented workers to live in the employers' home if this is established as a condition of employment. Those who are landed immigrants or citizens, however, would be released from the live-in requirement and would normally seek alternative employment other than domestic service.

Domestic workers interviewed for this study were all 'officially' live-in domestic workers; this was a precondition of qualification in the study. However, the respondents indicated that the 'live-in' feature for domestic service occupational status did not necessarily mean living with one's employer all week long; and in some cases, officially designated 'live-in' workers, actually lived out. In such a case this likely meant that they not only had a residence in the employer's home, but also maintained their own private or shared residence. Among the West Indian domestics, of the 24 who responded to this question, only four lived with their employer during the entire seven-day week (Q28). Thirteen lived with their employer during the five- or six-day working week only; five lived-out; and two had 'other' living arrangements that were not specified. Among the Filipinas, of the 24 who responded, only six lived with their employer all week. Sixteen lived with their employer during the working week only; and two lived out.

Regarding the live-in requirement of the FDM/LCP, the survey findings suggest that both employers and domestics are inclined to bend the full time live-in rule. This represents an important finding in the collective negotiating strategies of foreign domestic workers. The live-in requirement has been identified as one of the most oppressive features of the regulated policy in Canada.[328] Research internationally and over historical time has found that the single most important element in domestic workers' ability to negotiate or bargain for improvements in conditions of domestic service is the ability to live out, away from the dictates of the employing family.[329] Among both the Caribbean and Filipino domestic workers, the attraction to obtaining private, part-time residence away from the employer is clear. In addition to the restrictions and limitations associated with living with one's employer, who is also responsible for managing access to residence and work in Canada, the live-in requirement assumes that the employee has no family or personal life of her own. In spite of the potential risk of dire consequences, including termination and deportation, the rate of success in obtaining some degree of live-out arrangement apparent in our findings represents a significant accomplishment in negotiating citizenship rights for this non-citizen population. It may, however, also intersect with the desire on the part of the employer to not want the domestic worker in the home in all instances and to negotiate some 'family time' or 'personal time' away from the domestic employee.

The quality of accommodation reported by the domestic workers from both groups suggests another reason why attempting to live-out for at least part of the week is attractive. Among the West Indian domestics, 11 of 25 who responded reported that their room in their employers' house was in the basement (Q29); only seven of 25 had their own telephone (Q30D); ten of 24 who responded had no lock on their door (Q30E). Among the Filipino domestics, 16 of 24 who responded had a basement room; 16 of 23 had their own telephone; and fully 18 of 25 had no lock on their door.

While the quality of accommodation varies markedly, the living space for the majority of live-in domestics in Canadian middle-class homes is not designed to provide privacy and separation for live-in workers from employer's families. The resulting lack of privacy and constant employer (and employing family members') surveillance – whether by design or by default – inhibits domestic workers from having any private life of their own. The potential restrictions include barring intimate friendships and familial and sexual relationships, creating conditions that are in direct contradiction with the ideals of autonomous adulthood, so-called 'family values' and personal freedom in Canadian society. When asked what changes they would like to see in the LCP (Q36F), 18 of 25 West Indian domestics, and 16 of 23 Filipinas who responded said they favoured changes in the live-in requirement. The commonality of this response among both groups of workers in the interview sample is notable. Upon entering the country and experiencing the pressures of living with one's employer, both groups of foreign domestic workers in Canada encounter a commonly oppressive set of circumstances.

The live-in requirement has been identified in Canadian government policy circles as an essential feature of the foreign domestic worker programme. According to government explanations, the LCP exists due to a chronic shortage of labour from within the Canadian citizen employment market who are willing to provide live-in domestic service.[330] The LCP was enacted in 1992, following the earlier FDM policy of 1981, to address the purported need to recruit workers from out of the country for the sole purpose of filling this niche in the labour market.[331]

Our findings, however, suggest a different interpretation. From the standpoint of the employers, demand for live-in service is generally assumed to be high among those with small children, or in some cases elderly parents, who require care during all hours of the day and night. In the context of declining real incomes for the majority of income-earners, however, employers may in fact be more concerned to hire domestic workers who are willing to work for low wages and are subject to minimal regulation – whether they live in or live out. The purpose of recruiting foreign domestic workers may be motivated less by the necessity to compel an indentured, live-in labour force, as government policy has assumed, than to recruit a labour force kept in a sufficiently vulnerable position to compel them to accept low wages and poor working conditions. Our findings suggest that the compulsory live-in requirement is not as obvious a demand factor as government policies have earlier suggested. In either case, it is the interests of employer/citizens rather than those of employee/non-citizens that are considered as central to the policy. In sum, our findings indicate that among both West Indian and Filipino foreign domestic workers, arrangements for partially mitigating the live-in requirement through additional or alternative accommodation for one or more days per week appears to be far more common than acknowledged. Employers may be either compelled or willing to accept such a limitation to the live-in requirement even though this practice runs contrary to the terms and conditions of the LCP.[332]

Working conditions, wages and benefits

We have identified the temporary immigration status of foreign domestic workers in Canada, combined with the compulsory live-in requirement, as the main conditions that render them vulnerable to the arbitrary designs of their employers. These conditions are heightened by the personalistic nature of the employer/employee relationship characteristic of domestic service, and the differential impact of class, race and citizenship status. Among both West Indian and Filipino domestic workers, a substantial majority of respondents surveyed indicated that the two main areas of responsibility associated with their employment were caring for the employers' children, and cleaning the employers' house. For West Indian domestic workers, 22 of 24 respondents who answered this question identified care for the employers' children as part of their current job; among Filipinas, the 24 out of 25 who responded to this question all identified childcare.[333] Moreover, when asked to identify the frequency with which such care was provided (Q4A2A2), all 21 West Indian domestics who responded to this question answered seven days per week; all 24 Filipinas who responded offered the same frequency rate.

This is particularly interesting given the responses to the questions regarding accommodation. Though all of those who answered this question indicated they were expected to care for children seven days per week, a majority of respondents did not actually live in the employers' homes throughout the entire week. This suggests that employers' expectations were for the provision of care every day, every week; however, by arranging to live out for part of the week, workers were able to get some time off away from their childcare responsibilities.

The LCP is designed to provide affordable and flexible care for children, disabled persons and seniors for upper-middle-class and wealthy families. In order to employ a worker through the programme, the provision of personal care, rather than only the performance of other household duties such as house cleaning or gardening for example, must be part of the duties of the migrant worker. Thus, it is not surprising that virtually all Filipinos (most of whom entered through the programme) were engaged in childcare. What is more notable, is that all of the West Indians, most of whom did not enter through a government programme, were also engaged in childcare.

Not surprisingly, cleaning house was another major area of work responsibility characterizing the employment situation of West Indian and Filipino domestic workers (Q4A2C1).[334] For the former, the response rate of those who identified housework was 21 of 25; for the latter, 21 of 24. Other common tasks, indicated by at least 18 affirmative responses from both the West Indian and the Filipino respondents, were: serving guests (Q4A2K1); shovelling snow in the winter (Q4A2J1) and gardening (Q4A2L1). Thus, it was common for both Filipino and West Indian workers, hired as nannies, also to be expected to work simultaneously as housekeepers. This is consistent with the association of household labour with 'women's work', and defined as combining childcare and housekeeping as part of the same job description. It also indicates the tendency for women of colour to be expected to perform the duties of the employing 'woman of the house' in a gendered, hierarchical, heterosexual, nuclear family structure. When paid female domestic labour is employed in the private Canadian home, gendered divisions become altered by class divisions within the home. Women of means employ poor women to perform the domestic duties associated with women's labour; in the process a clear line of demarcation according to class and enforced by citizenship and race come into play. This pattern was common in the study whether the foreign domestic workers came to Canada from the West Indies or the Philippines.

The general expression of the citizenship divide within the household was notably uniform. However, when it came to breaking down the specific tasks involved in performing the duties associated with household labour, and the frequency with which they were executed, the responses became more varied, among both West Indian and Filipino domestic workers. For example, among West Indian respondents, 11 of 20 who answered this question (Q4A2C2) cleaned house once per week; eight did so every day of the week, and one only once per month. Eleven of 25 were involved in menu preparation (Q4A2D1), and the same number did so daily (Q4A2D2). Twelve of 14 who responded cooked meals for the children only (Q4A2E1), while ten of 25 who responded to a separate question (Q4A2F1) stated that they cooked meals for the household as a whole.

When we turn to the Filipino domestic workers, we see a pattern of responses that is equally diverse. Among 20 respondents for the question regarding frequency of cleaning house (Q4A2C2), 12 identified once per week, while eight noted that they cleaned the employer's house on a daily basis. Sixteen of 23 Filipinas who responded stated that their jobs included menu preparation; ten of 13 Filipinas who answered a separate question indicated that they prepared menus for meals every day of the week, while three did so once per week. Twelve of 22 Filipino domestic workers who responded indicated that they cooked meals for the children only, while 12 of 23 who responded to this question cooked meals for the entire household.

Doing the laundry appeared in the findings to be a task more universally included in the 'house cleaning' job description. Among West Indian domestic workers, 21 of 25 who answered this question (Q4A2G1) did the laundry; for Filipinas, the response rate was 22 of 24. Even here, however, when the question of frequency was asked, variations emerged again. Fourteen of 21 West Indian domestic workers who responded (QA2G2) did the laundry once per week; seven did the laundry on a daily basis. Among Filipinas, of 15 who responded, ten did the laundry once per week, while five did laundry daily. When a question was asked about ironing (Q4A2H1), all 25 of the West Indian domestics who were interviewed responded, among whom 13 indicated this task was part of their job description, performed once a week. For Filipino domestic workers surveyed, again there was a response rate of 100 per cent regarding the task of ironing: 22 indicated that ironing was a regular part of their expected duties. Sixteen of 18 Filipinas who responded indicated that they did the ironing once per week; one ironed every day; and one ironed only once per month.

What is most clearly indicated by these findings is the variation in the job descriptions and frequency of performing specific tasks associated with full time, live-in domestic labour. Not only are there great variations in the work performed – a characteristic in general of women's work in the home – but also in the frequency of the performance of those tasks within any given time period, and the hours of work in any given week.

Caring for and raising young children, maintaining the complex series of duties associated with household cleaning and maintenance, and serving the personal needs of adults in the private home, are forms of work notoriously invisible in modern capitalist societies. Household workers are often expected to perform several of these tasks simultaneously, even though performing one of these duties makes it difficult or indeed impossible to perform another. The expectations associated with the performance of these tasks are often unclear to the employee, as is the order of priority.

The characteristics of migrant domestic work that emerged in the findings of this survey are reflective of migrant domestic work in general, not only in Canada but internationally.[335] The absence of transparent standards according to which these tasks are performed indicates the lack of clarity associated with the replacement of paid for unpaid household work in the family unit. What is clear, however, is that such an absence of standardization supports the arbitrary, nearly accidental, norms of work imposed on paid live-in domestics. Work performed as personal service in the home is subject almost entirely to the discretion of the employing adult or adults, and usually the adult woman. The employing adults who own the home, hire the employee and supervise the performance of duties expect such work to be 'natural' for foreign domestic workers, and commonly communicate expectations in vague, inconsistent and personal terms. In addition, vulnerable immigration status and the live-in requirement associated with Canadian foreign domestic worker policy exacerbate exploitative conditions of work and the risk of abuse. For the employee to ask questions of clarification may be taken as a sign of incompetence or confusion; workers are more likely simply to perform the duties requested with minimal instruction, simply hoping to 'please' the employer.

Another feature of live-in domestic work is the spatially restrictive nature of the arrangement, where the employer is not only one's boss but also one's landlord. When the landlord is responsible for determining access not only to private residence but also to permanent residence in the country, the regulatory power of the employing family is augmented even further. Employers determine not only what the domestic worker is expected to do, but also what she is expected not to do, or denied access to do at all.

One finding that emerged in the survey data related to job description was conspicuous in this negative sense. A clear majority of respondents indicated that they were *not* expected to perform one duty commonly associated with household labour: grocery shopping (Q4A2I1). Among the West Indian domestic workers, of 25 who answered this question, 21 stated they did not do the grocery shopping; among Filipinas, of 24 who answered this question, 21 had the same response.

We believe this finding is suggestive of a pattern worthy of further exploration among foreign domestic live-in workers. Grocery shopping is unquestionably a task associated with household labour and with meal planning. However, given that there is no obvious correlation between the numbers of respondents responsible for menu preparation and the numbers who do the grocery shopping, this factor alone does not explain the high negative response rate. The survey does not suggest that domestic workers were not asked to plan the meals; what is indicated in the findings is only that they were not asked or expected to buy the groceries for the meals.

Alternatively, we suggest an interpretation of the labour of grocery shopping in relation to the household as a work site. Grocery shopping for a family on a regular basis suggests several forms of behaviour that may be considered distinct from other household duties. It compels fairly autonomous activity outside of the household. It requires transportation, in a car or taxi, that would logically be paid for by the employer, and assumes responsibility in managing this transportation to and from the household work site. It is also dependent upon financial exchange, sometimes in considerable amounts measured over a period of time, both for transportation and especially the purchase of the groceries. Indeed, the grocery bill for an employing family with two or more children, which is typical of employers of foreign domestic workers, may exceed the wages paid to live-in household workers. Given that most of the domestic workers cared for young children, it would also likely require that the children accompany the domestic worker in the activity, where responsibility on the part of the employee is increased. Moreover, as live-in domestics are expected to pay for their board out of wages paid them by the employer, the live-in domestic worker who buys groceries for her own consumption would, in a sense, be paying her own wages from the employer's funds. Grocery shopping is a duty that demands considerable individual discretion – choosing the best products, managing variation in price options, and so on. We believe that it is precisely because grocery shopping encouraged these features of autonomy, increased responsibility, physical distance from the household as a work site, control of family finances, and individual, mature discretion, that domestic workers tended not to be asked to perform this duty. Despite the small size of the interview sample, the uniformity of the responses among both West Indian and Filipino domestic workers is suggestive of the need for further investigation of this dimension of live-in domestic service.

Another set of survey questions regarding working conditions focused on the number of hours worked and the payment of wages. West Indian domestic workers interviewed worked an average of 51.3 hours per week; Filipinas worked an average of 49.2 hours per week. According to Ontario labour legislation, any work performed over 44 hours within a given week is overtime. Overtime pay for domestic workers is expected to be at the rate of $1\frac{1}{2}$ the hourly rate, and time off in lieu is required to be at the rate of one and one-half hours per hour of overtime worked.[336] In response to a question about payment for overtime, however, among 25 West Indian workers who answered this question, ten received overtime compensation, while 15 did not. Among Filipino domestic workers, of 22 responses, 16 received overtime compensation, while six did not.

There is sufficient discrepancy here to suggest a possible variation between the two groups, indicating that West Indian workers surveyed, who work an average of 2.1 hours more per week, are also less likely to receive overtime pay or time off in lieu for the work they perform. We interpret the discrepancy in overtime pay combined with the longer average work week to have resulted from the absence of security among these workers in demanding adequate compensation from thier employers. The larger number of undocumented workers among the West Indian workers surveyed would suggest greater vulnerability in the workplace, and less bargaining power to enforce compensation for overtime. However, the fact that six of 22 respondents among the Filipino workers, indicate lack of compensation for overtime pay is significant insofar as this national group of domestics is predominantly here under the LCP. Our survey indicates that both West Indian and Filipino domestic workers are vulnerable to extreme discrepancies in pay, in part due to the long hours of work associated with private service employment and the difficulty of enforcement of overtime compensation. The more vulnerable the immigration status of the worker, the more likely she is to be unfairly compensated, and the greater the margin of discrimination she is likely to suffer.

The measurement of hours of paid work in the home has long been a contentious and hard-fought issue among domestic advocacy organizations in Canada. In 1987, overtime pay or time off in lieu for domestic workers was recognized in Ontario law, a direct response to domestic workers' demands.[337] Subsequent studies indicate, however, that while a majority of domestic workers routinely work overtime, only a minority receive fair compensation for overtime work performed.[338] For the live-in domestic worker, enforcement of such a provision is dependent upon a separation of work performance in the home as a work site, from time off while resident in the same home as a site of respite from work. Our findings reflect this pattern of contestation surrounding hours of labour performed, a pattern suggested in the findings for both West Indian and Filipino workers.

We can now turn from number of hours worked, to hourly rates of pay. Here, again, there was considerable discrepancy, but the variations in pay were characteristic of both West Indian and Filipino domestic workers. There was wide variation in frequency of pay, with a majority expecting to receive a cheque every two weeks (Q4A122B); 12 West Indians and 14 Filipinas. Others expected to be paid monthly (Q4A12C): four among the West Indian domestic workers and eight among those from the Philippines. Still others expected to be paid weekly (Q4A12A): six in the West Indian group, three among the Filipinas.

While the frequency of pay is variable, this factor taken in isolation is not significant. However, when we combined information from responses regarding frequency of pay with hours of work per week and pay rates, we were able to approximate the hourly wages of West Indian and Filipino domestics in the survey.[339] Accordingly, West Indian workers were paid on average $4.53 per hour; Filipino workers in the survey were paid an average of $4.73 per hour. The 20 cent per hour discrepancy is a relatively small margin of difference given the number of undocumented workers among the West Indian group. What is more noteworthy is the fact that both the West Indian and Filipino workers received hourly wages considerably below the legal minimum wage in Ontario at the time ($5.40–$6.85 per hour).[340] Not only is the average earned demonstrably low, but it is also merely a statistical average. Among West Indian workers, the pay scale went as low as $2.14 per hour; for Filipino workers, the low end of the hourly pay rate was $1.91 per hour.

Our findings confirm and expose the highly unregulated employment standards applicable to foreign domestic workers in Canada, reflected in arbitrary and unaccountable rates of pay. Since 1987 full-time live-in domestic workers have been entitled to receive at least the minimum wage. Employers are allowed to deduct the costs of room and board, within standards provided in federal guidelines; however, the parameters for arbitrary pay rates are greatly increased by the live-in requirement of the FDM and LCP. The discrepancy in pay demonstrates the unregulated control placed in the hands of employers of live-in domestic workers in Canada. Moreover, the employee does not necessarily retain a formal record of payment for work performed. When asked if a pay slip was received with payment (Q4B4), among the 12 West Indian respondents who answered this question, only one received a pay slip with every payment; three received a pay slip once per year; and seven stated that they never received a pay slip. Among the Filipino workers, 14 responded to this question; three received a pay slip with every payment; 11 never received one. These findings are significant given that under the conditions of the LCP, the 'employer is required to include a statement of earning with [each] paycheque'.[341] Such a record of employment is necessary should the worker apply for employment insurance benefits, and as proof that the employee has worked the necessary length of time as set out in the federal regulations.[342] Our findings suggest that there is systematic non-compliance of employers with this pay slip requirement.

The survey investigated not only amounts and frequency of pay, but also workplace benefits. While the general conditions of work among the West Indian and Filipino domestic workers in the survey were similar, or similarly varied, certain benefits indicated a different pattern. Live-in domestics in Ontario are entitled to equal pay for equal work, pregnancy leave, paid public holidays, parental leave, regular payment of wages, vacation time, free periods away from work at designated intervals, termination notice and work details in writing.[343] They are also, like all Ontario workers, eligible for health care coverage, workers' compensation, certain tax benefits based on pay scale and employment insurance (formerly referred to as 'unemployment insurance' in federal legislation).

West Indian domestic workers were less likely to be guaranteed receipt of these benefits than Filipinas. Regarding health care benefits, among West Indian workers, of 25 respondents who answered this question (Q4A8A), 13 stated that they did receive benefits, eight did not, and four did not know. Among the Filipino workers, among 24 who answered this question, all received health care benefits. Regarding pension benefits (Q48B), of 24 West Indian respondents, four received benefits, 11 did not, while nine did not know. For the Filipino domestic workers, among 22 respondents, 20 did receive pension benefits and two did not. Turning to unemployment insurance (Q4A8D), of 23 West Indian domestic workers who answered this question, three received benefits, 17 did not, and three did not know. Among the Filipinas, of 22 respondents, 20 received unemployment insurance benefits while two did not. Finally, regarding the benefit of receiving a tax refund (Q4A8C), of 24 West Indian domestic workers who answered this question, 12 stated that they did, 11 did not and one did not know. For the Filipino domestic workers, of 22 respondents, 19 stated that they did receive a tax refund while one did not and two did not know.

Despite the small size of this study, these findings fall sufficiently along the lines of nationality to suggest further exploration. These benefits, when received, accrue to the employees from the government, whereas the necessary paper work and ensuring receipt of benefits rests with the employer. Unlike the payment of wages, there is not necessarily a direct cost to the employers in allowing these benefits to be accessed by the employees.[344] However, there are costs involved for the employer in the regularization of the employee/employer relationship, including paying the employer's contributions to various government funds. Given that we discovered that a significant number of the West Indian domestics interviewed had no documented migration status, one of the indicated effects is the inability to access benefits to which legal foreign domestic workers are entitled.[345] Despite the illegality of employing and harbouring an undocumented worker, the lack of regulation of the work process means that the employer gains even greater control and more work for fewer costs. It is likely that the significant gap in the access to employee benefits revealed in the findings is a feature of the undocumented status of many of the West Indian respondents.

Remittances and family support

Our survey also investigated the role of female domestic workers as the economic supporters of their own families. Immigration to Canada as a means to acquire remittances to support family members 'back home' for both groups of workers was a key issue of exploration. This is an important element of the negotiating strategy of migrant communities, particularly of women for whom compensatory paid work sufficient to support their families is limited relative to men in virtually every country in the world. The interviewees were asked to rank the importance – on a five-point scale with 'very important' at one end, ranging through 'important', 'neutral' and 'not very important', and with 'not important at all' at the other end of the scale – of a number of factors considered in their decision to come to Canada as a domestic worker. Each question was ranked separately.

For a significant number of women workers, among both the West Indian and Filipino groups, the decision to come to Canada was largely linked to their family's financial and social welfare. Among the West Indian domestic workers, of 25 who responded to the statement 'I wanted to immigrate to Canada', 24 ranked this as either important or very important (Q12A). Among 25 Filipino workers who responded, 20 ranked this statement in these categories. When asked to rank the statement, 'I wanted to bring over my family or certain family members to Canada' among 25 West Indian respondents, 15 placed this reason as important or very important; and among 25 Filipinos who responded to this question, 18 placed this statement in these categories (Q12B). When asked to rank the statement, 'I wanted to be able to earn money to send back home', 24 West Indian and 25 Filipino workers responded to this question. Among the West Indian workers, 17 placed this statement as important or very important, as did 19 Filipinas (Q12 H).

Another question, this one open ended, asked 'What are the major things you have gained, or hope to gain, in becoming a live-in domestic worker in Canada?' (Q31). Here, there was a differentiated emphasis between the West Indian and Filipino workers. The former stressed personal achievements associated with raising their standard of living, while the latter emphasized the importance of remittances. The largest number of West Indian domestics first mentioned furthering their education (ten of 25 who responded); the second most common answer was about integrating with others or getting to know Canada (eight responses); and the remaining responses were about raising their standard of living, acquiring landed immigrant status or bringing their family to Canada. The Filipino responses were different. Here, sending money home was the most common goal mentioned first (ten of 20 who responded); after this, the most common answers focused on bringing their family to Canada (six responses); and the remaining answers were scattered among educating their children, improving their standard of living and gaining a better job.

The role of remittances figures more highly in the concerns of the Filipina domestics interviewed than among the West Indians. In both cases, remittances are important, but the relative weight is different. When asked to rank their response to the question directly posed, 'For your family back home, how important do you feel it is that you send them money from your work in Canada?' (Q25), among 21 West Indians responding, 14 stated very important or important. Out of 25 Filipinas who answered this question, 19 stated very important or important.

This variation in emphasis may in part be reflective of the more recent migration flow of Filipinos to Canada, with more dependents remaining back home in need of overseas support. Around 15 per cent of households in the Philippines receive income from their relatives deployed abroad.[346] Further, the Philippine state is highly dependent upon overseas remittances as the main source of foreign currency, and for this reason often refers to its exploited female migrants abroad as national 'heroines'. There is a massive network of state and private interests encouraging overseas work for this purpose.[347] The West Indies are, however, also dependent upon overseas remittances. However, the culture of praising immigrants for sending back funds is not as pronounced as in the Philippine case. Another feature in explaining the difference in emphasis is the number of undocumented workers among the West

Indian interviewees. Sending money to another country that has been earned under the table is not only challenging, but highly risky to those both at the sending and receiving ends of the funds.

Despite the differences, an interesting similarity regarding remittance payments was also indicated in the survey. A majority in both the West Indian and Filipino groups did not send their remittance cheques to their husbands/partners back home, but to their mothers or other relatives. In answer to the question, 'To whom do you generally send remittance cheques?' (Q24), among 20 West Indian respondents, only three stated that money was sent to their husbands. Other responses included their mother (nine); combinations of relatives (six); or another relative or person (two). Among the 23 Filipino respondents who answered this question, only six stated that they sent money to their husbands. Other responses were their mother (nine); combinations of relatives (three); another relative or person (three); and eldest daughter (two).

Of note is the fact that among both groups of women, a greater number directed their remittance cheques to their mothers than to their husbands/partners, and to other relatives in general than to their husbands/partners. This is despite quite divergent marital patterns between the two samples (Q18). Of 25 West Indian domestics who answered a question about marital status, only three were in the category of married/ partner prior to arrival in Canada; one described herself in the category of separated/divorced/widowed; and 21 stated that they had never married. Among the 25 Filipinas who responded, roughly half (12) identified themselves as married/partner; two in the separated/divorced/widowed category; and 11 stated that they had never married. Therefore, there were a larger number of married/partnered Filipinas compared with the West Indian women.

This is a finding consistent with the divergent cultural norms related to the institution of marriage. In the Philippines, the majority of the population are practising Catholics and formal legal marriage is commonly expected of young women. In the West Indies, on the other hand, there is a common tradition of unions without formal marriage, and single-parent families headed by women are far from unusual.[348] In both groups, however, husbands were notably not the principle recipients of the remittance cheques.

This cross-cultural similarity in remittance patterns conforms to worldwide observations that women tend to work to support the basic needs of their families rather than for personal consumption. Moreover, it implies that there should be no automatic presumption that male partners or spouses are part of the familial picture; and if they are, there should be no automatic assumption that they are trusted to distribute the family earnings in accordance with the wishes of the women migrant wage-earners. As a strategy for negotiating citizenship, the financial independence of women workers is therefore an important factor in the process. This finding adds emphasis to the case for considering female migration patterns distinctly from male migration patterns and marital relations, even when considerations of family support as a motivation for immigration are highlighted.[349]

Conclusion

Despite the small size of this survey sample, certain discernible patterns are revealed in the findings. The citizenship divide on a global scale, enforced by gatekeeping mechanisms, is expressed within the private homes of Canadian families. Facing profound obstacles, women workers from the West Indies and the Philippines have negotiated strategies motivated overwhelmingly by the basic desire to support themselves and their families. Our study indicates that the restricted immigration status of both West Indian and Filipino domestic workers has a profound impact on their working and living conditions in Canada. More specifically, the greater the restriction faced at the border, the greater the risk of intense exploitation and discrimination. Our research suggests that the increased restrictions against West Indian workers has only served to increase the likelihood of illegal employment, without leading to any concomitant improvement in domestic service working or living conditions for those of Filipino origin. On the contrary, employers of domestic service continue to be subject to minimal regulation that might ensure a transparent standard of work expectation and enforcement of mechanisms to guarantee workers' legal rights.

The identification of the particular matrix of citizenship, class, race and gendered relations among foreign domestic workers in Canada that we suggest to be evidenced by our study is to our knowledge unique. While several studies have identified patterns of abuse, racism and exploitation, these have either traced general trends, or focused largely on a single racial/citizenship group. Rina Cohen has identified a more instrumental connection between race and job performance, tracing a pattern within domestic service where lighter-skinned workers were nannies, and darker-skinned workers were cleaners and cooks.[350] Our study indicates, alternatively, that there are indeed dramatic variations in the job descriptions and levels of compensation among domestic workers, but these variations are within a general spectrum of exploitation not directly reducible to the country of origin or racial identity of the domestic workforce. Instead, the sharp demarcation in class and citizenship status between the employers and migrant employees, supported by systemic factors in Canada and the world system, identified in previous chapters, fundamentally shape the relations of paid domestic labour. As Brigitte Young has aptly summarized:

> The flexibility of the labour market has produced greater equality between educated middle-class women and men while creating greater inequality among women. High value is placed on the integration of professional women into the formal economy while the 'paid' reproductive work of women in the informal economy (the household) continues to be undervalued; women's 'paid' work outside the home is not equal to women's 'paid' work inside it ... These changes have produced two categories of women within the household: professional women and maids.[351]

Our findings revealed the complexity of paid reproductive work performed by live-in household workers. Placed in the wider context of the global political economy, West Indian and Filipino women workers are part of a system that Parreñas refers to as the 'international transfer of caretaking'. In such a system, women from the Third World care for the children of wealthy women in the First World, and in turn support through their labour and remittances the provision of care for their own children back home. In the next chapter, we will turn to another dimension of the provision of such care, moving from private domestic service to the public realm of health care, and the specific contribution of West Indian and Filipino nurses.

6
Marginalized and Dissident Citizens: Nurses of Colour

Many of the problems faced by migrant domestic workers in attaining and exercising basic citizenship rights stem from their enforced confinement to employment within private households, where workers' rights remain unprotected or unregulated. Locating care occupations within the public sphere such as hospitals has not, however, rid the health care labour force of racialized and gendered ideologies, and class-bound structures, which have compromised the ability of migrant women of colour to exercise their full citizenship rights.[352] Historically, the nursing profession, health care administrators and immigration authorities vigorously promoted racial and cultural exclusivity in Canadian nursing.[353] The women in white tended also to be overwhelmingly white and, outside Quebec, of Anglo-Saxon origins. After the Second World War, formal colour bars were eliminated from nursing education for Black, First Nation and Asian women, and entry for migrant women of colour was facilitated by the liberalization of immigration policy in the late 1960s.[354] Since then, the nursing labour force has become increasingly ethnically and racially diverse, especially as a result of immigration from poorer countries in the Southern hemisphere.

Beginning in the 1950s, small numbers of Caribbean nurses were permitted into Canada only as 'cases of exceptional merit', and on the condition that hospitals, which gave them job offers, were made 'aware of their racial origin'.[355] Since the 1960s, Canada has imported nurses from poorer developing countries as one strategy to cut the costs of health care and to respond to fluctuating nursing shortages. By 1984, one in five immigrant nurses had migrated to Canada from Asia, Africa or the Caribbean.[356] The increased racial diversity of the Canadian nurse force has not eliminated a pattern of systemic racism experienced by Black nurses and other nurses of colour. Racial biases have been

107

found to exist in recruitment and hiring, promotion, supervision, work assignment, relationships with co-workers and patients, and disciplinary practices.[357]

Foreign nurses of colour encounter a variety of obstacles to equitable treatment. In the context of the 1990s and 2000s, restructuring in the health care system to reduce costs and increase deregulation has led to the deterioration of nurses' working conditions and a widely recognized crisis in the profession. In an atmosphere of a general assault on the recognition of the skills and abilities of nurses in Canada, management strategies have augmented the salience of racial, ethnic and citizenship differences among nurses. Migrating from impoverished circumstances in their countries of origin, Third World migrant nurses are compelled to endure working conditions, including those injurious to their health and dignity, assigned by management and rejected by Canadian-born and white nurses. While there have been cases of rising solidarity among white nurses and nurses of colour,[358] there has also been evidence of racism within the workforce. The necessity to struggle against racism has led nurses of colour to organize independently of the battles fought by some white nurse leaders focused on the efforts to achieve autonomy and full professional status. The barriers to effective unity among the nursing profession to resist the impact of restructuring has taken the form of a double challenge: in opposition to what remains a sexist and male-dominated hierarchy of physicians and hospital administrators, and to the racist legacy within the nursing profession itself, which has tended to scapegoat and marginalize nurses of colour.[359]

The mounting pressures on health care workers and on patients generated by restructuring, privatization and de-institutionalization by neo-liberal governments of the Canadian health care system since the mid-1980s have exacerbated discrimination experienced by nurses of colour. In efforts to cut costs, hospitals in all provinces have resorted to bed closures, inter-hospital amalgamations and reductions in full-time jobs.[360] Ontario, the province where this study is focused, has pursued an aggressive, cost-cutting programme in the health care sector, especially since the election in 1995 of the Progressive Conservative Government led by former Premier Mike Harris.[361] The introduction of new management philosophies of 'quality assurance' and 'patient information technology' has fundamentally altered the nature of nursing, reducing the time available for patient care, speeding up work and increasing surveillance, rendering nursing more fragmented and stressful, and leading to a rise in staff conflicts.[362] The new and intensified controlling mechanisms have fuelled a heightened sense of malaise, but have also provoked a new militancy among nurses who face job terminations, heightened job dissatisfaction and often lower pay.

The decline in quality of health care services and the deterioration in nurses' working conditions provide a structural context for the aggravation of disadvantage and marginalization among nurses of colour. The pervasive nature of systemic racism for black nurses and other nurses of colour was demonstrated by the landmark Ontario human rights settlement won in 1994 by seven Black nurses against Northwestern General, the metropolitan Toronto hospital which was found to have discriminated against them in employment practices and unjust firing decisions.[363] The fact that by the early 1990s, the Ontario Nursing Association (ONA), the union representing approximately 55 000 registered nurses in Ontario, reported being 'flooded' with racism complaints from all over Ontario was evidence that the findings of racism in Northwestern General were not an isolated case.[364] The ONA determined that nurses of colour were generally subjected to harsher discipline, over-supervision, more frequent termination and overall differential treatment.[365] In 1995, a conference organized specifically to address and challenge racism experienced by Black nurses in Toronto drew over 200 participants.[366]

As migrants and as women of colour, Black nurses and Filipino nurses face numerous obstacles to equitable employment and promotion in the workplace and within the profession. For many of them, their non-citizenship status presents a formidable barrier to entry into nursing itself, and many migrant nurses are forced to work as home support workers, nurses' aides and domestic workers. This sense of exclusion and disadvantage increases in the current climate of hospital restructuring and privatization, which foments unstable employment, fear of job loss and stress associated with increased workloads.

Migrant nurses from the Philippines and the Caribbean provide an interesting study of comparison and contrast with migrant household workers. Both groups of Third World female workers are in gendered 'care' occupations; both groups are located in an international labour market where there is a high degree of transnational mobility of workers. In spite of high demand, the Canadian Immigration Department assigns a zero occupational demand rating to both nurses and domestic workers. Both groups share vulnerability to workplace discrimination, and their access to their respective occupations is prone to regulation by stereotypes, which reflect intersections of gender, race and class ideologies, such as the very white, archaic icons for domestics and nurses of Mary Poppins and Florence Nightingale, respectively.

There is also overlap between the two groups: many trained nurses from developing countries have entered Canada through the foreign domestic worker programme, and worked as nannies and elder caregivers for two or more years, a trend which appears to be on the upswing. Filipino nurses have been particularly apt to migrate through the LCP to provide 24-hour home support services for the elderly and people with disabilities and illnesses. Grace Chang has commented on how 'there are 100 000 registered nurses in the Philippines, but almost none actually reside in the country'.[367] Many nursing schools were established in the Philippines in the 1980s, designed specifically for the export of nurses abroad, consistent with the overall thrust of the Philippine labour export policy. Countries such as the United States responded to nursing shortages by accepting migrant nurses with temporary H-1 visas.[368] The Canadian government attempted, without success, to develop specific arrangements with nursing schools in the Philippines, specifically for the purpose of exporting domestic workers.[369]

In Canada during the 1990s, temporary visas issued to foreign nurses disappeared with the move to retrenchment and hospital restructuring. The reinstatement of temporary visas has slowly returned in response to the nursing shortages that have characterized the larger health care crisis. Although there has clearly been an urgent demand for trained nurses that is not being met by the Canadian labour market in most parts of the country, the Department of Citizenship and Immigration denied that such a shortage existed by awarding zero points to nurses in the General Occupations List that determined eligibility for permanent, or landed immigrant, status.[370] This made it virtually impossible for foreign nurses to acquire sufficient points in order to enter as independent, landed immigrants. For many Filipino nurses wishing to migrate to Canada, the only available option has been to enter under the LCP.

For Filipino nurses, like their West Indian sisters in earlier decades, taking on live-in domestic work for a minimum of two years is a deskilling process. The foreign caregiver programme continues, despite various amendments, to create restrictions on the ability to access academic upgrading courses to refresh nursing skills. Long periods without application of nursing skills create delays in obtaining accreditation and passing the nursing exam required to practice in a Canadian province.

The Canadian Registered Nursing Examination, which must be written and passed in Canada, has been experienced as a major hurdle to accreditation for migrant nurses.[371] Indeed, in Ontario, the failure rate for foreign-trained nurses writing the licensing exam is 66 per cent.[372] The English-language test requirement is also perceived to be another obstacle, deemed unnecessary by Filipinas whose language of instruction is English in Philippine nursing schools and often throughout their formal schooling. In 1995, the Filipino Nurses Support Group (FNSG), based in Vancouver, formed to 'educate, advocate and organize' on issues facing Filipino nurses, particularly those who have entered through the LCP and have become confined by the restrictions of the domestic worker programme.[373]

Nurses who enter Canada as domestics endure a long, arduous and expensive process of gaining accreditation and entering the nursing profession in Canada. Others are permanently deskilled and continue to be employed for low wages as domestic workers, nursing aides, home care workers and other low-paying service-sector workers long after completing FDM/LCP requirements and attaining landed status.[374]

Notwithstanding these similarities and links, the situations of nurses and household workers from the Philippines and Caribbean are notably different. Foreign nurses more frequently enter Canada with landed immigrant status, a status which entitles them to many of the rights associated with Canadian citizenship.[375] Their work in the public sphere is embedded in an impersonal bureaucracy governed by more explicit contractual obligations and limits.[376] Although nurses have struggled unsuccessfully to attain the professional status accorded to many other health care occupations, there is little question that nurses enjoy higher status than domestic workers.[377] Unlike domestic workers, nurses are unionized with nursing unions often standing in the lead of public sector militancy and battles for higher standards of health and patient care.[378] While nursing is a highly supervised occupation, nurses are at least freed from the 24-hour-a-day surveillance by employers characterizing the situation of live-in domestic workers. Whereas domestics work in isolation, nurses are part of work groups upon which they depend for sociability and support. These important differences provide nurses with access to a degree of autonomy, working and living options, social welfare entitlements, and avenues for redress against discriminatory actions, deferred or denied altogether to foreign domestic workers who labour under temporary status in private family households. The question remains as to what extent these differences permit West Indian and Filipino nurses to experience full and meaningful citizenship given that both citizenship and nursing have themselves been constructed from exclusionary criteria based upon possession of the 'appropriate' race/ ethnicity, class and gender.

This chapter explores the immigration paths, workplace experiences of discrimination and perceptions of Filipino and Black West Indian nurses in Toronto in order to shed further light on the process by which Third World female migrants negotiate access to citizenship of labour-importing First World countries. Twenty-five Filipino nurses and 24 West Indian nurses working in Toronto hospitals, selected through a snowball sample, were interviewed with the use of questionnaires in 1994.[379] The analysis also relies on interviews with 'nursing gatekeepers' conducted between 1992 and 1999. These include two staff members from the Ontario College of Nurses (OCN), five directors of nursing recruitment in Toronto hospitals, a director of a nursing programme in a community college, four owners of nursing placement agencies and the vice-president of the Philippine Nursing Association in Manila. Further insights were derived from attendance at two anti-racist nursing confer-ences held in Toronto, organized by the Filipino Nurses Association in 1992 and the Congress of Black Women of Canada in 1995, respectively. Additional information was gathered in 2000–01 through correspon-dence with the Ontario Nursing Association.[380]

The survey dimension of the study parallels that conducted among West Indian and Filipina domestic workers discussed in the previous chapter. However, the differences in the living and working conditions, and immigration statuses, between foreign domestic workers and foreign nurses in Canada do not readily suggest a question-by-question compar-ison. The interviews for domestics and nurses were based on separate questionnaires, adjusting similar lines of investigation regarding the negotiation of citizenship rights to the particular realities of these two employment sectors of migrant women workers. A methodological model that artificially imposed direct comparability across employment sectors and citizenship status would have risked distortion or obfuscation of key factors in the lived reality of these migrant women's experiences and negotiating strategies.

Accepting this proviso, it is notable that the findings nonetheless sug-gest a distinct pattern in terms of the relationships among citizenship, class, gender and race. For foreign domestic workers, differences were suggested that reflected a structural and ideological bias against the recruitment of West Indian domestics. However, these distinctions were superceded by a generalized experience of exploitation as live-in domes-tic workers. Among nurses, a similarly if distinct socially constructed bias against the recruitment and accreditation of West Indian nurses relative to Filipinos was revealed in our findings. However, management prac-tices that discriminate against both groups of nurses are indicated to be meted out particularly harshly against those of West Indian origin. In a period of massive restructuring in the hospital sector, and where

West Indian and Filipino nurses work side by side, a strategy of managerial racial discrimination based on divide-and-conquer tactics is strongly suggested in our study.

A small number of writers have examined the issue of racism in Canadian nursing, chiefly as it has affected African Canadian/Black nurses, including immigrants from the Caribbean.[381] An unexplored question in the literature is to what extent the experience of racism in nursing, and specifically in hospitals, is similar or different for all nurses of colour. For instance, research by Agnes Calliste and Tania das Gupta on racism and anti-racist organizing among Black nurses suggests a racial hierarchy within nursing, where white nurses occupy the top ranks of desirable positions and Black nurses are at the bottom. This scholarship essentially leaves unexamined the question of how nursing is experienced by other nurses of colour such as Filipino nurses.[382] Our study, which includes both Black and Filipino nurses, permits us to compare the immigration patterns and experiences with workplace discrimination of two distinct groups of foreign-born nurses of colour. The intersection of race, gender and class with citizenship is here, as in the case of foreign domestic workers, the central focus of examination.

Canadian recruitment and regulation of migrant nurses of colour

Given high international demand for nurses, nursing degrees, whether obtained in First or Third World countries, have long been gained or utilized as passports to work abroad.[383] A study of nurse migration from 1960 to 1972 by the World Health Organization (WHO) estimated that about 5 per cent of the world's nurses were then working outside their home countries.[384] The directions of migrant nurse flows reflect international political economic realities of neo-colonialism, poverty and underdevelopment in Third World countries. These realities translate into wage differentials between labour sending and receiving countries. The considerable gap in employment levels and wages between underdeveloped countries and advanced industrial ones has provided a significant incentive for nurses to migrate from low-wage Third World to high-wage First World countries. Large-scale migration of nurses has occurred, however, with considerable regulation by labour-sending and receiving governments, private recruitment agencies and nursing regulatory bodies and professional nursing associations. It is with an eye towards increased remittances from their nationals working abroad, that some Third World governments have shown willingness to export their trained nurses, even when this emigration has resulted in major nursing shortages and diminished health care within these countries.

The volume of nurse migration is also significantly regulated on the receiving end, mediated by politically constructed demand for or surplus of nurses, and by racialized, gendered ideologies of suitability, or lack thereof, for particular types of work. Thus, Calliste points out how in 1963, the Barbadian government offered to meet Toronto's nursing shortage by sending 300 nurses to the city's hospitals. Toronto's District Superintendent declined this offer and relied upon racist and sexist stereotypes to conclude that these women were actually domestic servants, or at best nursing assistants.[385] In Canada as in the United States, a deep-seated identification of Black women with domestic servitude has been pivotal in shaping the experiences of nurses of colour. This racist stereotype has hindered the efforts of Black nurses from winning integration and acceptance in an occupation where white nursing leaders sought to create distance from the taint of domestic service.[386]

In the WHO study of nurse migration, the largest outflow of foreign nurses by far was from the Philippines, where annual losses amounted to 2000 or 8.7 per cent of the local nursing professional pool.[387] By the mid-1980s, the annual outflow of nurses from the Philippines exceeded 20 000 per year.[388] The expansion in nursing education in the Philippines during the 1970s and 1980s was detonated by the labour export policy of the Philippines government that encouraged its nationals to go abroad to earn foreign dollars. Indeed, the curriculum for these schools used US textbooks and emphasized procedures and equipment used in foreign countries, rather than training to serve the basic health needs of communities in the Philippines.[389] Many women and smaller numbers of men were motivated to earn credentials to work abroad and earn far higher wages by becoming overseas nurses. Although a moratorium was declared by the Philippines government in the mid-1980s on the opening of all new nursing schools, the fact that nursing schools had become such a lucrative business for the production of migrant nurses inhibited state authorities from enforcing the moratorium. IMF–World Bank structural adjustment policies hastened the deterioration and privatization of the Philippine health care system. With the closing of many government hospitals, nursing graduates are forced to volunteer, and even pay to volunteer in hospitals in order to gain work experience.[390] In 1990, it was estimated that 60 per cent (66 000) of the Philippines' total supply of nurses migrated to other countries, driven by the below-subsistence nursing wages and poor, often exploitative, working conditions in the country.[391] As the vice-president of the Manila-based Philippine Nurses

Association stated, 'most of our graduates go abroad. While we want to keep our nurses, there are not enough opportunities here. There is rapid turnover in hospitals where conditions are poor. Some nurses will stay six months to two years, but as soon as they get an offer abroad, they will leave even if they face a breach of contract.'[392]

Canadian demand for immigrant nurses grew after the Second World War when postwar prosperity permitted ordinary Canadians to afford health care services and facilitated the expansion of the publicly funded health care system.[393] An additional factor contributing to nursing shortages was the migration to the United States of Canadian nurses. Many Canadian nurses were compelled to leave Canada during the period of massive layoffs and continue to this day to be drawn by the higher wages, permanent job opportunities, and greater variety of specialized work available in the United States.[394]

Between 1953 and 1963, Canada admitted 15 359 immigrant nurses.[395] Between 1962 and 1968, nearly 20 000 graduate nurses immigrated to Canada, an average of 2800 per year.[396] But as Calliste points out, even in the context of nursing shortages, the racialized demand was for white nurses from Britain and from other 'white settler societies' such as Australia, New Zealand and South Africa. Largely through the spirited lobbying by Black community organizations and the support of unions and churches, 982 Caribbean nurses were admitted as landed immigrants between 1954 and 1965. Prior to recruitment by Canadian hospital administrators, some Caribbean nurses had first worked in Britain whose hospitals in large industrial areas attracted migrant nursing staff from New Commonwealth countries during the 1950s to the early 1970s. Caribbean nurses were obliged by law to inform their prospective Canadian employers that they were 'coloured'. Many were also required to upgrade their skills to be eligible for Registered Nurse (RN) status in Canada and in the interim were permitted to work as nursing assistants in Canadian hospitals. Additional barriers, such as the limited spots opened to foreign students within upgrading courses, left several of these nurses trapped in deskilled assistant positions. Hospitals were thus provided with well-trained captive low-wage labour.[397]

The experience of Filipino migrant nurses entering Canadian nursing was apparently more salutary in the 1960s and 1970s, when Canadian hospitals recruited nurses directly from the Philippines.[398] Other Filipino nurses arrived in Canada via the United States where hospitals had recruited them on temporary student visas. Virginia Levesque, one of the first Filipino nurses to migrate to Canada, arrived in 1961, after working for two years in a hospital in Rochester, New York. 'The borders were open. Canada welcomed us with open arms. All hospitals in Canada were willing to have us.'[399] Cecilia Dioscon, a registered nurse and organizer at the Philippine Women Center in Vancouver also found that when she migrated to Quebec in the 1970s, her credentials were readily accepted.[400] Like Caribbean nurses, however, some Filipino nurses were assessed to have less than fully adequate training and were required to pass an exam in paediatric nursing.[401]

Throughout the 1980s, employment of nurses increased significantly in Ontario hospitals. According to Ontario hospital nurse staffing surveys, the number of registered nurse full-time equivalent (FTE) positions increased from 35 903 in August 1983 to 44 500 by September 1989, peaking at 45 616 in March 1991.[402] To meet the increased demand for nurses, larger hospitals relied on overseas recruiting agencies operating in the United Kingdom, Philippines, Middle East, Asia and the Caribbean. Many of the nurses recruited from Britain were originally from English-speaking Caribbean countries and had completed their training in the United Kingdom, where they worked for several years prior to coming to Canada. The recruiting agencies offered to screen these nurses and promised to bring in trained RNs who would encounter no difficulties passing the nursing exams and getting licensed.[403] These overseas nurses entered Canada on one-year work permits, renewable every year.

A major problem for Ontario hospitals in recruiting from overseas was the time required to process nurse migrants through the Canadian Immigration Department. Immigration authorities required: (1) an offer letter, (2) eligibility letter (from the OCN) and (3) proof of identity. Delays occurred in obtaining the eligibility letter from the OCN, which required that academic records be sent directly from the schools attended by the migrant nurses. According to the Director of Nursing Recruitment at Toronto's largest hospital, nurses normally received their letter of eligibility within three to six months, depending upon the embassy applied from, but it was not unusual for the whole process to take up to 12 months. At the time of nursing shortages, hospitals would hold the positions open for the foreign nurses until they arrived.[404] Hospitals would also hire nurses who were waiting to obtain Ontario registration.

The federal Department of Immigration assisted hospitals in availing themselves of overseas contract nurses. During this period, a good rapport developed between hospital administrators and immigration authorities who would hold regular meetings to process temporary nurse employment. The Toronto Hospital, for instance, had a 'bulk agreement' with Immigration, requesting a bulk number of '2151's (temporary employment authorizations) for foreign employees. In 1990, when

Toronto Hospital experienced nursing shortages, it brought in about 250 graduate nurses on temporary visas, out of a total hospital staff of 2000 registered nurses.[405] To meet its shortages in nurses from the mid-1980s to 1990, Northwestern General Hospital hired nurses who had made direct applications from the Philippines, many of whom had already worked abroad in countries such as Saudi Arabia. Immigration Canada would readily renew the temporary employment authorizations of the migrant nurses, who would 'walk in two days before they expired'.[406]

Hospitals benefited from the temporary contract status of these nurses. Their temporary status hindered their ability to circulate freely in the labour market, and make transfers to employers offering more lucrative wages or more desirable positions. Their lack of mobility also meant that hospitals could assign them to high stress units such as haematology where burn-out rates were high.[407] Both employers and the Canadian state benefited from this migrant labour, as neither had to bear the costs of training that had already taken place in the poorer labour-sending countries. Nor did the Canadian state take responsibility for the health and education costs of maintaining the migrants' families who remained at home. As the loss of jobs for migrant nurses effectively meant a loss of residency in the country, the costs of unemployment would also be borne by the Third World sending country.

Despite nursing shortages and active overseas recruitment, barriers to licensure increased for Philippine-trained nurses migrating to Ontario. The wave of Filipino nurses who entered Canada in the 1960s and 1970s were not required to take English language tests such as the Test of Spoken English (TSE) or the Test of English Fluency (TOEFL). But by the 1980s, migrant nurses from non-English-speaking countries were required to pass TSE and TOEFL prior to submission of their applications for assessment by the OCN, the province's regulatory board for nurses. Even though many of the Filipino applicants spoke English, they would commonly fail these language tests, leading advocates to charge that the tests reflected cultural biases and were unnecessary impediments to the accreditation of nurses from the Philippines.[408] By 1992, the OCN adopted a new policy on language testing of foreign nurses in response to the lobbying efforts of the Toronto-based Filipino Nurses Association and the Coalition of Visible Minority Women. The College began granting exemptions from TOEFL and TSE to Filipino applicants who presented proof that English had been the medium of instruction of the school they attended.[409]

In 1990–91, the reduced financial transfers from the Ontario government to public hospitals precipitated new strategies of hospital management to control costs and operate 'more efficiently'.[410] As salaries accounted for about three-quarters of hospital budgets, staff lay-offs were regarded as 'inevitable'. Reducing the salaried workforce was achieved by contracting out services to the private sector, 'closing beds, shortening stays, performing more day surgery, contracting out, ... providing more treatment on an out-patient basis', shifting chronic patients into special care institutions and closing entire hospitals.[411] Nursing staff became particularly vulnerable to reduced employment levels as nursing salaries made up about one-third of hospital payroll costs.[412] In Ontario hospitals as a whole, registered nurse FTEs fell from 45 616 in March 1991, to 43 134 by March 1993, a level comparable to that which existed in 1988.[413] The first to be laid off were those whose immigration status was most precarious, namely migrant nurses on temporary employment authorizations. The Department of Immigration responded to the sudden 'over-supply' of nursing professionals by can-celling work visas for migrant nurses; and migrant nurses experienced a shift in the attitude of hospital administrators to their contract renewals from helpful to nonchalant. Interestingly, when hospitals no longer needed to recruit temporary migrant nurses, the assessment of the qual-ity of such foreign labour by hospital human resources managers tended to become less positive. In the words of one such manager,

> ... [T]he shortages [had] made us almost desperate. I don't want to say that the hospital was taking in warm bodies, but ... if you had a degree and passed the exam, you were guaranteed a job. This was a problem because on the 'soft scales' – compassion, problem resolution, response in an emergency, the nurses might be lacking.[414]

Ineligible for unemployment insurance, as migrant workers, these nurses were forced to leave the country.[415]

Each hospital dealt differently with diminished budgets, proceeding with more or less speed, with differing implications for recruitment and retention of nurses as a whole, and immigrant and migrant nurses specif-ically. Thus, one large downtown hospital, Mount Sinai, which is finan-cially better off due to sizeable community endowments, first laid off all of its Registered Nursing Assistants (RNAs) in April 1992 and tightened the qualifications for hiring nurses; only those with a Bachelor of Arts or Bachelor of Science (BA or BSc) degree, rather than college diploma, were now eligible. These policies adversely affected hospital workers from the Caribbean and the Philippines as an estimated 35 per cent of the RNAs were women of colour of these origins.[416] Some hospitals, like

Mount Sinai, initially retained the better paid, and therefore more expensive, RNs because professional regulations had made it necessary to employ them for certain types of work. Moreover, the increasing emphasis on hospital medical technology had made it difficult to substitute other workers with fewer qualifications.[417] In 1997, however, Mount Sinai Hospital laid off 94 RNs.[418] Toronto Hospital, the largest hospital in that city, laid off 322 nurses in 1996 and sought to save about $3.5 million by replacing its more highly trained and qualified RNs with lower paid, less experienced graduate nurses.[419]

Labour substitution – the process of breaking down nursing work into tasks allocated to other less expensive workers, and the replacement of nurses by medical technology such as monitors – has continued apace in Canadian hospitals throughout the 1990s.[420] Hospital administrations have in some instances found common cause with the increasing restrictions of professional nurses' accreditation bodies. In response to augmenting demands on downsizing and restructuring, these gatekeepers have redefined the entry price of admission and in so doing changed the job descriptions of those both inside and outside the gates. For example, graduate nurses only came under the jurisdiction of the OCN as a result of governmental review. Throughout the late 1980s and early 1990s, an exchange took place between the OCN and the ONA regarding the accreditation of graduate nurses. Originally, the College proposed to issue temporary certificates to graduate nurses to verify training and submit evidence of competence in Ontario. However, by the mid-1990s, following increasing pressure from a new government in the province under the Progressive Conservative leadership of Mike Harris, the College had tightened its restrictions and effectively barred graduate nurses from accessing registration accreditation, and lay-off notices started to be issued.

The College ultimately had decided to cease registration of nurses among current graduate nurses; graduate nurses who were already working in that category were not grandparented to allow registration. The differential impact of this policy on women of colour was obvious; according to the College of Nurses' own statistical profile of provisional nurses, 'the group of affected nurses are trained outside of Canada and are predominantly from racial minority groups. The largest individual group comes from the Philippines (30 per cent) and a number of those trained in Britain are racial minorities from other parts of the world such as the Caribbean'.[421] In 1995, the ONA initiated a complaint to the Ontario Human Rights Commission (OHRC) against the provincial College of Nurses, on the grounds that the College was in violation of the

Human Rights Code that made it illegal to discriminate on the grounds of disability, race or ethnic origin.

Another cost-cutting trend in the hospital sector has been the increased resort to part-time workers in nursing and allied health care occupations, and the casualization of the hospital workforce. A higher proportion of nurses are now part-time and work on a contract basis, for six to ten months, and for no longer than 12 months. In 1988, less than 57 per cent of the registered nurses working part-time in Canada did so by choice, whereas almost 18 per cent worked part-time because they did not find full-time work.[422] During the period of nursing shortages, hiring on a casual basis occurred through nursing agencies. Since then, hospitals have shifted from agency hiring to the less costly method of relying on casual staffing lists of their own. Nursing agency owners confirmed that by 1992, their volume of placement of nurses in hospitals had declined dramatically, and that the bulk of their business was now in the placement of health care aides and companions for nursing and retirement homes. The shift in demand from hospital-employed registered nurses to lower-paid health workers in other institutions has taken place at the cost of individual deskilling for many of the Filipino and other minority nurses who were not yet hired as permanent nurses in hospitals. No longer employed by hospitals, many of these nurses are hired out by health care agencies and forced by financial necessity to take on work for which they are overqualified. As one nursing agency owner stated, 'Three years ago [in 1989], RNs were in demand. We placed a lot of graduate nurses because hospitals were short of RNs ... Now they no longer ask for RNs. RNs register with more than one agency with contracts with different hospitals. The RNs are now taking RNA jobs just to have a job. But they're even cutting back on RNAs. I have heard that RNs are even taking jobs as health care aides and companions.'[423]

The rationalization of the health care system, hospital downsizing, and intensification of nursing work have been detrimental to nurses as a whole who are experiencing chronic overwork and 'burn-out' at unprecedented levels. These factors have had an especially adverse impact on migrant nurses of colour. First, the deep cuts in the hospital workforce led to a temporary halt to recruitment of overseas contract nurses, and the sudden 'disappearance' of migrant nurses on work authorizations reported by some hospital human resources officers. These trends illustrated the use by Canadian hospitals of foreign contract nurses as expendable commodities utilized to fill fluctuating and politically constructed shortages in nursing labour. Second, the downsizing and restructuring of the hospital nursing labour force has been accompanied by intensified and racialized surveillance and disciplinary practices which have rendered Black nurses and other nurses of colour more vulnerable to layoffs, demotions and dismissals. Such disciplinary practices are especially prevalent if nurses of colour resist racism and are labelled 'trouble-makers'.[424]

Survey findings: immigration histories and status

Twenty-five female nurses who were born in the Philippines, and 24 Black female nurses born in the West Indies were interviewed in Toronto in 1994 in order to ascertain their paths of migration and access to Canadian nursing. Of the West Indian nurses, 14 were from Jamaica, three from Barbados, two from Trinidad and Tobago, and one each from Anguilla, Grenada, Guyana, St Lucia and St Vincent.

Both Filipino and West Indian nurses are internationally mobile with many of these nurses having worked in another country prior to migrating to Canada. While 14 out of 25 Filipino nurses migrated directly to Canada from the Philippines, 11 had first worked as a nurse in another country. Of these, nine had worked first in the United States, one in the Middle East and one in Europe. West Indian nurses were equally likely to have worked in another country prior to migrating to Canada, with ten out of 24 having arrived in Canada after having completed a stint of nursing in Britain. The paths of migration to Canada for both groups of female migrants suggest that many of these nurses of colour are experienced international migrants, who have migrated twice or more to various destination economies. The difference in prior country of migration and work for the two groups reflects their location within distinct neo-colonial and imperial relations – between the Philippines and the United States, and between the English-speaking Caribbean and Britain. These different neo-colonial relations have also imprinted themselves in the educational systems of the Philippines and the Caribbean which have tended to follow the United States and United Kingdom, models respectively, thus facilitating the recognition of certain overseas credentials for the two groups of migrant nurses.

The survey data indicate that West Indian nurses have had to take more steps and navigate more obstacles in the transnational journey from training in nursing in their home countries to becoming registered nurses in Canada. While the numbers in this survey are small and therefore cannot be considered statistically representative, the qualitative findings are suggestive of a more varied pattern of experience. When asked what their first job had been in Canada, only ten out of

24 West Indian nurses first practised nursing, with full status as an RN. Five others took jobs within nursing, but with the probationary status of 'RN-pending'. The first Canadian job for two West Indian nurses was as an RNA. One West Indian woman first worked as a domestic worker, one worked in arts and crafts, and two were first employed as factory workers, one for seven years prior to becoming a nurse.

Filipino nurses were considerably more likely than West Indian nurses to have immediately worked as registered nurses upon arriving in Canada. The first job for 20 out of 25 Filipino nurses was in nursing. Of these, three worked with the status of 'RN-pending'. One Filipina worked as a health aide; another entered as a domestic worker, a job she held for three years. Thus, West Indian nurses were more likely than Filipino nurses to have entered Canada to take jobs that were either in lesser-skilled, and lower-paid health care positions, or in a smaller number of cases, in unrelated working-class occupations.

In regard to immigration status, however, both Filipino and Caribbean nurses who migrated to Canada in the late 1970s and early 1980s entered with a more secure immigration status than foreign domestic workers. Indeed, 20 out of 25 Filipino nurses entered Canada with independent landed status, five with a job offer and 15 without a job offer. The rest entered as sponsored immigrants, with the exception of one who migrated through Canada's foreign domestic worker programme. While West Indian nurses also were more likely than their counterparts in domestic work to achieve landed immigrant status upon entry into Canada, in comparison with nurses from the Philippines, they were more likely to have been sponsored by their family members. Thus, while 12 out of 24 entered through the independent category, ten arrived as sponsored immigrants. Until recently, immigrants in the sponsored category have been legally and financially dependent on their sponsors for up to ten years in most provinces in Canada.[425] Given that immigrants can apply for citizenship after three years residence, this meant that sponsored immigrants were not able to realize their full citizenship entitlements to such programmes as social welfare assistance for as many as seven years after they had legally taken out Canadian citizenship. This discrepancy left immigrant women vulnerable to various forms of abuse by their sponsor-spouses or other relatives and also deepened the poverty levels for poor immigrant families who are less entitled to access the social safety net than other Canadians.[426]

The greater impediments for Caribbean nurses to migrate through the more desirable independent status to Canada reflects the 'race anxiety' of Canadian immigration officials who were attempting to restrict entry of Black Caribbean immigrants to Canada.[427] Notably, this bias in immigration patterns parallels our findings regarding domestic workers.

The divergence in entry status may also be reflective of the higher educational qualifications of nurses from the Philippines: 14 of 24 Filipino nurses were university-trained registered nurses, and only five were practical, or diploma, nurses. The remaining five had attained Master's, doctoral or other degrees. These educational qualifications, are not, however, accidental. Nurses in the Philippines are consciously trained with a view to breaking through the gatekeeping requirements of the international labour market in the health care sector. The large proportion of Filipino nurses holding Bachelor's degrees in nursing reflects the fact that the Philippines had implemented a mandatory degree programme for nursing in 1981 which made Filipino nurses more 'desirable' labour exports to foreign countries.[428] The fact that most Filipino nurses have Bachelor's degrees in nursing at a time when the majority of nurses working in Canada had diplomas, and some arrived also with prior work experience in the United States, made them particularly attractive to Canadian hospitals.[429] Our findings are consistent with these general trends. Among West Indian nurses interviewed, in contrast, 21 out of 24 had diplomas in nursing and only three had university degrees in nursing.

Divergent migration motivations were evident in the different pattern of responses provided by Filipino and West Indian nurses to a question about the respondents' reasons for becoming a nurse in Canada. Nurses were asked how important various reasons were in their decision to become a nurse in Canada (Q32). Both groups of women showed almost equal commitment to work in nursing as a motivation for their immigration – 19 out of 24 Filipinas, and 18 out of 24 West Indians said that wanting to work in nursing was 'important' or 'very important'.

Filipino nurses and Caribbean nurses were not, however, equally motivated to immigrate to Canada. While 20 out of 24 Filipinas said that they wished to immigrate to Canada, only 14 out of 24 West Indian women gave this as a reason. Since the 1970s, the numbers of Filipinos migrating to Canada has accelerated tremendously, and the Philippines has become one of the top source countries for immigrants to Canada. The answers provided by Filipino nurses – such as 'I wanted to immigrate to the U.S. but it was easier to come to Canada' reveal that in several cases, Canada was not, however, their first choice for permanent settlement. For many Filipinos, the goal is to migrate to the United States, which retains a huge economic and cultural presence in the Philippines, rather than to Canada. There is also a long history of migration of Filipinos to the United States, beginning with the importation of Filipino indentured labour to work in plantations in Hawaii during the 1920s.[430] That many of the Filipino nurses migrated to Canada via the United States, which offered them only temporary status, also confirms Canada as a second choice for this migration.

For many West Indians, Canada's neo-imperialist relations with Caribbean countries through structures such as Canadian banks, in the context of the British Commonwealth nexus, has made Canada a probable choice for Caribbean migration.[431] As Helma Lutz suggests, in the de-colonization process after the Second World War, 'every Empire had created its own colonial system of hierarchical citizenship', which mediated the relative access of migrants to citizenship status and rights.[432] Beginning in the 1960s, immigration legislation was passed in Britain that differentiated between citizens of the Old Commonwealth and the New 'black' Commonwealth in order to deny 'black' migrants the legal right to settle in their former colonial 'motherland'.

Many of these unwanted settlers, who had been recruited for the relative cheapness of their labour, chose next to migrate to Canada. Prior to the Second World War, Canada had attained a pre-eminent position within the British Empire as a 'white' Dominion. Canada's abandonment of its official white immigration policy in immigration legislative reforms in 1967 and its demand for skilled labour opened the gates for migration from the Caribbean precisely at a time when Britain's gates were closing. Canada's history of nation-building as a white settler colony, however, meant that Black immigrants from Britain's former colonies would continue to be treated in immigrant selection processes as less than desirable future Canadian citizens.

While a greater proportion of Filipino than West Indian nurses indicated that an aspiration to immigrate to Canada was a reason for becoming a nurse in Canada, more West Indian than Filipino nurses had actually taken out Canadian citizenship. Eighteen of the 24 West Indian nurses had become Canadian citizens, while only 13 of the 25 Filipino nurses have taken out citizenship. At the time of the survey, however, all Filipino and West Indian nurses who were not Canadian citizens had obtained landed immigrant status. In comparison with domestic workers or visa nurses whose temporary status renders them vulnerable to employer reprisals including the threat of deportation, nurses with landed immigrant status and formal citizenship status are far less likely to fear such serious consequences. This security is important in creating a sense of confidence to challenge other barriers to full substantive citizenship rights, including actively resisting workplace discrimination.

The greater propensity for the West Indian than Filipino nurses in our study to have taken out legal citizenship may in part be a function of the length of time they have resided and worked in Canada. The West Indian nurses interviewed for this study had been working as nurses in Canada an average of three years longer than the Filipino nurses – 17 as compared with 14 years. While ten out of 25 Filipino nurses had been practising nursing in Canada for five years or less, only two out of 23 West Indian nurses have been nurses for as short a period of time. Fifteen out of 24 West Indian nurses had been practising nursing in Canada for at least 16 years, whereas only nine out of 25 Filipino nurses have been nurses in Canada for as long.

The decision of more Filipino than West Indian nurses to refrain from applying for Canadian citizenship, which is a choice available without compulsion for landed immigrants after a certain number of years, also suggests that the ties to their home country are stronger or more ongoing for Filipino nurses than for West Indian nurses. The restrictions on dual citizenship from the Philippines have until recently been greater than from the West Indies, and Filipino migrants have been forced to make greater sacrifices in rights to obtain Canadian citizenship than West Indian migrants.[433]

Another indicator of the density of these ties is the maintenance of transnational families through the regular circulation of goods, resources, individuals and information across national borders. Nurses were asked questions about the relative importance of remittances both as a reason for migrating to Canada and as a continued pattern of saving and transnational flows. Seven out of 24 Filipino nurses said that 'sending money back home' was an 'important' or 'very important' reason to become a nurse in Canada (Q29). In contrast, only one out of 24 West Indian nurses identified this as a reason for becoming a nurse in Canada. When asked directly whether they 'regularly send money to members of their family in their country of origin' seven out of 25 Filipino nurses answered affirmatively, but only one out of 13 West Indian nurses who answered this question indicated that she regularly sent remittances home. Six other West Indian nurses indicated that they 'occasionally sent money home through the mail' or 'on special occasions'. This pattern of remittances is similar to that established among domestic workers. Among both groups of workers, remittances figured more highly in the concerns and financial activities of Filipino women than among West Indian women. The establishment of nursing schools by the Philippines government was largely motivated by the anticipated foreign remittances from nurses working abroad, as remittances are a major plank of the Philippines state strategy for dealing with its severe balance of payments problems.

Notwithstanding this government objective, Filipino nurses are less likely than Filipino domestic workers to cite remittances as an important reason for migrating to Canada. Filipino nurses have on average lived in Canada far longer than Filipino domestic workers, and as landed immigrants are more likely to have been accompanied by or reunited with members of their immediate families in Canada. They are less likely than domestic workers to remit their wages home to support dependent members of their families. As one Filipino nurse stated, 'My family is here and right now we can't afford to send money to parents or sisters and brothers in the Philippines.'

Nurses were asked two open-ended questions about what they felt were 'the major things they have gained, or hope to gain, in coming to live and work in Canada' (Q44) and 'what things did they feel they gave up by coming to Canada' (Q45). Several respondents gave multiple responses to these questions. In answers that show a notable consistency in revealing the economically driven nature of migration from the Philippines, 21 out of 23 Filipino nurses who responded to Q44 said that they had gained financial security or independence. Other financial goals were also met through migration as reflected in the response of one Filipina who said: 'I was able to help pay for my parents' medical expenses and for the building of a house for them.' Other gains cited by Filipinas included: higher education, advancement in their career, travel, and the ability to bring their family members to Canada. When asked what they had given up by coming to Canada, the most frequent response of the 19 Filipino nurses who responded was family ties (mentioned by nine respondents). Other responses included their roots, love life and social life, work and money (one respondent who stated that she had lost her job through discrimination), career (teaching in a university-training hospital serving the poor) and slower pace of life. Three Filipinas who mentioned that they had given up their family ties indicated that this loss was temporary, as they were eventually reunited with their family members in Canada.

The pattern of gains cited by West Indian nurses was different and more heterogeneous. West Indian nurses were less likely than Filipino nurses to mention financial security as something gained through immigration to Canada, although it was the third most frequent response to this question. Only six out of 23 said that they had made financial gains ('more money', 'higher finances', 'financial security') through becoming a nurse in Canada. West Indian nurses were more likely to view their gains in terms related to their nursing job, with eight nurses mentioning such benefits as 'more nursing experience', 'job status' and 'career advancement'. In addition, three specifically mentioned that they had earned a nursing diploma or further nursing education in Canada.

The most frequently mentioned gain by West Indian nurses was 'exposure to other (or different/Canadian) culture(s)', cultural diversity and multiculturalism, remarked upon by ten out of 23 nurses.[434] Some of the West Indian nurses assessed their gains in terms of knowledge of other cultures and multiculturalism, or in one nurse's words, their learned 'ability to adapt and adjust to other cultures'. While some of the West Indians saw their gains in Canada in terms of the 'opportunity to work and live within a multicultural society', others explicitly made mention of the racial discrimination which encounter with different cultures in Canada is associated. Indeed, in response to the question about what gains they had made in coming to Canada, three West Indian nurses cynically observed the benefits of migration to Canada in terms of their novel apprehension of racism, discrimination and prejudice. These responses, and the much lower propensity of West Indian than Filipino nurses to mention 'financial security' as something achieved through immigration to Canada can further be accounted for by the higher levels of work-related discrimination reported by West Indian than Filipino nurses. Systemic racism has led to job immobility, termination and unemployment and imperiled the capacity of Caribbean nurses to achieve financial security. It is important to note here that multiculturalism and cultural diversity mentioned in these responses did not refer to the benign or superficial 'saris, samosas and steel-bands' variety with which official multiculturalism policy is often associated.[435] Rather the experience of cultural diversity was accompanied by racism, which many critics, including vociferous Caribbean immigrants, argue has been soft-pedalled and depoliticized within Canadian state multicultural policy.[436]

Among those things which the West Indian nurses surveyed felt that they had lost in immigrating to Canada were: their 'connection with community', their culture, freedom and autonomy, a less stressful way of life, historical and geographical knowledge of birth country, and beautiful climate. Seven of 22 West Indian nurses who responded to this question mourned the loss of close, and often extended, family life.

Some of the noted qualities of life left behind in the West Indies, with the exception of the climate, are considered to be vital characteristics within liberal and communitarian conceptions of citizenship. Thus, freedom and autonomy have been emphasized within liberal frameworks as prerequisites for citizenship. Communitarian theorists, who view citizens as individuals embedded in their communities, focus on membership and a sense of belonging within a community where social relations transcend the individual, and regard citizenship as a vehicle for nation-building. Viewed within the context of either liberal or communitarian frameworks, these migrant women have not simply traded allegiance from one sovereign state to another. In the fraught process of negotiating and formally gaining Canadian citizenship through immigration and naturalization, migrant nurses of colour have relinquished many valued facets of their citizenship within their home countries. These citizenship values have not been substituted with an equivalent package of newly obtained citizenship goods in Canada. Filipino nurses consistently reported the gains from migration in terms of economic resources in line with the emergent globalized concept of citizen as 'consumer', and the losses in terms emphasized within communitarian perspectives on citizenship. For Black nurses, material gains of First World citizenship have been less tangible.

Discrimination findings

For each nursing job they had worked in, Filipino and West Indian nurses were asked whether they had experienced any discrimination on the basis of their race, colour, gender or other grounds (Q9). The majority of both groups of nurses had experienced discrimination in at least one of their nursing jobs; however, based on their self-reports, West Indian nurses expressed facing greater discrimination than Filipino nurses. While 14 out of 24 Filipino nurses who responded to this question said that they had experienced job-related discrimination, 19 out of 24 West Indian nurses remarked that they had been discriminated against in one or more nursing jobs. When asked what or who were the sources for this discrimination, management topped the list. Nine of 14 Filipino nurses and 13 of 19 West Indian nurses attributed discrimination to management.

Another finding from the survey suggests a pattern of management discrimination. When asked about work related to training on-duty staff, our findings indicate somewhat higher involvement in this among West Indian than Filipino nurses. However, when asked about formal recognition of their performing administrative duties, the pattern is reversed, with a suggestion that Filipinos are somewhat more readily recognized as administrators than West Indian nurses. In other words, while both West Indian and Filipino nurses experience unfair conditions of promotion and skill recognition on the job, there is a suggestion of a systematic pattern of divide and conquer tactics, where one visible minority group, in this case Filipino nurses, are placed in a hierarchy above another, Black West Indian nurses. For West Indian nurses, in their current job in Canada at the time of the interview (Q9C4E1), 13 of 15 who answered this question were involved in training on-duty staff. For Filipina nurses, seven of 14 who answered this question trained on-duty staff.

Another finding suggests that this discrepancy is consistent, regardless of years of experience. When we turn to a question about their history of nursing employment in Canada, West Indian nurses indicated that in their first nursing job (Q9A4E1), 15 of 22 who answered this question trained off-duty staff. However, only ten of 22 Filipino nurses who answered this question indicated that they trained on-duty staff. For their second nursing jobs in Canada (Q9B4E1), the pattern is less obvious, as the numbers of Filipinas who answered this question declines. However, there were still a significant number of West Indian nurses who indicated that they were involved in on-duty staff training. Thus, ten of 20 West Indian nurses who answered this question were involved in training, as opposed to 12 of 13 Filipinas.

However, when asked about employment in formal administration (Q9C4G1), the responses indicated that Filipinas were somewhat more likely to be recognized. For West Indian nurses, only four of 15 who answered this question were involved in administration; for Filipino nurses, seven out of 11 had administrative duties. Again, the findings suggest that there is a systematic pattern here, enduring over time. For first nursing jobs in Canada (Q9A4G1), two of 23 West Indian nurses had administrative posts; this was proportionately lower than for the eight of 25 Filipinas. For second jobs (Q9B4G1), among West Indian nurses, two of 19 were involved in administration; for Filipino nurses, six of 15 responded affirmatively to this question.

Research to date on nursing has revealed a pattern in Canadian hospitals where nurses of equal skill are divided by managerial strategies that promote white nurses over the heads of qualified Black nurses. Experiences where disciplinary measures are taken out against Black nurses, but are overlooked when white nurses perform in the same manner, have also been identified.[437] Our findings, however, suggest that there are further divisions cultivated by management between West Indian and Filipina nurses, that pit one group against the other. In a period of restructuring, and one of increasing militancy among nurses, ensuring that nurses are pitted against one another through racial and ethnic hierarchies could prove to be a useful form of collective discipline.

In addition to management strategies of discrimination, there were also reports of co-worker discrimination. This was perceived to be a problem by nine of 19 West Indian nurses and five of 14 Filipino nurses. Patients and/or patients' families were also perceived to be a source of discrimination for ten of 19 West Indian nurses and five of 14 Filipino nurses. The type of discrimination attributed to the different sources varied. Thus, patients and families of patients were reported to verbally assault Caribbean and Filipino nurses. Nurses would be called a whole range of racial epithets and would be told by white patients 'to go back to where you came from' or to other countries where the majority of the population is non-white. Patients and patients' families would question the competence of Black nurses and some would refuse to be treated or cared for by nurses of colour. In some cases where patients would be under the care of nurses of colour, patients' families were reported to bypass their authority and approach white nurses to inquire about their relative's status. Left unchecked, discriminatory behaviour by patients and their families can endanger nurses of colour, who may be subjected to racially motivated threats and physical attacks for alleged neglect of patients.[438]

Verbal harassment and discriminatory treatment by patients became part of one hospital's work environment when hospital management chose to ignore such discrimination, or warned nurses of colour that they should expect to encounter racist name-calling and insults from their patients. One of the most common forms of discrimination reported by Caribbean and Filipino nurses in this study, practised by management, head nurses and in-charge nurses, involved workload assignment. Nine West Indian nurses and six Filipino nurses reported having been assigned heavier and more difficult work than that assigned to white nurses. Common complaints would be that these nurses of colour were always asked to work on the floors associated with the heaviest physical labour, the least desirable shifts, and with the most critically ill and difficult patients. They would also report being system-atically excluded from positions that involved exercising leadership or supervision over other nurses. Thus one Jamaican-born nurse who had worked for 28 years as a nurse in Canada stated that she was 'the most senior nurse on the floor and yet was never allowed to be in charge. The head nurse would place a junior white nurse in charge.'

Racialized, gendered ideologies of Filipino and Black women, which we had earlier identified as key discourses in the relegation of these groups of migrant women to private domestic service, also facilitated their assignment to some of the most physically and mentally adverse nursing work. The stereotype of the Filipino women as nurturing and self-sacrificing in the service of others has also served a similar allocative function. Thus, one Filipino nurse stated that, 'I am assigned the most difficult patients and the worst shift. They think I am more compassionate and patient, being a Filipino.'[439] Comments made by white staff in Northwestern General Hospital about people of colour stereotyped Black employees as 'very slow', and nurses trained in Jamaica as arriving with 'below average standards' and in need of extra training.[440] Calliste has persuasively argued that stereotypes of Black women arising out of slavery and colonialism have constructed them as inherently suitable for the more boring and dead-end jobs in nursing that involve heavy physical labour, rather than intellectual and executive skills.[441]

The report by the OHRC into the firing of six Black nurses at Northwestern General in 1990 confirmed that workload assignment in that hospital systematically discriminated against Black nurses. Specifically, the report stated that 'methods of appointing people to positions within the staff showed "favouritism and denial of equal opportunity" '.[442] As a result, Black nurses were streamed to heavy-workload units such as chronic care, and away from acute care areas such as surgery. The OHRC found that 85 per cent of staff in the heavy-workload units at the Northwestern General was Black in a hospital whereas about 55 per cent of the nurses were people of colour.[443] While white nurses with similar qualifications were permitted to choose the floor they worked on, Black nurses were denied this consideration.[444] The consignment of nurses of colour to heavy-workload units provides fewer opportunities for further training and advancement. The strenuous physical labour associated with the heavy-workloads units also makes staff more prone to injuries that can be seriously disabling.[445] This bias reproduces a hierarchy where white nurses are placed on a mobility track to the top of the nursing hierarchy in administrative positions and in high specialty and high technology areas. In contrast, Black nurses and other nurses of colour tend to be allocated to the most injurious, least desirable forms of nursing, which can lead to disability and offer no opportunities for further advancement.[446]

The Manager of Human Resources at Northwestern General confirmed that the head nurses at that hospital were all white, arguing that for such positions, one needs at least 15 years of experience. By this logic, overwhelmingly white nurse leadership is the product of the historical scarcity of nurses of colour working in Canadian cities such as Toronto.[447] Yet nurse migration from the Philippines and the Caribbean to Canada has occurred for over three decades. The historical argument of benign systemic discrimination also does not take into account a key finding of the OHRC investigation into the complaints of the Black nurses fired from Northwestern General – namely that nurse managers used their discretionary power to systematically favour white nurses and discriminate against Black nurses and other nurses of colour. Moreover, a consultant's report into racism at Northwestern General reported an actual decline in nurse managers who were nurses of colour from 1989 when three out of ten were persons of colour, to 1993 when only one of ten was a person of colour.[448]

Our interviews with Filipino and Caribbean nurses, who had worked in several Toronto area hospitals, provided evidence of racially biased management practices consistent with this pattern. Nurses of colour reported that they were extensively questioned when they took sick leave, and were made to provide documentation, whereas white nurses would be free of such scrutiny.[449] White nurses would receive preferential treatment when it came to days off and vacation leave. One Jamaican nurse complained that 'special privileges and recognition were given and shown to my white colleagues but not to myself'.[450] One of the most common forms of racial bias in management practices involved differential documentation and discipline or what Agnes Calliste terms 'the racialization of surveillance practices in nursing'.[451] An instance of this was described by a Filipino nurse who spoke of an accumulation of negative documentation by her supervisor which eventually led to her termination.

> My supervisor accused me of derogatory behaviour towards patients (such as commenting to a patient in the OR that he was big and talking to a patient in the hallway with my gloves on) and incompetence. I got verbal consent but forgot to get written consent on which hand (right or left) should be operated. I tried to rectify but the patient was already pre-medicated. But the file went through four nurses, and I was the only one charged. Other nurses were guilty of what she accused me of but I was the only one disciplined. When I asked to be transferred, she found more fault with me. I was terminated without notice before I was supposed to go on maternity leave.[452]

In comparison to the relative leniency shown towards white nurses who made similar or more serious errors in patient care, Black nurses and other nurses of colour have been subject to excessive monitoring, differential documentation and disciplinary action by hospital management.[453] A Barbadian-born nurse who had worked in the same hospital job in Toronto for 21 years reported:

> I was wrongly accused of a situation by a white nurse who had herself created the situation. She told the white supervisor who acted

without first seeking clarification or hearing my side of the story ... A meeting was held and both the nurse and the supervisor apologized, but the white nurse was not penalized in any other way.[454]

A striking difference in the reports of discrimination by Filipino and West Indian nurses pertained to their responses to these discriminatory practices and incidents. The vast majority of Filipinas did not file complaints or grievances with their union or take any formal action. Some said that they refrained from complaining because they were naive or unknowledgeable about racial discrimination. Two Filipino nurses who faced racial slanders from patients worked as psychiatric nurses and felt that as the patients were elderly people and had psychiatric problems, little could be done about their offensive behaviour. Two other nurses whose first nursing jobs in the 1960s were in small towns in northern Canada where there were no other people of colour, described how they were subjected to the intolerance and racial slurs of townspeople. They had been brought there in a group of 20 Filipino nurses recruited by an agency in the Philippines. Both nurses described how they resigned from their jobs in order to escape the racism of the townspeople, the harsh winters and the remoteness of the communities to which they had been assigned. One of these nurses found that in her second job in nursing in a downtown Toronto hospital, she was assigned the most strenuous duties and the most difficult hours. Unaware of any avenues for redress, she left the practice of nursing and went into nursing education. Another Filipino nurse stated that in her first job working in 'post-operation', she was assigned the most difficult jobs and hours and was subjected to the verbal assaults of patients, especially seniors. Rather than reporting the discriminatory behaviour, she opted to leave this job after working there for only seven months, in order to join a Filipino-owned clinic. Only one of the 14 Filipino nurses who reported discrimination filed a grievance with her union.

Caribbean nurses were considerably more likely to seek assistance from their union, the ONA, and to file grievances against their employer to obtain redress for their subjection to discrimination. A Jamaican nurse who had been denied time off for a vacation, which was given instead to a junior white nurse, filed a grievance with her union and was subsequently given the time requested. A nurse from Grenada reported a similar bias in allocation of time off: 'The nurse manager encouraged a senior white nurse to apply for the same time period I had requested off so that she could use seniority to give the time to her instead of to me. She also made derogatory remarks about my race.'

With the assistance of the union, the time off requested was given to her and the nurse manager was made to apologize for the racist remark.

Given the systemic character of racism within hospitals, the pursuit of redress through the union grievance process did not always lead to a satisfactory result. Thus, a Barbadian nurse who had worked for 14 years in obstetrics grieved a case of management discrimination that went to arbitration and was settled. However, the 'hospital breached the settlement; hence there is another grievance pending after four years'.

A small number of West Indian nurses also indicated that they received help from managers and supervisors in dealing with their cases of discrimination. One Trinidadian nurse said that when her co-workers would 'fail to treat her as a fellow RN', her supervisor called a meeting. The outcome was that 'the biased attitude of co-workers was curtailed somewhat but not really changed'. In another case, where a white patient told a Jamaican nurse that 'she did not want any Black nurse looking after her', the supervisor intervened to inform the patient that the nurse assignment would not be changed and the patient eventually made an apology.

While co-worker harassment in multiracial nursing teams was part of the 'poisoned environment' of hospitals identified by nurses of colour, four of the West Indian nurses who had faced discrimination spoke of the moral support provided by co-workers. Thus, a Jamaican nurse spoke favourably of the help she received from her co-workers when she faced the resentment of white patients who would refer to her as 'the Black nurse'. 'Talking with other co-workers, we share experiences and support each other emotionally, and give each other reassurances to continue to do our work well.'[455] The presence of work groups in public institutions such as hospitals differentiates the capacity of nurses to resist demeaning treatment, from domestic workers who work in isolation. Structural trends in hiring and employment within hospitals during the current regressive political climate, however, are undermining the extent to which work groups offer an alternative system of workplace values than those imposed by management. One such trend is the shift in nurse-hiring patterns by hospitals from full-time to part-time and casual nurses. This structural change undermines teamwork and group morale that previously might have aided in building a sense of solidarity across, or indeed within, racial and ethnic lines. Threatened by a sense of solidarity among nurses, particularly among nurses of colour who were outspoken about the hospital's racist practices, hospital managers have required nurses, including nurses of colour, to act as spies on other nurses and report to management, or face retribution.[456]

Five of 19 West Indian nurses mentioned the OHRC as a source of assistance in dealing with their cases of discrimination, although none elaborated on the type of assistance provided. Most of these cases involved complaints of systemic discrimination that had not yet been resolved at the time of the survey. Both the ONA and the OHRC had initially been reluctant to deal with nurses' complaints of systemic racism in Toronto hospitals. While the ONA characterized the complaints as within the domain of 'human rights' rather than union issues, the OHRC viewed these complaints as labour-management problems that were better dealt with by the nurses' union.[457] It was not until antiracist organizations from the Black women's community began a campaign of organizing, protest and lobbying of the nurses' union and the OHRC that the Commission and the ONA began to take complaints of systemic racism in hospitals seriously.

The early to mid-1990s witnessed a flurry of organizing by the Black Congress of Women, out of which was formed the Coalition for Black Nurses, and by the Nurses and Friends Against Discrimination (NAFAD), a multiracial organization of nurses and community supporters. These antiracist associations organized demonstrations and rallies, held press conferences in the office of the OHRC, organized conferences on racism in health care, and attended members' labour arbitration hearings.[458] A key focus of the campaigns by these organizations was the pursuit of inquiries into systemic racism in hospitals and other health care institutions.[459] A key victory of this antiracist movement in nursing was the 1994 precedent-setting human rights agreement won by seven Black nurses who were discriminated against and unfairly dismissed by their employer, Northwestern General Hospital, four years earlier. In addition to the monetary settlement of $320 000, including $10 000 paid to each nurse for mental anguish, the settlement called on the hospital to implement new structures, policies and race-related training designed to rid the institution of racism.[460] However, the implementation of the terms of the settlement and the achievement of fundamental changes in the processes of systemic racism within the hospital has proven to be a challenge.[461] The campaigns of antiracist community coalitions which had accused the nurses' union of collaborating with employers in race-related grievances for the sake of 'good working relationships', successfully pressured ONA to adopt antiracist policies, structures and processes to deal with a 'flood' of complaints of racism from all over Ontario.[462]

Three of the West Indian nurses and one Filipino nurse in our survey stated that they had joined the community organization, NAFAD, in pressing the union, the OHRC, and the hospital to bring about antiracist reforms. These nurses permitted their own grievances to become test cases of systemic hospital racism and displayed courage and patience in withstanding the process, which took several years to wend its way through the investigative and mediation machinery of the Ontario government. The activism of these nurses of colour in participating in oppositional practices of community antiracist groups in order to contest the prevailing arrangements of power in institutions such as hospitals, human rights commissions and even class-based organizations such as trade unions is illustrative of the practice of 'dissident citizenship'.[463] Lacking responsive institutionalized channels of redress to their grievances within hospitals, and holding subordinate positions within nursing hierarchies, these nurses resisted the complex marginalization that they face because of their race, gender and class by creating their own effective organs of resistance, and in turn disrupting and reforming these institutional practices themselves.

Conclusion

In comparison with their counterparts who work as domestic workers, migrant women from the Philippines and the Caribbean who work as nurses collectively enjoy much readier access to both formal citizenship status, and citizenship rights and entitlements in Canada. A key difference is that while domestic workers are recruited into a programme whose temporary status and compulsory live-in condition leave them vulnerable to extreme exploitation, foreign nurses arrive in Canada with a variety of immigration statuses. Those who arrive with temporary employment visas encounter some of the same deficits in rights as foreign domestic workers, such as the inability to refuse assignment to the least desirable, most injurious units, and loss of legal status in the country following hospital consolidations and job termination. The majority of nurses in our Toronto-based survey, however, arrived with landed status, and as such are included within employment standards, social security and human rights legislation. In addition, working in public institutions, albeit often faced with huge bureaucracies, has afforded migrant nurses access to information, union rights, work support groups, grievance procedures and other means of seeking justice and equality – all mechanisms that are out of reach for the vast majority of domestic workers isolated in private family households.

Yet at the same time, there are significant commonalities that warrant attention among the experiences of West Indian and Filipino non-citizen domestic workers and nurses. The efforts of non-citizen nurses to acquire rights is linked to broader citizenship concerns shared by a wider constituency, stemming from the neo-liberal restructuring of the welfare state and specifically the privatization and crisis-ridden character of the health care system. The Canadian Nurses Association has predicted that, by 2011, Canada will have an acute shortage of 113 000 nurses.[464] As with foreign domestic workers, foreign-trained nurses from developing countries are being recruited to fill the 'caring gap' in hospitals, clinics, nursing homes, extended-care facilities, and in delivering home care. These pressures are also impacting on the domestic service industry. Private childcare and elder care are increasingly the only options available to families, and the state increasingly plays a policing role. While it metes out inadequate public services according to more and more restrictive criteria, it encourages citizens to see themselves as individuated consumers of child, elder and health care services that are increasingly transferred to the private sector. The state's neo-liberal policies have been detrimental to the rights of immigrants, workers and citizens. The renegotiation of citizenship rights associated with nursing, considered a highly skilled profession, and its bridged association with domestic care, considered a low-skilled profession, indicates the complex terrain of the citizenship divide.

By migrating to take up positions in Canadian nursing, Third World nurses of colour enter an occupation whose standards have been established in part according to norms of white femininity and the struggles for professional autonomy waged by white nursing leaders. This too is changing as nurses increasingly see themselves as workers subject to increasing exploitation through an appeal to the 'labour of love' they are expected to perform.[465] However, the enduring myth of professional autonomy has only served to intensify the alienation of nurses of colour. Faced with racist stereotypes which construct them as deficient in qualities required for executive positions and more specialized fields of nursing, Caribbean and Filipino nurses have encountered the persistent effects of systemic racism from management, co-workers, patients and the larger community. By preventing them from enjoying the benefits of their formal membership within Canadian citizenship, and in daily assaulting their sense of competence, dignity and equality with Canadian-born white nurses, systemic racism has eroded the substantive benefits of Canadian citizenship for nurses of colour.

Within our survey, the engagement within practices of dissident citizenship, to pressure a reluctant union and human rights commission, and resistant hospitals, to address systemic racism in nursing was more evident among West Indian than Filipino nurses. Beginning in the

1960s and until the 1980s, nurses from the Philippines were actively recruited for their English-language skills, and university training, with many having attained prior work experience in the United States. The immediate recognition of their qualifications, attainment of landed status and recruitment with a job offer facilitated the integration of these nurses into Canadian hospitals and the larger society on more equitable terms. In contrast, West Indian nurses entered more often with a sponsored immigrant status, which denied them access to many social programmes even years after becoming naturalized citizens, and had a more arduous time in attaining employment as registered nurses. They also reported greater levels of discrimination in hospitals. However, as racist practices that challenge the rights of Filipino nurses became widespread, it is clear that no nurses of colour are immune to racism. On the contrary, the difficulties encountered by West Indian nurses set a discriminatory standard that also limits the rights of Filipino nurses. Alternatively, the collective actions taken by West Indian nurses in challenging racist practices, as in the case of Northwestern General Hospital, indicate important precedents for all nurses of colour in combating systemic racism in the health care sector.

Many Filipino nurses who entered Canada as domestic workers through the LCP, have been sought out to provide a highly qualified but easily exploitable labour force to provide elder and home care.[466] In spite of a growing recruitment crisis in Canadian nursing, CIC persisted for many years in refusing to grant nurses any occupational points when assessing the merits of nursing applications for independent immigration status.[467] This obstacle within Canadian immigration policy, coupled with the high costs of immigrating with independent status (including the condition that applicants must have $10 000 in savings), has effectively denied the possibility of obtaining immediate landed status for many nurses from the Philippines. This is especially the case as many Filipino nurses are earning below-subsistence wages in the Philippines.

New immigration regulations accompanying the new IRPA of November 2001 removes 'labour shortages' from the eligibility criteria for independent immigrants, who are assessed according to a revised points system that places greater emphasis on 'transferable skills sets'.[468] The extent to which the new regulations will facilitate recruitment of foreign-trained nurses is as yet untested, although the Canadian Nursing Association expressed confidence that the revised points system would support the migration to Canada of foreign-trained qualified nurses.[469]

While these immigration reforms may facilitate nurse migration, Canadian nursing gatekeepers have introduced new restrictions that will render the transnational journey to becoming a nurse in Canada more difficult for migrant nurses from many developing countries. Thus, the OCN passed a motion to recommend to the government that by January 2005, all new RN registrants would be prepared at the baccalaureate level in order to keep pace with the specialized knowledge required in light of new technologies. This would effectively bar from entry into Canadian nursing many of the nurses from our West Indian survey who had entered Canada having completed diploma programmes.[470]

The irony is that even in the midst of an acknowledged nationwide nursing shortage fed by budget restraints and neo-liberal policies in health care, the perceived economic advantages of a 'variable' nursing workforce prevail, including a Third World migrant nurse population constructed as non-citizens.[471]

7

The Global Citizenship Divide and the Negotiation of Legal Rights

The transition from non-citizenship to citizenship status for Third World migrants in First World states entails successfully navigating various legal, institutional, financial and ideological barriers that are established by a range of gatekeepers. Recent critical scholarship on citizenship has tended to neglect the centrality of these gatekeepers in regulating access to formal, juridical citizenship, based on the argument that democratic rights are 'purely formal' in the face of massive social inequalities. Dismantling legal restrictions on the enjoyment of rights is seen to be unlikely to ensure real advances in human autonomy and democracy without concomitant measures to reduce material inequalities.[472] As Bridget Anderson has pointed out, citizenship debates have thus 'rather taken for granted the right to citizenship in the formalized sense of what passport a person holds and an individual's right to be present and work in a particular nation state'.[473]

From the vantage point of migrant non-citizens, however, formal, legal citizenship is exceedingly important in accessing an array of rights, including what continues to be state-defined rights to remain in a given country. The importance of the nation-state in extending, or alternatively withholding, rights to non-citizens is also evident when we turn to strategies undertaken by non-citizens to contest the oppression and exploitation that stems from their non-citizenship status. A central challenge in organizing for migrant rights is that gatekeepers evade or completely disclaim responsibility for the legal rights of these workers, or for their own role in establishing barriers to citizenship rights. Migrant workers, as individuals and in collective organizations, face various levels of restrictions in accessing rights. They are further compelled to challenge gatekeepers' ideological justifications for the marginalization of Third World non-citizens. Such justifications, often based on racist stereotypes and patriotic claims to protect national-citizens, are often treated as 'common sense' and beyond negotiation.

In participating in either individual challenges or in political activism that opposes the prevailing relations of power in the global citizenship divide, migrant workers can be viewed as engaging in what Holloway Sparks terms, 'dissident citizenship'.[474] By 'dissident citizenship', Sparks is referring to 'the practices of marginalised citizens who publicly contest prevailing arrangements of power by means of oppositional democratic practices that augment or replace institutionalised channels of democratic opposition when those channels are inadequate or unavailable'.[475] Sparks offers a rich analysis of forms of citizenship practices of 'marginalised citizens' that involve dissent and an ethic or political courage. The analysis is, however, silent on the question of the absence of formal citizenship status among some groups of dissidents, such as temporary or non-citizen migrants. The practices of these non-citizen activists are nonetheless central in contributing to a redefinition and expansion of citizenship within and beyond the borders of the nation-state. The literature that investigates emergent forms of transnational or global citizenship, specifically popular activist networks transcending borders, also tends not to problematize the legal–juridical status of 'global citizens'.[476] Indeed, the literature on transnationalism often assumes that mobile people enjoy dual or multiple citizenships.[477] Unlike citizens of advanced capitalist states, poorer non-citizen migrant workers are legally barred from participating in certain forums of citizenship deliberation and participation such as voting or otherwise engaging in electoral, parliamentary or other forms of established politics. For non-citizens struggling to obtain full citizenship rights, formal channels through which to make claims to such rights are themselves limited. Moreover, as discussed in Chapter 2, access to full citizenship rights within advanced capitalist states, even for those who enjoy full legal citizenship status, is itself a restricted and partial experience, especially if they face exclusions based on class, racialized and gendered criteria.

Within these constraints, the limited formal, legal channels that are available for non-citizens to attempt to gain increased citizenship rights within advanced capitalist states take on, we maintain, increased importance. If we consider the case of foreign domestic workers in Canada, their non-citizenship, non-resident status is defined by immigration legislation, rendering the non-citizenship of these migrant workers inherently unstable. It is subject to a continual and dynamic process of both reproduction and renegotiation. Such negotiation on the part of domestic workers includes navigating the obstacles to their entry as landed immigrants, or even as temporary domestic workers, that exist at the border of the receiving state. For instance, our Toronto-based survey of domestics from the Caribbean found that in order to circumvent the anti-Caribbean and anti-Black biases among Canadian immigration gatekeepers and private domestic placement agencies, West Indian women were more likely to enter as visitors rather than through the LCP. They then would remain to work illegally in domestic service.[478]

At the micro-level of private family-household, domestic workers engaged in a multitude of small acts of resistance, often on a daily basis, to the indignities stemming from their employers' denial of their autonomy, privacy and status as paid workers. For instance, household workers will resist their employers' attempts to define them as 'one of the family', which obliterates both their legal status as a worker, and their own obligations and responsibilities as members of their own families.[479] In order to obtain some privacy and distance from employers, many live-in workers co-rent small apartments with other domestic workers in order to gain an autonomous private living space, cook their own food, and socialize during their days off. Ultimately, if workers assess that the costs of staying with demanding or abusive employers are too high, they may choose to leave. Such a decision is not taken lightly, however. Leaving the job also means losing one's place of residence. It necessitates quickly finding other live-in employment that may not always be readily available. Ultimately, such a decision risks jeopardizing the worker's status in the country and future chances of permanent residence, and the concomitant sponsorship of family members and citizenship rights.

Obtaining legal recognition for residence and mobility rights, even in partial and highly conditional ways, can make a major difference in the lives of individual non-citizens and at the same time challenge the legitimacy of state practices of exclusion. Yet non-citizens are far less likely to use legal channels, given that a nation-state's laws will inevitably reflect a bias towards citizens and against non-citizen 'aliens'. Poorer migrants also lack the economic capital that permits wealthier transnational migrants to negotiate flexible terms of entry and entitlements from advanced states. Sparks's discussion of dissident citizenship considers 'unconventional forms of democratic engagement and opposition'.[480] But in the case of non-citizens, the very act of protesting the policies and actions of a state that tolerates their presence within its borders only if they acquiesce to considerable constraints on their freedom, is itself a form of 'unconventional' and dissident practice. The fact that dissidence against the national laws of the receiving society can jeopardize their legal status in the host country, and future prospects of attaining legal citizenship status, is testimony of the courage of migrant activists in contesting unjust immigration, citizenship and labour laws.

From this perspective, this chapter examines the role of the Canadian courts as an arena of contested citizenship, in both circumscribing and providing a means to advance the rights of foreign domestic workers under the LCP. Given that courts are particularly wrapped in the veil of universality, equality and fairness, they are of particular interest in considering the negotiating strategies of excluded non-citizens. The courts have offered individual non-citizens one arena to battle the non-observance by immigration authorities of some rights that had been ceded to migrant domestics in past battles. Legal strategies to win rights, however, must contend with the justifications that exist in both international and national law permitting discrimination in immigration policy. The law not only permits, but also enforces the ontology of state sovereignty, the deference of the judiciary to the sovereign power of the national state to assert control over its borders, and over its non-citizen residents within these borders. Given that the courts provide an arena where the norms of civic justice and human rights are, however, expected to prevail, they also offer a locus of transparency for the extreme abuse often endured by foreign domestic workers. These cases reveal in stark relief the hiatus that marks the citizenship divide. They also expose the contradiction between the inclusive rhetoric of citizenship and the exclusive reality for the non-citizen seeking inclusion.

Negotiating rights through the courts

The Canadian courts represent one arena where citizenship rights are contested and negotiated. Despite appearances, the courts are not a neutral arena. To date, most jurisprudence involving domestic workers has consisted of cases brought by the state against individual foreign domestic workers, rather than cases initiated by domestic workers to press for their legal rights, or to legally challenge the foreign domestic worker programme itself. Some of the mandatory conditions of the LCP, the contravention of which has led the Department of Citizenship and Immigration to reject workers' applications for permanent residence, include: the condition that caregivers not take additional work outside their caregiving duties; the compulsory live-in requirement; mandatory successful medical examination of family members and the requirement that foreign caregivers work 24 months within a three-year period from the time of residence and work in Canada. A few cases will be discussed here to illuminate the role of the courts in challenging or alternatively reinforcing the legitimacy of immigration authorities to deprive foreign domestic workers of citizenship rights. Other cases have been precipitated by domestic workers' failure to meet the regulations of the LCP, breaches that are then regarded by immigration authorities as just cause for denying permanent residence to these workers and seeking their removal from the country. Although the use of litigation on behalf of domestic workers' rights has not been extensive, the cases fought in the courts by workers and their advocates are significant. Individual domestic workers have used the courts to stay deportation orders brought against them in order to remain in Canada to work, and/or to be eligible for permanent residence. Several cases came before the Canadian courts in the late 1970s and 1980s involving the issue of marital and family misrepresentation.

'Misrepresentation' cases reveal the manner in which state policies of both receiving and sending states criminalize migrant women in a dual strategy of importing cheap household labour and inhibiting permanent migration. The emergence of cases involving misrepresentation of marital status and family obligations is a legacy of the Caribbean Scheme of the 1950s and 1960s, and the 1973 Temporary Employment Authorisation Program. These earlier programmes explicitly disqualified married women, women in common law relationships and/or women with dependent children from coming to Canada as domestic workers.[481] Immigration authorities attempted to forestall the settlement and reproduction of families and communities of colour through the legal fiction that Third World domestics imported to look after Canadian families had no family attachments themselves.

The Foreign Domestic Movement retained the incentive to conceal marital status and family commitments. It negatively linked the presence of 'dependent family members residing outside of Canada who may be coming to Canada to join the applicant' to the assessment of the future ability of the low income applicant to become 'self-sufficient'.[482] A failure to demonstrate self-sufficiency would prevent the applicant from successfully obtaining landed immigrant status in Canada.

In the 1979 case, *Lodge v. M.M.I.*,[483] the Federal Court of Appeal ruled that it had no jurisdiction to prevent the removal of 'seven Jamaican mothers' previously admitted as landed immigrants while their complaints of discriminatory treatment were pending before the newly established Canadian Human Rights Commission.[484] The grounds for deportation were that the women had misrepresented their marital status and family commitments when applying to enter Canada. The familial relations of the seven women were subsequently revealed when they sought to sponsor their spouses and children and bring them to Canada as permanent residents. This case became a rallying point for a major campaign publicizing the Canadian government's racist and sexist policies against foreign domestics. It drew the support of domestic advocacy associations, Canada's Black community and antiracist organizations. While unsuccessful in their litigation, the sympathetic publicity the case attracted ultimately won the Jamaican women re-admission to Canada and landed status through the provision of Minister's Permits. The latter is an exceptional intervention available to Cabinet Ministers, in cases such as these, on humanitarian grounds. Such intervention does not alter the nature of the law in general.

In the 1989 case, *Fernandez*, reported on by Macklin, 'an inquiry under the *Immigration Act* was ordered to investigate the allegation that Ms Fernandez, *qua* visitor, was in violation of section 27(2)(g)' which speaks of 'fraudulent or improper means or misrepresentation of any material fact'.[485] The adjudicator in *Fernandez* ruled that misrepresentation of marital or family obligations are 'material' only in the evaluation of immigrants, not, as in Ms Fernandez' case, of visitors. Ms Fernandez' order of deportation was consequently overturned.[486] *Fernandez* was a victory for foreign domestics who felt pressured to conceal their marital and family ties, and who were often actually counselled to conceal them by employment agencies in their respective countries,[487] but for whom such disclosure is ultimately a condition for immigration to Canada.

Notwithstanding the legal victory for foreign domestics in *Fernandez*, the institutionalization of the right to remain in the LCP, and thus in Canada, despite having misrepresented one's marital and/or family status, occurred only as the product of persistent lobbying and pressure by domestic worker associations. Thus, the West Coast Domestic Workers Association (WCDWA) reported in October 1989 that divergent practices of dealing with marital misrepresentation were followed in the Vancouver and Toronto Immigration offices. In Vancouver, domestics with misrepresented marital status were taken to immigration hearings and ordered to leave Canada. In Toronto, immigration officials permitted domestic workers to write to the federal government to disclose their true marital status. The change in the Toronto policy was reported to result from meetings between domestic worker advocates and Immigration representatives.[488] Following a meeting between WCDWA representatives and immigration authorities in Vancouver, the practice of handling misrepresentation in that office was made consistent with that of the Toronto office. Subsequently, misrepresentation of marital and family status by foreign domestics was to become relevant only at the time of application for landed status.[489]

The uneven process by which the new policy on misrepresentation came into practice and has been administered reveals two essential aspects of immigration policy, of which foreign domestic worker policy forms a part. First, immigration policy involves a very wide berth of discretion on the part of individual immigration officials. This allows for the exercise of many arbitrary and prejudicial biases that systematically disfavour constituencies who do not fit the ideologically constructed notions of 'real' and 'desirable' immigrants. Second, as Deborah Cheney describes it, 'immigration law, which consists of both legislation, non-statutory rules, and administrative practice, is less an entity in or of itself that can be fixed and "read" than a shifting array of expressions which confuse and disorientate'.[490] Foreign domestic policy in particular has developed as a mutating patchwork of administrative rules and regulations. Given this fact, immigration officers who are asked to administer such policy both in Canada and abroad have acted with inconsistent understandings of the policy. The inclination to turn to stereotypes and discriminatory past practices rather than to a standardized body of legally accountable criteria is endemic.

The case of *Eugenio v. Canada (Minister of Citizenship and Immigration)*[491] focused on misrepresentation of the domestic worker's identity. Edith Mabini Eugenio had applied from the Philippines to be a domestic helper in Singapore. While boarding the plane to Singapore, she noticed that the passport provided by her recruiting agent was not in her name but under the name of Erlinda Angeles Ullero. The agent explained that he had arranged for her to take the place of another nanny who had been approved but who subsequently could not travel. The financial survival of her family (her husband and four children) was the major motivating factor for Ms Eugenio to accept overseas work under a false identity. Approximately two years later, in 1990, still using the false passport, Ms Eugenio successfully applied from Singapore to enter Canada under the FDM. While in Canada, she continued to use her false identity to acquire official documents including employment authorizations, a driver's license, passport, US visas and social insurance number. In 1993, she was granted landed status under the assumed name. After being injured in an accident that prevented her from visiting her family in the Philippines, the appellant decided to reveal her true identity to immigration authorities.

When an immigration inquiry was conducted, an adjudicator ordered Ms Eugenio deported. Ms Eugenio was found to be a person described in Section 27(1)(e) of the *Immigration Act*, that is, a person 'who was granted landing by reason of possession of a false or improperly obtained passport, visa or other document pertaining to his [*sic*] admission or by reason of any fraudulent or improper means or misrepresentation of any material fact whether exercised or made by himself [*sic*] or by any other person'. Ms Eugenio's appeal contended that the issuance of the deportation order under Section 27(1)(e), which applies to permanent residents, stopped the Minister from denying that the appellant was a permanent resident. The Minister, relying on Section 27(2)(g) of the Act, argued that Ms Eugenio was not landed, did not have status as a permanent resident, and thus had no right to appeal. Mr Teitelbaum, the adjudicator at the Appeal Division hearing, rejected the arguments of the appellant's counsel that an agent, rather than Ms Eugenio herself, had concocted the false identity, and also disregarded the accomplishments of Ms Eugenio during her five years in Canada. 'No amount of sympathy or taking into account her contribution to Canadian society alters the fact that Ms Eugenio does not exist in Canada.'[492] The Appeal Division adjudicator also represented Ms Eugenio as a criminal, who 'once having started in the cloak of another ... perpetuated the fraud by obtaining a variety of documents to sustain the charade'.[493] In the view of the adjudicator, she had 'committed an act of impersonation punishable under the Criminal Code' and was 'liable to imprisonment for a term not exceeding fourteen years'.[494]

The reasoning of the Immigration adjudicators in *Eugenio* is premised on a liberal model of individual autonomy and responsibility. Such a perspective is blind to the international political economy that drives Third World women to leave their families and endure years of servile labour overseas in isolating and fearful circumstances. The citizenship divide requires these women to become enmeshed in various layers of restriction, regulation and inevitably deceit, in the process of obtaining even minimal rights within Canada. But deceit is itself treated by differential criteria depending upon which side of the citizenship divide is affected.

Domestic worker migration is compelled by broader socio-economic and political forces, and operates largely through the coercive and often fraudulent practices of intermediaries such as recruitment and placement agencies. These aspects of the domestic worker business are ignored within immigration hearings where domestic workers are treated as individuals assumed to exercise judgements within a liberal

framework of freedom and choice. Third World women who seek redress
in their quest to obtain citizenship rights are treated with suspicion, as
individuals wilfully breaking the law. Appellants become criminalized
as persons who commit indictable offences, rather than being seen as
'emotionally complex human beings trapped and manipulated within
the pressures of a wider socio-political framework', the international
political economy, and the restrictions of particular state policies.[495] The
fear among foreign domestics of disclosure of a fraudulent identity
imposed by a recruitment agency is the same fear that inhibits workers
from seeking redress against employers whose employment practices
violate federal immigration and provincial employment standards.
Domestic workers often accurately perceive that they will be punished
for failing to observe immigration regulations and policy, while their
employers will escape all sanctions.

The liberal myth of legal-administrative equality between citizen-
employers and non-citizen employees was challenged in the ruling
made in *Bernardez v. Canada*.[496] *Bernardez*[497] involves a case of a Filipino
woman who was admitted to Canada as a live-in caregiver and who was
required by her employer to work in the employer's family business, a
variety store some distance from the employer's home. She was asked to
clean, attend to customers and perform other chores associated with
maintaining store operations. Ms Bernardez did not receive additional
payment for her work at the store, but acquiesced to the extra work in
the belief that her refusal would lead to her removal back to the
Philippines. A deportation order was issued against Ms Bernardez following the finding of an immigration adjudicator that her employment
in the store was not a legitimate extension of her domestic duties under
the LCP, but rather unauthorized employment in a completely different
job. In his decision, the adjudicator reasoned that Ms Bernardez' behaviour was reasonable under the circumstances given to 'obedient domestic servants'. He also exonerated the employers from blame, arguing that
they made an understandable error in regarding their business as an
extension of their home. Nevertheless, the domestic worker was issued a
deportation order while the employer's actions were not penalized. The
adjudicator characterized Ms Bernardez in the following way:

> *You are an obedient domestic servant.* The employer asked you to work
> in their place of business as well as the home and you in pursuit of
> the objectives which are readily apparent to everyone were *obedient*
> and carried out these duties. It may very well be and probably is that
> the employers were acting in good faith. They probably considered

this place of business to be an extension of their home, but nevertheless they [*sic*] are quite separate. It would be perhaps a little different
if the household, as *often is in ethnic situations* [*sic*] is located in the
same building, perhaps above the store and things like this might get
fuzzy, but here it's a quite clear-cut difference.[498]

The value of obedience is reinforced here and in other parts of the
adjudicator's decision as an appropriate attitude to be displayed by Third
World female domestic servants towards their employers. Obedience is an
attribute commonly linked with pre-capitalist relations between masters
and servants/slaves, in contrast with the more impersonal, contractual
workplace relations associated with modern capitalism. Yet, because this
obedience led the servant, Ms Bernardez, to carry out unauthorized
employment contrary to Section 27(2)(b) and (e) of the Immigration Act,
the adjudicator issued a deportation order. The Federal Court of Canada
(Trial Division), however, overturned this decision. In the judgement of
Jerome A.C.J., the immigration adjudicator had neglected to take into
consideration the exploitation of Ms Bernardez who was compelled 'to
submit to her employer's reasonable demands to clean their family
store'.[499] The judge argued that the question of the employment under
Section 2 of the Immigration Act depended on the 'circumstances in
which it is performed' which in this case included the 'lack of collusion
with the employer, the fact that no surplus money or benefits were
received by the applicant, and the fact that this foreign domestic feared
potential dismissal and was ignorant of her right to refuse the unautho-
rised work'. Associate Chief Justice Jerome also brought attention to the
coerced nature of work performed by foreign live-in workers in suggesting
that it is questionable that the work of 'a domestic who is coerced or compelled to perform duties for her employer can truly be considered to be
employed in that capacity'. In failing to consider these issues, Mr Justice
Jerome concluded that the adjudicator committed an error of law. He also
argued that fairness was lacking in the Immigration Department's failure
to advise the applicant that she was engaged in unauthorized conduct in
order to afford her 'opportunity to correct the impugned behaviour prior
to being expelled from Canada'. Citing Jerome's own previous judgement
in *Turingan v. Canada*,[500] Jerome in *Bernardez* argued that:

> ... the purpose of the Live-in Caregiver Program is to *facilitate the
> attainment of permanent resident status* for foreign domestic workers
> and, therefore, it is incumbent on the Immigration Department
> to adopt *a flexible and constructive approach* in its dealing with the

program's participants. Failure to do so undermines the purpose of the program.[501]

Such decisions on the part of the Federal Court overturning Immigration and Refugee Board decisions, reflect a contextualized liberal approach to justice in evaluating the restrictions on live-in caregivers' capacity to act as autonomous subjects, and the necessity of the Immigration department to honour the stated 'balance of objectives' in the LCP that are to benefit both employers and employees, rather than citizen-employers alone. In other words, the court explicitly recognized the limitations of a purely individualist ontology of liberal law, which ignores the inequality of power between employers and employees in unfree conditions, and the absence of choice on the part of unfree workers that is in fact mandated by Canadian immigration law in the form of the LCP.[502] In these cases, the universalistic promise of citizenship has come up against the underlying reality of the exploitation of non-citizen domestic workers.

The court here also invokes the view that one of the legitimate purposes of the foreign domestic worker programme is to facilitate the attainment of permanent resident status for migrant workers. This was an objective that had been incorporated into the migrant domestic programme only after vociferous protest and advocacy by domestic organizations against the previous domestic worker programme (1973–81) that had offered no opportunity whatsoever to cross from temporary to permanent resident/citizenship status.[503] Several other Federal court judgements admonish the Immigration department for failing to facilitate the fulfilment of this goal and for its use of technical grounds to issue deportation orders against domestic workers who have breached LCP or FDM regulations.[504] In other words, the courts have in a handful of instances permitted migrant household workers to compel immigration authorities to treat them in accordance with their probationary status for the prize of citizenship in Canada, rather than as merely highly exploitable and expendable surplus labour.

The judicial branch of the state, however, if at times receptive to arguments that formally recognize certain legal rights of foreign domestic workers, stands in stark contrast to the intransigence of immigration authorities. The latter have continuously defined technical breaches of the LCP as deportable offences. In the highly publicized case of Leticia Cables, an Edmonton-based Filipino nanny, the Immigration Minister, Elinor Caplan, refused to stay the deportation order against Ms Cables despite the widespread support and sympathy she had received from opposition Members of Parliament, the mainstream press, the Alberta labour movement, churches, the Filipino community and immigrant women's groups. Ms Cables, who sought sanctuary in an Edmonton church, became known as the 'nanny who worked too much' after it had been revealed that she had violated the LCP rules by working simultaneously for more than one employer. She subsequently left Canada in March 2000, and an opposition MP sarcastically remarked that the Minister had refused to 'set a precedent in Mrs Cables' case [which might cause] the entire live-in caregivers program [to] collapse'.[505]

The case of *Baker v. Canada*[506] differs from the other judicial rulings considered thus far in that the appellant did not enter Canada under the foreign domestic worker programme. Nor does this case refer specifically to the obligations of the Canadian Immigration Department to participants in such programmes. In *Baker*, the wider issue of migrant workers' rights in relation to international law in general, governing the rights of children in particular, comes into focus.

Mavis Baker, a Jamaican citizen and a mother of four children, came to Canada from Jamaica in 1981. She supported herself illegally as a live-in domestic worker for 11 years. Ms Baker entered Canada as a visitor and took up domestic work, as have many tens of thousands of Caribbean women, at a time when legal entry as domestics from this region had been foreclosed by Canadian immigration authorities. She had another four children in Canada. Following the birth of her last child, she suffered from 'post-partum psychosis' and was diagnosed with 'paranoid schizophrenia'. While Ms Baker was receiving treatment, two of her children were placed in the custody of their father and the other two went to foster care, though these two children were returned to her when her health improved. Her 1993 application under Section 114(2) of the Immigration Act for leave to make an internal application for landing was dismissed on the basis of insufficient humanitarian and compassionate (H and C) grounds. A deportation order was issued and served to Ms Baker in May 1994. Notes made by the subordinate reviewing officer (Lorenz) and subsequently used by a senior officer (Caden) when reaching the decision to deport Ms Baker included the following passages:

> PC is unemployed – on Welfare. No income shown – no assets. Has four Cdn.-born children – four other children in Jamaica – HAS A TOTAL OF EIGHT CHILDREN ... [...] This case is a catastrophy [sic]. It is also an indictment of our 'system' that the client came here as a visitor in Aug. '81, was not ordered deported until Dec. '92 and in

APRIL '94 IS STILL HERE! ... The PC is a paranoid schizophrenic and on welfare. She has no qualifications other than as a domestic. She has FOUR CHILDREN IN JAMAICA AND ANOTHER FOUR BORN HERE. She will, of course, be a tremendous strain on our social welfare systems for (probably) the rest of her life. There are no H and C factors other than her FOUR CANADIAN BORN CHILDREN. Do we let her stay because of that? I am of the opinion that Canada can no longer afford this kind of generosity ...[507]

The Federal Court of Canada (Trial Division) ordered the stay of the deportation order. Justice Rouleau cited the argument of the applicant's counsel that Ms Baker's removal would be in violation of the Canadian Charter of Rights and Freedoms (presumably Section 7, 'life, liberty and security of the person', although the specific section was not cited). However, the Federal Court of Appeal dismissed Ms Baker's application for judicial review. The Motions Judge also certified a question concerning the international Convention on the Rights of the Child. At issue was whether Ms Baker's deportation order should be stayed given the interests of her four Canadian-born children, who were citizens in Canada.[508]

The Supreme Court overturned Ms Baker's deportation order and accepted her appeal, which meant that the matter would be returned to the Minister for re-determination by a different immigration officer. The Supreme Court justices concluded that the principle of procedural fairness had been violated in this case insofar as there was a reasonable apprehension of bias in the making of the decision. Justice L'Heureux-Dubé pointed out that given the great importance to the individuals affected by the decisions taken by immigration officers, a special sensitivity and openness to diversity is required of these officers. Instead, the immigration officer's notes reveal a predisposition to stereotypes regarding Baker's mental illness, her training as a domestic worker, and her status as a single mother with several children. The officer's frustration with the 'system' was also noted to have interfered with his duty to act impartially.

The lower courts in the *Baker* case had forwarded the question of the approach to be taken to the interests of children when reviewing an H and C decision. The Supreme Court found that the decision to deport Ms Baker was unreasonable insofar as the immigration officer had been completely dismissive of the interests of Ms Baker's children. The immigration officer had failed to take a contextual approach to statutory interpretation of Section 114(2) of the Immigration Act governing H and C considerations, which requires close attention to the interests and needs of children. The court held: 'Children's rights, and attention to their interests, are central humanitarian and compassionate values in Canadian society.'[509] The ruling thus recognizes that non-citizens with children born in Canada in fact do have human rights in Canada.

While the Supreme Court decision to overturn the deportation order of Ms Baker was unanimous, judges were divided as to whether international conventions ratified by Canada had any legal effect if they had not been incorporated into domestic law. The view of the majority was that the values reflected in international human rights law 'may help inform the contextual approach to statutory interpretation and judicial review', whereas a minority disagreed. Writing for the minority, Justice Iacobucci argued that the Court should not give 'force and effect within the domestic legal system to international obligations undertaken by the executive alone that have yet to be subject to the democratic will of Parliament'.[510] Given that the Convention on the Rights of the Child was not part of the law of Canada, Justice Iacobucci argued that it had no application to this case. This interpretation suggests that even where international rights conventions offer a greater range of rights to migrants, the doctrines of state sovereignty and parliamentary supremacy might be invoked by some Canadian judges to limit the application of international norms, rights and obligations.

Nevertheless, the majority in *Baker* accepted that international law constitutes 'a part of the legal context in which legislation is enacted and read'. Insofar as is possible, therefore, 'interpretations that reflect these values and principles are preferred'.[511] The *Baker* case thus raises important questions about the strategic uses of international conventions in Canadian courts to broaden access of foreign domestic workers to certain rights, including the right to remain within the country legally. It is notable that the IRPA that received Royal Assent in the Fall of 2001 did indeed, state the need for immigration policy to take into account the children's rights convention.[512] The international convention for which domestic worker advocates have vigorously though unsuccessfully sought Canada's signature and compliance has been the International Convention on the Protection of the Rights of All Migrant Workers and Members of their Families.[513]

Baker also indicates that the courts can serve to render visible the complex human dimensions of the migration of Third World female workers to Canada. These workers may remain for many years, bear children who establish ties with Canada, and then, like any individual, become ill and incapacitated – all costs to the Canadian state which a 'temporary worker' programme such as the FDM/LCP were designed to prevent and to export to the migrant worker's home country.

The cases considered thus far pertain to purported migrant worker transgressions of the domestic worker programme's or wider Immigration rules and regulations, with the attendant consequence of deportation from the country. That very few reported cases involve employer abuses of their institutionalized power over non-citizen, live-in caregivers, is in itself significant. One exception is *Mustaji v. Tjin and Tjin*[514] which was decided by the B.C. Supreme Court, and unsuccessfully appealed by the defendants. This case involved an extreme instance of exploitation of Sarmini Mustaji, a domestic worker held virtually prisoner in the Vancouver home of her employers, Khi Yeong and Rosna Elly Tjin. After working for the Tjins as a nanny for their four children in Indonesia and Singapore, in 1989, Ms Mustaji accompanied her employers to Vancouver, as a participant in the FDM programme. Ms Mustaji and Khi Yoeng Tjin signed a document provided by Immigration Canada outlining Ms Mustaji's work duties, her monthly wages of $883 for a 40-hour week, and room and board deductions of $225 per month. The plaintiff testified that after her arrival in Vancouver she worked for the Tjins as their live-in servant and nanny for three years and three months, over 15 hours a day, seven days a week, and 365 days a year. For this work she was paid $40 or $50 every two to three months.

Her employers kept Ms Mustaji a virtual prisoner, denying her use of the telephone, the freedom to go out on her own or the opportunity to invite friends home. Her isolation was aggravated by her inability to speak or read English, and her lack of both friends and money. By approaching a stranger, Ms Mustaji was placed in contact with the WCDWA. The WCDWA appointed a lawyer, assisted her in fleeing her employers and helped her file a claim for wages with the B.C. Employment Standards Branch. Ms Mustaji successfully recovered $5000 for the last six months of her employment. The B.C. Supreme Court ruled that the Tjins had a duty not to exploit Ms Mustaji and upheld a jury award totalling $250000 – the highest amount ever awarded in a domestic worker case.[515] The Tjins lost their appeal of the B.C. Supreme Court decision. They were ordered by the Court to pay Ms Mustaji about $75000 in lost wages and $175000 in damages for breach of fiduciary duty.

Mustaji serves as a warning to employers that limitless exploitation of foreign-born household workers may result in hefty monetary damages to be paid to their super-exploited domestic employees. It also shows that Canadian courts and juries regard the enslavement of foreign domestic workers as an unacceptable practice. Aspects of this case, however, such as the extreme nature of reported abuse, the exceptional wealth of the employers, and the fact that the employers were, like their domestic employee, also foreign-born Asians – limit the general application of this legal victory to the broader category of foreign domestic workers. The *Mustaji* case could be read as an isolated case of a notoriously bad, and not incidentally foreign, employer. In effect, it falsely marks as exceptional the case of the 'bad employer'. And the case indicates that where there are such 'bad employers', they are the exception, and they are brought under the discipline of a wider, and benevolent, legal structure within the state. Yet the evidence overwhelmingly indicates that the majority of live-in nannies in Canada continue to be paid less than is legally required and continue to work and live under substandard conditions (usually) employed by white Canadian citizens. The Canadian government's liability for establishing these conditions for domestic worker exploitation, and for failing to protect the limited rights available to these vulnerable workers, was never raised in *Mustaji*.

Conclusion

Courts have generally been sympathetic to upholding domestic workers' procedural rights on an individual basis to stem the unjust deportation of these workers from Canada. Litigation has challenged the unfairness and restrictive technical reasoning deployed in immigration hearings to deny continued legal presence in the country, or permanent residence, to individual foreign domestic workers who have done their time in the purgatory of live-in domestic service. Thus, domestic workers and their advocacy associations that have sought vindication of domestic migrant rights in the courts have engaged in 'accountability politics, or the effort to hold powerful actors to their previously stated policies or principles'.[516] However, the majority of cases of abuse do not reach the stage of legal action. And there has been no judicial review of the federal domestic worker programme(s) in general.[517]

   At the heart of the judiciary arm of the state's reluctance to challenge even the most blatantly discriminatory aspects of immigration policy, lies its structural and ideological subordination to the entrenched priority in maintaining authority over border regulation as a keystone to the defence of its sovereignty. There is profound anathema to the idea of bringing the administration of the Canadian immigration system under scrutiny using any section of the Charter of Rights and Freedoms.[518] The exceptions have tended to be in refugee cases, where Section 7 of the Charter has been invoked, and where in contrast to immigration cases, the right to liberty and security of the person could be seen to be at stake in decisions made by Canadian immigration officials.[519] In contrast, the Federal courts have refused to apply the Charter to immigrant selection decisions by visa officers, the representatives of the Immigration Department abroad.[520]

Critical immigration lawyers aptly characterize immigration law as 'unnecessarily arbitrary, unfair and discriminatory'.[521] Immigration law is compared with the Hydra, the monstrous serpent of Greek myth. This Hydra 'turns a number of faces toward those who come before it', but, when successful court cases of legislative amendments 'strike off one of the heads ... new heads replace it'.[522] Immigration law is based on the fundamental belief that sovereign states can accord 'aliens' access to mere 'privileges' rather than 'rights', and that such 'privileges' exist at the pleasure of the state. While states may make available a share of the bounty to 'guests' that they more readily provide to their citizens, they hold to the belief that they alone decide which guests have access to their territory and to which of the state's resources. States are especially loathe to constitutionally enshrine claims for rights to 'guests' who are imported to provide labour in 'menial', low-paid jobs, such as private child and elder home care.

It is significant, however, that in light of recent global and regional trade agreements – such as the WTO, NAFTA and negotiations towards the FTAA – states are themselves increasingly subject to international juridical rulings when they are seen to enact legislation that could inter-fere with the 'rights' of multinational corporations to unfettered profit earnings.[523] At issue then, is not only the role of the elected representa-tives of the state as the highest decision-making body, but also the non-elected opinions of court adjudicators. What we see is another indication of the hierarchical differentiations in citizenship, where corporate rights are on the ascendancy in terms of juridical authority, while the rights of foreign workers are largely ignored, and granted only under duress and in exceptional cases. It is in light of this systemic real-ity that migrant workers have turned increasingly to the negotiation of citizenship rights based on collective strategies of resistance. This is the subject of the next, and concluding, chapter of this study.

8
Dissident Transnational Citizenship: Resistance, Solidarity and Organization

The preceding discussion has taken as a premise an imperialist world system in which citizenship is a negotiated process, a relationship that reflects and reproduces an array of social differentiations, including the global divide between citizens of the economic North and South. We have attempted to trace the negotiation process of Third World women of colour as they encounter various obstacles and challenges in their efforts to acquire First World citizenship rights.

In recent years, the hegemony of corporate globalization has meant that the designated 'rights' of capital to travel freely across borders have increased, while the mobility and citizenship rights of people, particularly the poorest and most vulnerable people, have tended to decline. Canada, as an advanced capitalist state, has actively led in the promotion of the neo-liberal, pro-corporate agenda both at home and internationally. Its immigration policies have reflected neo-liberal principles in favouring investor immigrants and those skilled in the information technology sector over migrants whose skills are in caring for people, and in the heavy enforcement emphasis evident in the regulation of non-business migrants and asylum-seekers. In this context, we have focused on the experiences of two distinct groups of migrant women workers, domestic workers and nurses, originating from two Third World regions, the Philippines and the West Indies, for the purpose of tracing the patterns of negotiating citizenship through the various dimensions of gatekeeping that exist in the global system. We have attempted to demonstrate that modern citizenship is a process that combines the promise of accessing a wide range of often-fundamental rights, with the creation and reproduction of inequality among individuals and groups in the context of contemporary globalization.

While structural adjustment programmes have tended to create pressures within Third World states for increasing out-migration, First World states have tended to tighten the controls on immigration and limit the access to citizenship rights of those who are able to enter. Canada's increasing restrictions on the ability of foreign domestic workers and nurses to gain access to landed immigrant, or permanent, residence status in the country is a case in point. While nurses are normally permitted entry as landed immigrants, racialized criteria have constrained access for nurses from Third World countries, and limited their rights within the nursing profession. Foreign domestic workers, however, have been subject to unique and extraordinary regulations, including the current federal LCP. We maintain that though Canada's foreign domestic policy is commonly identified as a model of fairness, in fact the requirements of a compulsory live-in relationship with the private employer, and temporary residence status in the country, deny foreign domestic workers basic citizenship rights.

A central point of the analysis presented here is that negotiation of citizenship rights includes a complex process of navigation of contested relationships with various gatekeepers. These include state actors in both sending and receiving countries, including immigration and emigration personnel, and professional and educational accreditation institutions. Our study has focused on the gatekeeping role of specific governmental policy, the private placement agencies and the particular legislation that regulates the terms and conditions of foreign domestic service.

More specifically, our survey of domestic workers and nurses indicates certain patterns that have not been previously identified in the literature. Our findings suggest that there are differences between West Indian and Filipino domestic workers regarding immigration status, with a higher concentration of illegal migrants among the West Indian group. However, among the domestic workers, the commonalities in the experiences of these two groups were greater than the differences, indicating patterns of employer/citizen exploitation and lack of adherence to even minimal employment standards.

We also consider the citizenship negotiation processes and strategies among Filipino and Black West Indian nurses in Canada. Immigrant nurses are more readily accepted by the Canadian state as landed immigrants, and their workplace environments are subject to more accountable public regulation than foreign domestic workers. Thus, the citizenship experiences of immigrant nurses have generally been more positive than the experiences of migrant nannies and domestic workers.

However, our findings demonstrated that racism, sexism and the impact of severe cutbacks in the health care sector have impacted seriously on the citizenship rights of nurses of colour.

For foreign domestic workers, differences were suggested that reflected a structural and ideological bias against the recruitment of West Indian domestics. However, these distinctions were superseded by a generalized experience of exploitation as live-in domestic workers. Among nurses, as in the case of domestic workers, our findings revealed a socially constructed bias against the recruitment and accreditation of West Indian workers relative to Filipinos, though both groups experienced discrimination. In a period of major restructuring in the health care sector, a strategy of managerial racial discrimination based on divide-and-conquer tactics, pitting one group of women of colour against another, is suggested by the findings.

As discussed in this final chapter, citizenship is indeed gradational, imposing greater obligations and restrictions on some and providing more abundant rights to others who, because of wealth and other social characteristics, are deemed more legitimate. However, the inequities of citizenship are also subject to some measure of contestation and reform involving the organizing and negotiation strategies of those located in disadvantaged positions in the citizenship hierarchy. Our concluding discussion shines a searchlight, in theory and in experience, on the collective strategies of organization, resistance and dissident citizenship among migrant women workers in the global system.

Filipino migrant workers have been at the forefront of the most recent wave of political activism advancing the rights of domestic workers and nurses in Canada. This movement has politically linked the issue of migrant rights to the anti-imperialist strategies of social movements and organizations contesting global capitalism in the Philippines. Transnational networks, connecting the country of origin to the country of residence and promoting democratic participation in both places, have challenged the notion of single allegiance to one national political community. They also pressure labour-receiving states to adopt policies that recognize the existence of mobile, transnational networks and reflect at least some dimensions of post-national, or perhaps what could be more accurately termed transnational citizenship. States that benefit economically from migrant labour, as well as from neo-colonial relations with labour sending states, have been pressured to extend citizenship entitlements to transnational communities, so that their most vulnerable migrant members might gain autonomy and resources to contest inequitable social structures and unjust practices.

Transnational citizenship practices

The literature on transnational migrant experiences and diasporic communities draws attention to the growing evidence of the simultaneous involvement of immigrants in the social and political life of more than one nation-state.[524] Some observers have pointed to how advances in electronic technology, especially the internet, and the lowered costs of air travel and communication are facilitating the ability of migrants and immigrants to sustain 'multi-stranded social relations that link together their societies of origin and settlement/residence'.[525] States of origin also have been proactive in their attempts to incorporate diasporas into a form of deterritorialized state and definition of the nation, in large part to encourage remittances and capital investment brought 'home' by migrant communities.[526] It is not just immigrants, however, with permanent resident if not formal citizenship status in receiving states, but also non-citizen migrants, who live their lives across borders and are actively engaged in the politics and nation-building processes of two or more nation-states. As Riva Kastoryano observes, migrants who have perceived their sojourn in foreign countries to be temporary have long tended to spontaneously maintain multiple links with their country of origin.[527]

While this study focuses on the experiences of both West Indian and Filipino migrant women in Canada, the two migrant communities differ in the extent of deployment of transnational organization in their respective negotiating strategies. Because the largest West Indian migrant flows arrived earlier, dissident strategies have tended to focus on anti-racist activity within Canada. There is now a long established tradition of anti-racist organization in which first generation West Indian activists frequently play a central and leading role.[528] While transnational family and community ties continue, many West Indian immigrants have successfully established a legitimate and recognized role in advocating for greater citizenship rights within Canadian social, economic and political structures. This has not meant that full citizenship rights have been achieved; rather West Indian activists have provided a leadership role in the exposure of intense racism through community organizing at various levels of governance and across many institutions – including the police force, education and health care.

In contrast, as part of a more recent immigrant community, Filipino migrant organizations in Canada are enmeshed in a dense network of North–South people's organizations, many of which continue to be rooted within the Philippines itself. These organizations have sought to end the exploitation of Filipinos at home in export-processing zones, and the abuse of Filipino migrants abroad as cheap, expendable labour – including the abuse of sex workers, domestic workers, health care workers and mail-order brides. They have internationalized the movement in the Philippines to challenge imperialist globalization and the export-led development strategies that have compelled such extraordinarily high numbers of Filipinos to leave their homeland. The structural subordination of the Philippines within the world economic system is regarded to be at the root of the 'hemorrhagic flow of migrant Filipinas to all corners of the globe'.[529] The migrant organizations have also globalized citizenship struggles of Filipino migrants by asserting their rights wherever they may find themselves working and living.[530] Thus, significantly, the migrant campaigns have highlighted the need within a transnational context for migrants to win mobility citizenship rights in labour-receiving countries, but also to fight for their rights as Filipino citizens to radical transformation and restructuring in the Philippines that would allow them to remain at home.[531] For the purposes of considering migrant dissident strategies for negotiating global citizenship rights, we will examine some Canadian campaigns of Filipino migrant nurses and domestic workers, and their transnational links with Filipino peoples' networks.

Filipino migrant nurses have connected the campaign to reform the obstacles to the practice of nursing in Canada with larger issues involving globalization and neo-liberal restructuring in health care. For example, campaigns have targeted policies defined as threatening the rights of migrant workers and denying Canadians high quality health care. The Vancouver-based FNSG, whose objective is to advance the full rights and welfare of Filipino nurses in Canada, provides an instance of this challenge. The FNSG has vociferously lobbied the Canadian Department of Immigration to eliminate the LCP, and to permit migrant nurses, many of whom are forced to enter Canada as domestic workers, in order to gain admission into the country to enter as landed immigrants. It has also petitioned the Philippines government. That government's slow process of verification of nurses' board exam results through the Philippine Regulatory Commission has contributed to migrant nurses' lengthy process of accreditation. The FNSG has sought public support for its campaign for citizenship rights for migrant nurses by connecting the oppression of Filipino and other foreign-trained nurses to the broader public's concern with a decline in social citizenship rights through 'clawbacks' in the social welfare system. Specifically, the FNSG has drawn attention to 'bed closures, critically long waiting lists, overflowing emergency rooms, [and] burnt out health workers'.[532] While the nursing shortage is conveyed as part of the problem with the ailing health care system, the availability of 'a gold mine' in B.C.'s backyard of 'hundreds of Filipino nurses in B.C. numbering to thousands across Canada', who could assist in filling the gaps in the nursing profession, is presented as part of a solution.

The inability of Filipino nurses doing domestic work to practise their profession is seen as racist oppression on the part of public and private gatekeepers, all of whom disclaim responsibility for the injustices experienced by these non-citizens; but it is also understood as a waste of human resources in the context of a nursing shortage, resonating with the public's anxieties over the deterioration of public health care. The FNSG has sought to influence the policies of the Registered Nurses Association of British Columbia (RNABC) and the B.C. Nurses' Union (BCNU) in order to render them more sensitive to the needs and barriers faced by Filipino nurses. This process has not been without its challenges, and there have been strategic arguments between the nurses' union and the FNSG regarding specific demands.[533] However, it is through this process of negotiating increased rights for migrant workers, and challenging the legacy of protectionist policies within the labour movement, that an effective movement for increasing rights for all citizens ultimately depends.

Filipino domestic worker politics have been more explicitly transnational than the movement asserting Filipino nurses' rights. Domestic organizations have coupled activity in Canada with challenges to the Philippine government and vigorous protests appealing to the international community. The political message that is carried aims to demystify the causes of migration from the Philippines. Pressure has been placed on the Philippine government, through mass protests, lobbying, alternative media networks and so on. The demand is to shift public resources from servicing debt to the IMF and World Bank through structural adjustment programmes, towards developing resources in rural infrastructure and social services such as primary health care, education and housing.[534]

Virtually all Filipino migrant organizations in Canada have strong ties with organizations headquartered in the Philippines with affiliates in every country where there has been significant Filipino migration. *Migrante*-International is a transnational alliance of Filipino migrant organizations, formed in 1994. While headquartered in Manila, it has a presence in at least 18 countries. *Migrante* aids in consolidating and strengthening the organizational efforts of Filipino migrants and immigrants across the Asia-Pacific, Europe, Middle East and North America. In the Philippines,

Migrante critiques state compliance with export-oriented development favoured by institutions like the World Bank and IMF, which are regarded as responsible for pushing people out of the Philippines. Alternatively, the aim is to work towards 'meaningful development' that will allow Filipinos to build a livelihood in the Philippines.[535] *Migrante's* politics are thus part of the country's militant left movement that 'contests the Philippine state's project of economic development and the ways in which it is inserted into the global economy'.[536] Another target for global campaigns has been 'state extractions' – the hefty fees Filipinos must pay the Philippine state migration bureaucracy as a condition of seeking overseas employment, and the 'double taxation' of Filipino migrants by their home and host states.[537]

Gabriela-Philippines, a national alliance of women's organizations in the Philippines, is part of a transnational network of *Gabriela* affiliates in Canada, the United States, Europe and Australia. While organizations such as the Toronto-based *Migrante* Women's Collective, the Montreal-based *Pinay*, and the Vancouver-based Philippine Women Centre, focus on organizing migrant workers and advocating for an end to oppressive Canadian immigration laws and exploitative Philippine emigration policies, their organizing activities are also part of the movement to advance the rights of Filipino citizens in their home country. These organizations have been particularly prominent in protesting against and seeking justice in extreme cases of abuse of Filipinas working abroad, including life threatening violations of human rights.[538] Such groups also agitated, via internet campaigns, rallies in front of Philippine embassies, petitions and other means, in 'People's Movement II' to oust the corrupt Joseph E. Estrada from the Philippines presidency. Estrada was held responsible for the continued export of Filipinos abroad into deskilled and racist conditions.[539] As Rodriguez points out, the politics of Filipino migrant networks challenge conventional notions of citizenship by seeking transnational justice and rights that contest the role of working Filipinos as degraded and mobile servants under global capitalism. However, the alternative form of transnational citizenship evidenced in this movement remains linked to an emergent form of Filipino nationalism that has an anti-imperialist character. It repudiates both the 'modern-day slave' status provided by labour importing wealthy states and the discourse of the Philippine state that defines Filipino migrants as 'national hero(ines)'. A central feature of this alternative citizenship is 'Filipinos' right to return "home", and to reclaim the Philippines around an alternative nationalist project that privileges the rights of the working class and the dispossessed'.[540]

Domestic advocacy organizations in Canada have brought attention to the relationship between the treatment by the Canadian government of migrant household workers as expendable commodities, and the structural processes that produce a seemingly endless supply of exploitable migrant labour. This connection was forcefully illustrated in the campaign to stop the deportation of Melca Salvador. Melca Salvador, a domestic worker from the Philippines, was ordered by immigration authorities to leave Canada when she had been unable to complete the 24 months of work over a three-year period designated by the LCP. The employer who sponsored her terminated Ms Salvador when it was discovered that she was pregnant. Ms Salvador's pregnancy affected her 'marketability'; her subsequent attempts to obtain live-in employment consisted of an endless spiral of rejections and refusals from immigration authorities.

Ms Salvador's application in February 1999 for ministerial exemption on humanitarian grounds, that included arguments about the best interests of her Canadian-born son, was rejected. Her case illustrates how the LCP deprives migrant women of a significant pool of rights associated with what has been termed 'reproductive citizenship' rights for women.[541] While advanced states, concerned with falling birth rates and ageing populations, encourage higher rates of reproduction of their national populations, this concern focuses on parents of the 'right' race/ethnicity and class position. Defined solely in terms of their relationship with their employers, however, migrant domestic workers are not permitted to bring their families to Canada or, in practice, to become pregnant if this impedes their ability to tend to the needs and demands of their employing families.

A 'Campaign to Stop the Expulsion of Melca Salvador' obtained wide support from Filipino community organizations and attracted media attention across Canada. Led by *Pinay*, a Philippine women's advocacy organization in Montreal whose membership includes many live-in caregivers, the campaign was also supported by solidarity organizations in the movement for global justice in Canada.[542] The campaign drew attention to the global trade in human labour that is oiled by the discriminatory policies of labour-exporting and labour-importing states. Thus, the campaign highlighted the Labour Export Policy of the Philippines government, that has 'mastered the art of trading its people' in order to receive millions of dollars in remittances, yet refuses to come to their defence as promised, because 'there are hundreds of thousands more where [Melca] came from'.[543] The campaign to stop Ms Salvador's expulsion also demanded that foreign nannies be allowed to obtain permanent residency status upon arrival in Canada, 'something ... all other immigrants get as a matter of course when they arrive in Canada to work'.[544]

In May 2001, supporters of Ms Salvador had cause to celebrate when the Department of Citizenship and Immigration awarded her an open visa with the possibility of landed immigrant status after one year. Filipino domestic advocacy organizations were quick to point out, however, that Ms Salvador's victory in resisting deportation did not translate into structural reform of the LCP, which continues to provide 'a revolving door of cheap labour'.[545]

Another notable example of transnational dissident citizenship involving the political agency of migrant domestic workers is the 'Purple Rose Campaign'. This transnational campaign was hosted by *Gabriela*-Philippines and launched through *Gabriela* affiliates in labour-importing countries. It combines in a single network Filipino migrant organizations in international education and action against the trafficking of Filipino women in Canada, the United States, Australia and Europe. The campaign has focused its publicity on sex trafficking and the parallel migration of mail-order brides. The Vancouver launch, however, also added domestic workers to the categories of Filipino women trafficked in Canada, reflecting the strength of the domestic migrant movement for rights. Taking its name from the exotic purple rose, bred by horticulturalists for pleasure and profit, the movement works through educational forums, public rallies, internet campaigns and cultural events to draw attention to the devastating effect of the global trafficking of Filipino women and children as exoticised objects of pleasure and sources of profits.

In conclusion

Despite the emergence of discourses about cosmopolitan and post-national citizenship, the nation-state remains the major organizer, arbiter and guarantor of major fundamental rights, but the citizenship role of particular states is heavily conditioned by the international political economy. Citizenship is a relationship. While liberal democratic states define their citizenship as an equality-enhancing form of membership, in fact, national citizenship is conditional, partial, particularistic and generates inequality. It is not linear, static or thing-like, but a negotiated set of rights, obligations and practices, structurally embedded in global capitalist relations, and enforced and protected by powerful state and non-state gatekeepers. In this sense, citizenship is expressed and negotiated through an elaborate network of relations formed between the complex of state and non-state institutions, organizations and apparatuses.[546] Yet it is a relationship that crystallizes many other sets of social relations, including the unevenness among states in the global economy, and the inequities stemming from social class, racism and sexism. Because states bestow citizenship on the basis of an imagined national community, one that welcomes only those persons with the 'appropriate' attributes at any given historical point in time, citizenship simultaneously has inclusionary and exclusionary dimensions.

Conceived of as a relationship, citizenship is also subject to active negotiation, and is therefore unstable. It is constructed and re-constructed in given historical contexts. Individuals, collectivities, private organizations and interests, and state institutions can enter into such negotiation, which can occur in various locations. The effectiveness of diverse negotiation strategies varies, but as we have indicated, the global citizenship divide can be, and is continually, challenged by the dissident citizenship practices of determined non-citizen activists, who draw upon social capital such as transnational networks. In an era when neo-liberal globalization has seen nation-states endorse and embrace markets and multinational corporations, powerful and affluent states have declined to sign international human rights agreements that would, at least formally, protect vulnerable groups such as poor migrants on the grounds that such agreements would 'violate' their own national sovereignty. Thus, Canada and most labour-receiving states have refused to sign the 1990 United Nations' International Convention on the Rights of all Migrants and Members of their Families.[547]

Despite over two decades of organization, education and agitation on the plight of foreign domestics in Canada, it is fair to assess the actual reforms to domestic worker policies, especially at the national level, to have been relatively modest. Foreign household workers are still indentured to a purgatory of a minimum two years live-in service, foregoing their own freedoms and family relations, and on probation for Canadian permanent residence and eventually legal citizenship. The state's role in these arrangements is to assist Canadians of economic means in privately realizing their citizenship entitlements, such as childcare, elder care and other forms of home care, in a context where these services have been eroded by the state's own neo-liberal policies.

Current Canadian government policy restrictions have indicated that access to the LCP for foreign domestic workers is declining. The reasons for this decline are not stated. Certainly, demand for live-in domestic care for pre-school age children, and for care for the elderly, are on the increase. There is, however, another unique element of the LCP, one that runs counter to the current pattern of increased restrictions on the rights of immigrants in Canadian and international immigration legislation; this is the opportunity for foreign domestic workers to apply for permanent resident status, from inside Canada, after the successful completion of the two year live-in requirement within a three-year period. As we have noted, the right to move from virtual indenture to legal landed immigrant status was won by domestic workers as a result of mass collective organizing in the 1970s. In the current context, the Canadian government's efforts to all but eliminate the policy by dramatically restricting the numbers who are allowed entry under its terms, needs to be seen as a further encroachment on the rights of a vulnerable section of migrant workers. Our research suggests that the impact of the increasing restrictions to access to Canada through the LCP has been to augment the numbers of undocumented domestic workers. These undocumented workers, denied any legal or public status at all, are then placed in positions of even greater vulnerability to exploitation and deportation than those who enter through the LCP.

The entrenchment of neo-liberalism has proven fertile ground for the rise of ideologies of privatization, familialism and anti-immigrant sentiment that justify attaching different moral significance to the treatment of citizens and aliens. Thus, despite the proliferation of transnational institutions, as Jacqueline Bhabha suggests,

It is arguable that being a citizen has become more rather than less important as a qualification for rights enforcement ... Although the relationship between state and individual citizen has changed and continues to change in the era of globalisation, the power of the state as an enforcer of individual rights and as a conduit to entitlements, political, economic or social, is still unrivalled.[548]

Despite the enormous constraints foreign household workers face in terms of time, resources, lack of autonomy and vulnerability to threats of deportation, many have displayed tremendous courage in contesting the unjust laws and social arrangements that have threatened to imprison them. Their efforts to win rights from the receiving state's institutions can be read as dissident citizenship practices aimed at breaking the conventional nexus of relationships among citizenship, sovereignty, territoriality and nationality, and thus advancing a new regime of transnational citizenship. At the same time, the political practices of these non-citizen actors, connected as they are in transnational networks of solidarity that include the meaningful development of the rights of poor citizens of their country of origin, are working to bring about the material conditions that will end the forced migration of their nationals and the inequities of unfree social contracts forged across the global citizenship divide.

Notes

1 Introduction: Negotiating Citizenship

1. Peter Stalker, *Workers Without Frontiers: The Impact of Globalization on International Migration* (Boulder, Colo.: Lynne Rienner Publishers, 2000).
2. The specific details regarding research methodologies are documented in each chapter in which the data is addressed.
3. A recent Royal Commission recommended significant expansion of funding for the Canadian health care sector. While the federal Liberal government has promised to implement these recommendations, specific commitments have not yet been implemented. See *Building on Values: The Future of Health Care in Canada*, Commissioner Roy Romanow (Ottawa: Government of Canada, 2001), <http://publications.gc.ca/control/publicHomePage?lang=English%20>.
4. See House of Commons, Canada, Bill C-11, 'Immigration and Refugee Protection Act', <http://www.parl.gc.ca/37/1/parlbus/chambus/house/bills/government/C-11/C-11_3/90141bE.html#1>.
5. Amnesty International, *Brief on Bill C-11: An Act Respecting Immigration to Canada and the Granting of Refugee Protection to Persons who are Displaced, Persecuted or in Danger*, March 2001, <http://www.amnesty.ca/Refugee/Bill_C-11.PDF>.

2 Negotiating Citizenship in an Era of Globalization

6. On this point, see the exposition by Jacqueline Bhabha, 'Embodied Rights, Gender Persecution, State Sovereignty, and Refugees', *Public Culture*, 9 (1996), 3–32.
7. As an example of this official ideology on citizenship, the Canadian government department charged with immigration and citizenship matters asks in a 'Fact Sheet' on 'Citizenship' the question, 'What does it mean to be a Canadian citizen?' In its response, Citizenship and Immigration states that Canada, and thus Canadian citizenship, are defined in terms of the following characteristics: multicultural, two official languages and equal treatment of its citizens. Citizenship and Immigration Canada, 'Citizenship: Fact Sheet', June 1997 <http://www.cic.gc.ca/english/newcomer.fact_09e.html>.
8. Robert Menzies, Robert Adamoski and Dorothy Chunn, 'Rethinking the Citizen in Canadian Social History', in Robert Adamoski, Dorothy Chunn and Robert Menzies, eds, *Contesting Canadian Citizenship* (Peterborough, Ontario: Broadview Press, 2002), 13.
9. Menzies, Adamoski and Chunn, 'Rethinking the Citizen', 12.
10. Menzies, Adamoski and Chunn, 'Rethinking the Citizen', 19. Particularly noteworthy in this regard are the perilous and 'potentially obliterative'

consequences of citizenship in settler states for indigenous peoples. Menzies, Adamoski and Chunn, 'Rethinking the Citizen', 31. On the consequences for indigenous peoples of settler state citizenship, see James (Sákéj) Henderson, '*Sui Generis* and Treaty Citizenship' *Citizenship Studies*, 6: 4 (December 2002), 415–40.

11. Our framework addressing the articulation between migration and citizenship is not meant to capture all of the complexity of contemporary global migration, much of which is South to South, particularly movements of peoples displaced by war, drought and immiseration.

12. As elaborated in our analysis of the role of placement agencies in racializing the labour market for private domestic service, there are many private interests that play a role in negotiating the package of citizenship rights, entitlements and exclusions for domestic workers. These include labour brokers in sending and receiving countries, with many working illegally.

13. Post-national theorists include Yasemin Soysal, David Jacobsen, James Holston, Arjun Appadurai and Damian Tambini. See Yasemin Nuhoglu Soysal, *Limits of Citizenship: Migrants and Post-national Membership in Europe* (Chicago: University of Chicago Press, 1994) and 'Changing Citizenship in Europe: Remarks on Post-national Membership and the National State', in D. Cesarini and M. Fulbrook, eds, *Nationality and Migration in Europe* (London: Routledge, 1996); David Jacobsen, *Rights Across Borders: Immigration and the Decline of Citizenship* (Baltimore: Johns Hopkins University Press, 1996); James Holston and Arjun Appadurai, 'Cities and Citizenship', *Public Culture*, 8 (1996), 187–204 and Damian Tambini, 'Post-national Citizenship', *Ethnic and Racial Studies*, 24 (2001), 195–217. David Held elaborates a model of 'cosmopolitan democratic citizenship'. David Held, *Democracy and the Global Order: From the Modern State to Cosmopolitan Governance* (Cambridge: Cambridge University Press, 1995).

14. Hélène Pellerin and Henk Overbeek, 'Neo-Liberal Regionalism and the Management of People's Mobility', in A. Bieler and A.D. Morton, eds, *Social Forces in the Making of the New Europe* (Basingstoke: Palgrave, 2001), 137.

15. J.F. Hollifield, 'Immigration and Republicanism in France: The Hidden Consensus', in W.A. Cornelius, P.L. Martin and J.F. Hollifield, eds, *Controlling Immigration: A Global Perspective* (Stanford: Stanford University Press, 1994).

16. Richard Falk, Lester Edwin J. Ruiz and R.B. Walker, 'Introduction: The International and the Challenge of Speculative Reason', in Richard Falk, Lester Edwin J. Ruiz and R.B. Walker, eds, *Reframing the International* (New York: Routledge, 2002), x.

17. Joseph H. Carens, 'Aliens and Citizens: The Case for Open Borders', *The Review of Politics*, 49 (1987), 251–73. See also R. Brubaker, 'Commentary: Are Immigration Control Efforts Really Failing?' in W.A. Cornelius, P.L. Martin and J.F. Hollifield, eds, *Controlling Immigration: A Global Perspective* (Stanford: Stanford University Press, 1994) and J. Isbister, 'Are immigration Controls Ethical?' *Social Justice*, 23: 3 (1996), 54–67.

18. Holston and Appadurai, 'Cities and Citizenship', 188.

19. Holston and Appadurai, 'Cities and Citizenship', 189.

20. Holston and Appadurai, 'Cities and Citizenship', 192.

21. C. Joppke, 'Review of Thomas Faist, David Jacobsen and Marco Martiniello', *Contemporary Sociology*, 26: 1 (1997), 66.

22. Ellen Meiksins Wood, *Democracy Against Capitalism* (Cambridge UK: Cambridge University Press, 1995), 201.
23. T.H. Marshall, *Citizenship and Social Class* (Cambridge: Cambridge University Press, 1950), 19.
24. Marshall, *Citizenship*, 18. Marshall qualified this statement by arguing that citizenship can also permit and even encourage social stratification through inequalities fostered by education and occupation. See *Citizenship*, 39.
25. Jost Halfmann, 'Citizenship, Universalism, Migration and the Risks of Exclusion', *British Journal of Sociology*, 49: 4 (1998), 519.
26. Marshall, *Citizenship* (italics added), 24.
27. Marshall argues that social services are important for providing a 'general enrichment of the concrete substance of civilized life, a general reduction of risk and insecurity, an equalization between the more and the less fortunate at all levels ...' *Citizenship*, 33.
28. Helma Lutz, 'The Limits of European-ness: Immigrant Women in Fortress Europe', *Feminist Review*, 57 (Autumn 1997), 98.
29. See Ward Churchill, *A Little Matter of Genocide: Holocaust and Denial in the Americas 1492 to the Present* (San Francisco: City Lights Books, 1997).
30. See Daiva Stasiulis and Nira Yuval-Davis, eds, *Unsettling Settler Societies: Articulations of Gender, Race, Ethnicity and Class* (London: Sage, 1995).
31. Cited in Peter H. Schuk and Roger M. Smith, *Citizenship Without Consent: Illegal Aliens in the American Polity* (New Haven: Yale University Press, 1985), 51.
32. 'After several years of controversial debate, the Federal Republic introduced a new law on citizenship (*Staatsangehörigkeitsgesetz*) on 1 January 2000, which clearly marks a departure from the traditional ethno-cultural notion of citizenship by embracing a more inclusive concept common in many other European countries. The most important changes include the introduction of the *jus soli* principle in the citizenship law and the easing of the requirements for naturalization'. Christian Lemke, 'Citizenship Law in Germany: Traditional Concepts and Pressures to Modernize in the Context of European Integration' <www.sociology.su.se/cgs/LemkePaper.doc>, accessed 21 April 2003. As Lemke details, significant barriers (e.g., exclusion of dual citizenship, residency requirements) exist in the new citizenship legislation that would prevent the majority of foreigners of non-German origin in Germany from naturalizing.
33. Edward Broadbent, 'Citizenship Today: Is There a Crisis?', in Dave Broad and Wayne Antony, eds, *Citizens or Consumers? Social Policy in a Market Society* (Halifax: Fernwood Press, 1999), 25.
34. Anthony Giddens, *Profiles and Critiques in Social Theory* (London: Macmillan, 1982); M. Roche, 'Citizenship, Social Theory and Social Change', *Theory and Society*, 16 (1987), 363–99; Bryan S. Turner, 'Outline of a Theory of Citizenship', *Sociology*, 24: 2 (May 1990), 193–4; Saskia Sassen, *Losing Control? Sovereignty in an Age of Globalization* (New York: Columbia University Press, 1996), 38–9.
35. Saskia Sassen, *Losing Control? Sovereignty in an Age of Globalization* (New York: Columbia University Press, 1996), 39; Janine Brodie, 'Citizenship and Solidarity: Reflections on the Canadian Way' *Citizenship Studies*, 6: 4 (December 2002), 377–94. With reference to Canada, Jane Jenson argues that

there has been a shift from the postwar to neo-liberal 'citizenship regime'. A citizenship regime is defined by its 'institutional arrangements, rules and understanding that guide and shape state policy; problem definition employed by states and citizens; and the range of claims recognized as legitimate'. Jane Jenson, 'Fated to Live in Interesting Times: Canada's Changing Citizenship Regimes', *Canadian Journal of Political Science*, XXX: 4 (December 1997), 631. See also Jane Jenson and Susan Phillips, 'Regime Shift: New Citizenship Practices in Canada', *International Journal of Canadian Studies*, 14 (1996), 111–35. For dissenting views that argue for a more limited and conservative notion of social citizenship in the postwar era, and a continuation rather than rupture with postwar policies, see Martin Powell, 'The Hidden History of Social Citizenship' *Citizenship Studies*, 6: 3 (2002), 229–44 and Janet Siltanen, 'Paradise Paved? Reflections on the Fate of Social Citizenship in Canada' *Citizenship Studies*, 6: 4 (2002), 397–414.

36. We would interpret the public outpouring of sentiment over the death of former Canadian Liberal Prime Minister, Pierre Elliott Trudeau in September 2000 as in part expressing nostalgia for the heady days of entitlement of citizens and a host of social movements in the Trudeau era of the late 1960s and 1970s fostered by the expansion of the Canadian welfare state.

37. Susan Boyd, 'Challenging the Public/Private Divide: An Overview', in S. Boyd, ed., *Challenging the Public/Private Divide: Feminism, Law, and Public Policy* (Toronto: University of Toronto Press, 1997), 11.

38. Claude Denis, ' "Government Can Do Whatever it Wants": Moral Regulation in Ralph Klein's Alberta', *Canadian Review of Sociology and Anthropology*, 32: 3 (1995), 365–83. Perhaps ironically, the governments implementing neo-liberal and conservative policies in the 1980s and into the new millennium have not always been of the New Right variety. Thus, in the United States, a Democratic President, Bill Clinton, signed into law Republican-style welfare 'reforms' that introduced workfare, turned responsibility for welfare over to the states and cut off welfare to legal immigrants. In Canada, the Liberal Government of Jean Chrétien has cut social programmes more drastically than the more ideologically right-wing Conservatives under Prime Minister Brian Mulroney. In Britain, the Labour Party 'cloned important elements of Conservative policy' and took up the old conservative refrain about 'personal responsibility'. J. Simpson, 'Conservatism by Any Other Name', *Globe and Mail*, Toronto (29 March 1997), D4. In France, the Socialist government of Jospin that took office in 1997 privatized more state enterprises than his two conservative predecessors combined. Peter Schwarz, 'Vote for National Front leader heightens political crisis in France', <http://www.wsws.org/articles/2002/apr2002/fran-a23.shtml>.

39. Barry Hindess, 'Neo-liberal Citizenship', *Citizenship Studies*, 6: 4 (June 2002), 140.

40. Denis, 'Government Can Do Whatever it Wants'.

41. Melanie White, 'Neo-Liberalism and the Rise of the Citizen as Consumer', in D. Broad and W. Antony, *Citizens or Consumers? Social Policy in a Market Society* (Halifax: Fernwood Press, 1999), 63.

42. Janine Brodie, 'The Politics of Social Policy in the Twenty-First Century', in D. Broad and W. Antony, *Citizens or Consumers?*, 39.

43. For instance, the World Trade Organization (WTO) Dispute Settlement permits trade bureaucrats to decide on violations of WTO rules. These bureaucrats have little appreciation of domestic legislation or government responsibility to protect workers, the environment or human rights. Working Group on the WTO/MAI, 'A Citizens' Guide to the World Trade Organization', July 1999. See also Maude Barlow and Tony Clarke, *Global Showdown* (Toronto: Stoddart, 2001); Lori Wallach and Michelle Sforza, *The WTO: Five Years of Reasons to Resist Corporate Globalization* (New York: Seven Stories Press, 1999).

44. Brodie, 'The Politics of Social Policy', 41.

45. B. Denitch, 'Democracy and the New World Order: Dilemmas and Conflicts', *Social Justice*, 23: 1–2 (1996), 21–38.

46. Ralph Miliband, 'The New World Order and the Left', *Social Justice*, 23: 1–2 (1996) 15–20. In addition, as Denitch argues there are at least three forces in the EU militating against unfettered forms of international capitalism and ideologies of unfettered individualism: (1) powerful trade unions allied to the social democratic parties that have a plurality in the European Parliament; (2) the Catholic Church, and Social Christian parties it dominates, which raise moral objections to socially damaging practices of corporations; and (3) the increasingly influential 'Eurocrats' or bureaucrats in the powerful commissions of the European Community in Brussels who are 'economic and social interventionists', technocratic statists – anything but free marketeers'. B. Denitch, 'Democracy and the New World Order'.

47. Mustafa Koc, 'Globalization as a Discourse', in Alessandro Bonnan *et al.*, eds, *From Columbus to ConAgra: the Globalization of Agriculture and Food* (Lawrence: University Press of Kansas, 1994).

48. Brodie, 'The Politics of Social Policy', 39.

49. The non-state sectors include the private, for profit sector, the family household and the volunteer sector.

50. See Carole Pateman, *The Sexual Contract* (Cambridge: Polity Press, 1988); Nira Yuval-Davis, *Gender and Nation* (London: Sage, 1997).

51. Pateman, *The Sexual Contract*; Lindsey German, *Sex, Class and Socialism;* Lise Vogel, *Marxism and the Oppression of Women* (London and New York: Pluto Press and Rutgers University Press, 1983).

52. Raia Prokhovnik, 'Public and Private Citizenship: From Gender Invisibility to Feminist Inclusiveness', *Feminist Review*, 60 (Autumn 1998), 87.

53. Boyd, 'Challenging the Public/Private Divide', 4.

54. Boyd, 'Challenging the Public/Private Divide', 13.

55. For an insightful analysis of the ways in which citizenship excludes persons with disabilities, see Helen Meekosha and Leanne Dowse, 'Enabling Citizenship: Gender, Disability and Citizenship in Australia', *Feminist Review*, 57 (Autumn 1997), 49–72.

56. Thus, the nineteenth-century Canadian 'tort of seduction' meant that employers could sue for damages against men who seduced their female servants. Master and servant legislation, however, did not supply an obligation on the part of masters to provide medical care or the necessities of life to servants, thus defining the relationship as one of contract, rather than familial obligation. Judy Fudge, 'Little Victories and Big Defeats: The Rise and Fall of Collective Bargaining Rights for Domestic Workers in Ontario', in

A. Bakan and D. Stasiulis, eds, *Not One of the Family: Foreign Domestic Workers in Canada* (Toronto: University of Toronto Press, 1997), 122.

57. Annie Oakly, *Subject Women* (New York: Pantheon Books, 1981), 182.
58. Pat Armstrong, 'Restructuring Public and Private: Women's Paid and Unpaid Work', in Susan B. Boyd, ed., *Challenging the Public/Private Divide* (Toronto: University of Toronto Press, 1997), 37–61.
59. Brodie, 'The Politics of Social Policy,' 43.
60. Armstrong, 'Restructuring Public and Private'.
61. Bridget Anderson, *Doing the Dirty Work?, The Global Politics of Domestic Labour* (London: Zed Books, 2000), 162.
62. Anderson, *Doing the Dirty Work*, 162.
63. Aida Hurtado, 'Relating to Privilege: Seduction and Rejection in the Subordination of White Women and Women of Color', *Signs*, 14: 4 (1989), 849.
64. Peter Stalker, *Workers Without Frontiers: The Impact of Globalization on International Migration* (Boulder, Colo.: Lynne Reinner Publishers, 2000), 17.
65. J. Vickers, *Women and the World Economic Crisis* (London: Zed Books, 1991), 4.
66. Per capita income differentials between migrant receiving and sending countries are substantial. In 1992 they were 12 : 1 between Germany and Turkey, and 7 : 1 between the United States and Mexico. P.L. Martin, 'The United States: Benign Neglect Towards Immigration', in W.A. Cornelius, P.L. Martin and J.F. Hollifield, eds, *Controlling Immigration: A Global Perspective* (Stanford: Stanford University Press, 1994), 207. In 1998, the wage differential between Germany and Ukraine was 100 : 1 and that between Germany and Poland, 10: 1. Anderson, *Doing the Dirty Work?*, 182.
67. Anderson, *Doing the Dirty Work?*, 29. According to the International Labour Organization, by the end of 1998, approximately 900 million people around the world were underemployed, i.e., working substantially less than full time and wanting to work longer, or were earning less than a living wage. Cited in Peter Stalker, *The No-Nonsense Guide to International Migration* (Toronto: New Internationalist Publications, 2001), 37.
68. Discourses of migrant workers as 'new national heroes' are particularly salient in the Philippines. Robyn M. Rodriguez, 'Migrant Heroes: Nationalism, Citizenship and the Politics of Filipino Migrant Labor', *Citizenship Studies*, 6: 3 (2002), 341–56.
69. For example, the government of the Philippines has historically referred to its female overseas workers as the 'new heroines of the Philippines'. Originally viewed as a temporary answer to the Philippines' unemployment and severe balance of payment problems, labour export, and in particular international migration of female domestics and entertainers, male seafarers and predominantly female nurses has become an integral aspect of the Philippine economy, promoted by all administrations since that of Ferdinand Marcos. Remittances from Salvadoreans working in the United States have become critical in sustaining the Salvadorean economy, amounting to at least $1 billion a year, far higher than coffee export earnings. S. Jonas, 'Rethinking Immigration Policy and Citizenship in the Americas: A Regional Framework', *Social Justice*, 23: 3 (1996), 74. In Egypt, migrant remittances have 'at times generated as much foreign exchange as tourism, oil exports, and the income of the Suez Canal combined'. Stalker, *The No-Nonsense Guide*, 109. The top five developing country receivers of

remittances in 1999 were India, Philippines, Mexico, Turkey and Egypt. Of these five, remittances represent the highest percentage of GDP (8.9 per cent) in the Philippines. Some small countries are particularly dependent on remittances: in Yemen, they represent 25 per cent of GDP. Stalker, *The No-Nonsense Guide*, 109.

70. See J. Salt, 'The Future of International Labor Migration', *International Migration Review*, 26: 4 (1993), 1077; International Organization for Migration, *World Migration Report* (New York: United Nations, 2000), 31. Salt's estimate of the value of migrant remittances in 1993 was US$67 billion, whereas Stalker suggests that if one allowed for funds that pass through unofficial channels, an estimated half of all migrant remittances, the global flow of remittances to developing countries may exceed $100 billion. Stalker, *The No-Nonsense Guide*, 109.

71. Cynthia Enloe, *Bananas, Beaches and Bases: Making Feminist Sense of International Politics* (Berkeley: University of California Press, 1989), 185.

72. H. Overbeek, 'Towards a New International Migration Regime: Globalization', in D. Thranhardt and R. Miles, eds, *Migration and European Integration: The Dynamics of Inclusion and Exclusion* (London: Pinter, 1995), 15.

73. M. Rodriguez, 'Migrant Heroes', 355.

74. M. Rodriguez, 'Migrant Heroes', 353.

75. Pellerin points out how regional efforts to coordinate migration policies, such as the Regional Conference on Migration in Central and North America, take as their goal 'ordered migration' rather than reduced migration. Hélène Pellerin, 'The Cart Before the Horse? The Coordination of Migration Policies, in the Americas and the Neo-liberal Economic Project of Integration', *Review of International Political Economy*, 6: 4 (Winter 1999), 481.

76. Jacqueline Bhabha, 'Enforcing the Human Rights of Citizens and Non-Citizens in the Era of Maastricht: Some Reflections on the Importance of States', *Globalization and Identity: Dialectics of Flow and Closure* (Oxford: Blackwell, 1999), 101.

77. Hélène Pellerin, 'The Global Governance of International Migration in the 1990s', in C. Turenne-Sjolander and J.F. Thibault, eds, *On Global Governance* (Ottawa: University of Ottawa, forthcoming).

78. A. Borowski, A. Richmond, J. Shu and A. Simmons, 'The International Movements of Peoples', in H. Adelman *et al.*, eds, *Immigration and Refugee Policy: Australia and Canada Compared*, Vol. 1 (Toronto: University of Toronto Press, 1995), 65. See also Anthony Richmond, *Global Apartheid: Refugees, Racism and the New World Order* (Toronto: Oxford University Press, 1994).

79. D. Moisi in Glen St J. Barclay, 'The European Union and the Maghreb: A Clash of Civilisations', in *Australia and World Affairs*, 25 (Winter 1995), 5–17.

80. Yasmeen Abu-Laban and Christina Gabriel, *Selling Diversity: Immigration, Multiculturalism, Employment Equity and Globalization* (Peterborough: Broadview Press, 2002), 86, 91.

81. Anthony Richmond, *Global Apartheid*, 211.

82. Mustafa Koc, 'Globalization as a Discourse'.

83. It is significant that in the mid-1990s, the MSI, the neofascist party in Italy, could garner 30 per cent of the vote in local elections (Miliband 1996: 10) and that polls in France in early 1997 showed the national support of the National Front at 30 per cent (*Globe and Mail*, 26 February 1997).

84. Abu-Laban and Gabriel, *Selling Diversity*, 86.
85. Chapter 7 examines some legal cases in Canada where the judiciary has sought to protect the rights of foreign household workers rejected and ordered to be deported by the immigration administration.
86. States are more heavily policing the entry into their territories of travellers such as visitors, thus imposing more visa restrictions on a greater number of countries, and denying visas to people from countries which are feared to produce undocumented migrants.
87. Hélène Pellerin, 'Crisis? What Crisis? The Politics of Migration Regulation in the Era of Globalization', in G. Young and E. Kofman, eds, *Globalization, Theory and Practice* (London: Pinter, forthcoming).
88. H. Amerfoort and R. Pennix, 'Regulating Migration in Europe: the Dutch Experience, 1960–92', *Annals of the American Academy*, 534 (1994), 132–46; W.A. Cornelius, P.L. Martin and J.F. Hollifield, eds, *Controlling Immigration*.
89. N. Rodriguez, 'The Battle for the Border: Notes on Autonomous Migration, Transnational Communities and the State', *Social Justice*, 23: 3 (1996), 21–37; K. Calavita, 'U.S. Immigration and Policy Responses: The Limits of Legislation', in W.A. Cornelius, P.L. Martin and J.F. Hollifield, eds, *Controlling Immigration: A Global Perspective* (Stanford: Stanford University Press), 55–82.
90. N. Rodriguez, 'The Battle for the Border', 31.
91. Jonas, 'Rethinking Immigration Policy', 75.
92. D. Bacon, 'For an Immigration Policy Based on Human Rights', *Social Justice*, 23: 3 (1996), 137–53.
93. S. Diamond, 'Right-wing Politics and the Anti-immigration Cause', *Social Justice*, 23: 3 (1996), 159.
94. Jonas, 'Rethinking Immigration Policy', 72.
95. Jonas, 'Rethinking Immigration Policy', 75.
96. Jonas, 'Rethinking Immigration Policy', 75.
97. Bhabha, 'Embodied Rights', 3–7.
98. In addition to subjecting refugees to arbitrary arrest, detention, denial of social and economic rights and closed borders, states have violated *non-foulement*, the most fundamental principle of refugee protection, and have forcibly returned refugees to countries where they face persecution and possible death. Human Rights Watch, 'Refugees and Displaced Persons', <http:www.hr.org/refugees/>.
99. Jonas, 'Rethinking Immigration Policy', 75.
100. Bacon, 'For an Immigration Policy Based on Human Rights', 150.
101. Human Rights Watch U.S., 'We Are Not the Enemy', <http:///www.hrw.org/us/indix.php>, accessed 5 January 2003.
102. The Canadian government took the lead in introducing a new refugee policy sensitive to the gendered forms of persecution experienced by women. The new guidelines on gender-related persecution broadened the interpretation of 'social group' to include women fleeing from female-specific forms of violence and persecution. These have included rape, female infanticide, genital mutilation, bride-burning, forced marriage, domestic violence, forced abortion and compulsory sterilization. Canada, Immigration and Refugee Board, *Guidelines on Women Refugees Fleeing Gender Related Persecution* (Ottawa, 1993), 7. Canada's new IRPA, which received royal assent in November 2001, and its

regulations, while overwhelmingly restrictive, have also introduced some changes benefiting those immigrants who are able to gain entry. Positive measures included a reduction in spousal sponsorships from ten to three years that would prove beneficial to vulnerable female migrants, reduction of the period of sponsorship for children under 22 years to ten years, of age 25 (whichever is shorter), and the creation of a new category of conjugal partners (partners separated by immigration who are unable to cohabit) that is particularly significant for same-sex partners. Canadian Council for Refugees, 'Canadian Council for Refugees Reacts to Publication of Immigration Regulations, 11 June 2002 <http://www.web.ca/~ccr/regsrelease.html>.

103. The elimination of a right to appeal for asylum seekers and the fact that refugees' fates were now to be decided by a single decision maker were particularly challenged by refugee advocates. 'Refugees were promised the right to an appeal', said Kemi Jacobs, President of the Canadian Council for Refugees. 'Now at a time when borders are increasingly being closed to refugees, refugees are to be denied a right as basic as a review of a life-and-death decision ...' Canadian Council for Refugees, 'Canadian Council for Refugees Reacts'.

104. Louise Langevin and Marie-Claire Belleau, *Trafficking in Women in Canada: A Critical Analysis of the Legal Framework Governing Immigration Live in Caregivers and Mail-Order Brides* (Ottawa: Status of Women Canada, October 2000), 33.

105. Bill C-31 and Bill C-11, different versions of the Chrétien government's proposed overhaul of the immigration and refugee legislation introduced to the Canadian Parliament in June 2000 and February 2001, respectively, were characterized by a heavy enforcement emphasis which the Canadian Council of Refugees suggested would 'promote negative stereotypes about refugees and immigrants and caters to xenophobia and racism within Canadian society'. The announcement of Bill C-31 by then Immigration Minister Elinor Caplan framed the overall objective as one of 'closing the back door to those who would abuse the system' in order to keep the front door open. Canadian Council for Refugees, 'Comments on Bill C-31: An Act Respecting Immigration to Canada and the Granting of Refugee Protection to Persons Who are Displaced, Persecuted or in Danger', Montreal, July 2000, 2, 7. Bill C-31 died on the order paper when the November 2000 federal election was called, but most of its provisions were reintroduced in Bill C-11, the basis for Canada's 2002 IRPA. Canadian Council for Refugees, 'Bill C-11 Brief', 25 March 2001.

106. In Canada, permanent residents have enjoyed many social rights, including public health care, education, welfare and almost all of the political and civil rights of Canadian citizens, except for voting and standing in elections or being eligible for high security positions in the civil service.

107. Canadian Council on Refugees, 'C-11 Brief'. For instance, permanent residents 'face losing their right to appeal to the Immigration Appeal Division "to review circumstances surrounding their loss of status or deportation when their case is based on broad grounds of inadmissibility, such as criminal acts" '. 'Serious criminality' is defined as a crime punishable in Canada by a sentence of at least two years. Canadian Bar Association quoted in Abu-Laban and Gabriel, *Selling Diversity*, 83.

108. Abu-Laban and Gabriel, *Selling Diversity*, 85.
109. J.F. Hollifield, 'Immigration and Republicanism in France', 143–76.
110. Hollifield, 'Immigration and Republicanism in France', 170–1.
111. Craig Whitney, 'Criticism of Bill Angers French', *Globe and Mail*, 26 February 1997, A-13A.
112. Peter Schwarz, 'Vote for National Front leader heightens political crisis in France', 23 April 2002, <http://www.wsws.org/articles/2002/apr2002/fran-a23.shtml>.
113. Hollifield, 'Immigration and Republicanism in France', 166, 171.
114. Hollifield, 'Immigration and Republicanism in France', 173.
115. Yasemin Soysal, *Limits of Citizenship*, 131.
116. Lemke, 'Citizenship Law in Germany', 7.
117. Lemke, 'Citizenship Law in Germany', 8.
118. P. Martin, 'Germany: Reluctant Land of Immigration', in W.A. Cornelius, P.L. Martin and J.F. Hollifield, eds, *Controlling Immigration: A Global Perspective* (Stanford: Stanford University Press, 1994), 210.
119. Martin, 'Germany', 194.
120. Martin, 'Germany', 220.
121. Martin, 'Germany', 214.
122. Jacqueline Bhabha, 'Enforcing the Human Rights', 109.
123. Yasmeen Abu-Laban, 'Reconstructing an Inclusive Citizenship for a New Millennium', *International Politics*, 37: 4 (December 2000), 512, 521. While NAFTA allows for the expedited cross border travel and temporary residence of business people and professionals, it does not provide regional citizenship for the citizens of countries that are signatories to this regional agreement. This is unlike the 1993 Maastricht Treaty, which created a new regional European citizenship between countries of the EU.
124. J.F. Hollifield, 'Immigration and Republicanism', 167; A. Rea, 'Social Citizenship and Ethnic Minorities in the European Union', in M. Martiniello, ed., *Migration, Citizenship and Ethnic Minorities in the European Union* (Aldershot: Avebury, 1995), 180. While Article 13TEC of the Amsterdam Treaty provides a legal basis for EU action to combat discrimination based on sex, racial or ethnic origin, religion or belief, disability, age or sexual orientation, it excludes nationality as a ground for discrimination, thus permitting discrimination against third-country nationals on the basis of their nationality. Jan Niessen, 'Third-country Nationals and the Legal Basis for Community Action Against Discrimination', MGP [Migration Policy Group] – EP Hearing on Anti-discrimination', E:\WPDOC\AUDITION\2000\23–24 mail\ Contributions\EXPERTS\Speech – Niessen EN.doc, 17 May 2000.
125. Bhabha, 'Enforcing the Human Rights', 113.
126. Bhabha, 'Enforcing the Human Rights', 115.
127. Bridget Anderson, *Doing the Dirty Work?*, 175.
128. See e.g., Benjamin B. Ringer, *We the People and Others* (New York and London: Routledge, 1983).
129. Marshall, *Citizenship*.
130. Michael Murphy and Siobhán Harty, 'Reconstructing Citizenship: Self-Determination in a Post-National Era', Paper presented at the Annual Meeting of the American Political Science Association, San Francisco, 30 August–2 September 2001, 2.

131. Murphy and Harty 'Reconstructing Citizenship', 2.
132. Peter Nyers, 'Forms of Cosmopolitan Dissent', Paper Delivered at the Citizenship Studies Symposium, York University, 15 January 2003.
133. For some works that have argued that nation-state power has given way to the power of global institutions, multinational corporations and global regulatory arrangements, and that global governance and law is increasingly independent of states, see Susan Strange, *The Retreat of the State: The Diffusion of Power in the World Economy* (Cambridge: Cambridge University Press, 1996); Robert J. Holton, *Globalization and the Nation-State* (London: Palgrave, 1998); and Christoph Schreuer, 'The Waning of the Sovereign State: Toward a New Paradigm for International Law?' *European Journal of International Law*, 4 (1993).
134. For a discussion of the shortcomings of the current international lawmaking system and international law compliance system, see Andrew L. Strauss, 'Overcoming the Dysfunction of the Bifurcated Global System: The Promise of a Peoples Assembly', in Richard Falk, Lester Edwin J. Ruiz and R.B.J. Walker, eds, *Reframing the International: Law, Culture, Politics* (New York: Routledge, 2002), 83–106.
135. Liza Schuster and John Solomos, 'Rights and Wrongs Across European Borders: Migrants, Minorities and Citizenship', *Citizenship Studies* 6: 1 (March 2002), 48.
136. The sovereignty of states with respect to power over entry is absolute and is recognized in all international conventions including the 1952 UN Convention on Refugees and the 1990 UN Convention on the Protection of the Rights of Migrants and Members of their Families.
137. *Nishimura Ikiu v. United States*, 142 US 651, 659, cited in Jeannette Money, *Fences and Neighbors: The Political Geography of Immigration Control* (Ithaca: Cornell University Press, 1999), 21.
138. Bhabha, 'Embodied Rights', 6.
139. Aiwa Ong, *Flexible Citizenship: The Cultural Logics of Transnationality* (Durham: Duke University Press, 1999), 6, 112.
140. Schuster and Solomos, 'Rights and Wrongs', 50.
141. L. Basch, N.G. Schiller and C.S. Blanc, *Nations Unbound: Transnational Projects, Postcolonial Predicaments, and Deterritorialized Nation-States* (Amsterdam: Gordon and Breach, 1994).
142. Rodriguez defines 'autonomous international migration' as 'international migration defined by workers, their families and communities independent of intergovernmental agreements' (1996: 23). He argues that the goal of current US restrictionist policies towards migrants is designed to end the self-directed migration pursued by many migrant families across the US–Mexican border as a transnational survival strategy. N. Rodriguez, 'The battle for the Border', 23, 31.
143. Micheline Labelle and Franklin Midy, 'Re-reading Citizenship and the Transnational Practices of Immigrants', *Journal of Ethnic and Migration Studies*, 25: 2 (April 1999), 214.
144. As Rodriguez argues, transnationalism is not only constituted by migrants' practices, but these transnational practices are also shaped by the deterritorialized nationalist projects of their home state (such as the encouragement of immigrants to invest in economic development projects at 'home').

Rodriguez notes the significance in the Philippine state of changing the nomenclature around migrants, identifying them as 'overseas Filipino workers' rather than 'overseas contract workers'. The new discourse 'emphasizes the Filipino-ness, or the nationality of workers in the diaspora'. Rodriguez, 'Migrant Heroes', 343, 347.

145. Rhacel Salazar Parreñas, *Servants of Globalization: Women, Migration, and Domestic Work* (Stanford: Stanford University Press, 2001), 11–12.

3 Underdevelopment, Structural Adjustment and Gendered Migration from the West Indies and the Philippines

146. This chapter draws upon Abigail B. Bakan and Daiva Stasiulis, 'Structural Adjustment, Citizenship, and Foreign Domestic Labour: The Canadian Case', in Isabella Bakker, ed., *Rethinking Restructuring: Gender and Change in Canada* (University of Toronto Press, 1996). We are grateful to Anne-Marie Murnaghan for her valuable research assistance.

147. See e.g., Kevin Danaher, ed., *Democratizing the Global Economy* (Philadelphia: Common Courage Press, 2001); Michel Chussodovksy, *The Globalization of Poverty: Impacts of IMF and World Bank Reforms* (New Jersey: Zed Books, 1999); Susan George, *The Debt Boomerang: How Third World Debt Hurts us All* (Boulder: Westview Press, 1992); Kathryn Ward, ed., *Women Workers and Global Restructuring* (Ithaca: Cornell University Press, 1990); Paul Harrison, *Inside the Third World* (Harmondsworth: Penguin Books, 1993), especially 448–85; Paula Sparr, ed., *Mortgaging Women's Lives* (London: Zed Books, 1994).

148. For background on the theoretical and empirical context to this phenomenon, see e.g., Parreñas, *Servants of Globalization*; Saskia Sassen-Koob, 'Labour Migrations and the New International Division of Labour', in June Nash and Maria Patricia Fernandez-Kelly, eds, *Women, Men and the International Division of Labour* (Albany: State University of New York Press, 1983), 175–204.

149. See Nigel Harris, *The New Untouchables: Immigration and the New World Worker* (Harmondsworth: Penguin Books, 1995), 60.

150. See George, *The Debt Boomerang*, 110–35.

151. Etienne Balibar, '*Es Gibt Keinen Staat in Europa*: Racism and Politics in Europe Today', *New Left Review* (March/April 1991), 186: 18.

152. 11 September 2001 is the date when the US World Trade Centre in New York City and the Pentagon building in Washington DC were the targets of extensive terrorist attacks. The full implications of this historic event go beyond the scope of this study. However, it should be noted that in virtually every major receiving country in the world, racialized criteria in the selection and rights of immigrants were increased and given greater official license. On the historical context, see Robin Cohen, *The New Helots: Migrants and the International Division of Labor* (Vermont: Gower Publishing Co., 1987).

153. See e.g., Brigitte Young, 'The "Mistress" and the "Maid" in the Globalized Economy', in Leo Panitch and Colin Leys, eds, *Socialist Register, 2001: Working Classes, Global Realities* (London: Merlin Press, 2001); Sylvia Chant,

Women and Survival in Mexican Cities: Perspectives on Gender, Labor Markets and Low-income Households (New York: Manchester University Press, 1991); L. Lim, 'Women's Work in Export Factories: the Politics of a Cause', in I. Tinker, ed., *Persistent Inequalities* (New York: Oxford University Press, 1990).

154. Diane Elson, 'Male Bias in Macro-economics: The Case of Structural Adjustment', in Diane Elson, ed., *Male Bias in the Development Process* (New York: Manchester University Press, 1991). On the specific implications of gender to the international division of labour and the global process of capital accumulation, see Ward, ed., *Global Restructuring*; Swasti Mitter, *Common Fate, Common Bond: Women in the Global Economy* (London: Pluto Press, 1986); Thanh-Dam Truong, *Sex, Money and Morality: Prostitution and Tourism in South-East Asia* (London: Zed Books, 1990) and Vickers, *Women and the World Economic Crisis*.

155. Enloe, *Bananas, Beaches and Bases*, 177.

156. Canada, the focus of this study, is a case in point. While costs and quality of care vary considerably, and there are no national standards by which to measure cost per service, 'the typical cost of a regulated child care space for a three-year-old is between $4000 and $6000 per year (even higher in Ontario) ... [P]arents ... in 1988 were found to be spending about 8 per cent of the family's pre-tax income, or nearly 18 per cent of the mother's pre-tax income on child care costs'. 'Introduction' to *Our Children's Future: Child Care Policy in Canada*, eds, Gordon Cleveland and Michael Krashinsky (Toronto: University of Toronto Press, 2001), 9.

157. Ludmilla Kwitko, 'Filipina Domestic Workers and the New International Division of Labour', Paper presented at the Asia in the 1990s: Making and Meeting a New World Conference (Queen's University, Kingston, 1993), 1, 21.

158. Bridget Anderson, *Britain's Secret Slaves: An Investigation into the Plight of Overseas Domestic Workers* (United Kingdom: Anti-Slavery International and Kalayaan, 1993).

159. Kathy McAfee, *Storm Signals: Structural Adjustment and Development Alternatives in the Caribbean* (London: Zed Books and Oxfam America, 1991), 7.

160. On the relationship between the changes in production and the role of domestic service in the family with the emergence of western capitalist societies, see e.g., Rhonda Rapoport and Robert Rapoport, 'Work and Family in Contemporary Society', in John N. Edwards, ed., *The Family and Change* (New York: Knopf, 1969): 385–408; L.A. Tilly and J.W. Scott, *Women, Work and Family* (New York: Holt, Rinehart and Winston, 1978) and Mary Romero, *Maid in the USA* (New York: Routledge, 1992), 47–70.

161. Romero, *Maid in the USA*, 64–5.

162. Linda Martin and Kelly Segrave, *The Servant Problem: Domestic Workers in North America* (Jefferson NC: McFarland, 1985), 69.

163. This phrase, taken from a somewhat different context, belongs to Phyllis Palmer. See 'Housewife and Household Worker: Employer–Employee Relationships in the Home, 1928–1941' in Carol Groneman and Mary Beth Norton, eds, *'To Toil the Livelong Day': America's Women at Work 1780–1980* (Ithaca: Cornell University Press, 1987), 180.

164. Elizabeth Clark-Lewis, 'This Work had a End ...', in Carol Groneman and Mary Beth Norton, eds, *'To Toil the Livelong Day': America's Women at Work 1780–1980* (Ithaca: Cornell University Press, 1987), 197.

165. See Shellee Colen, ' "Housekeeping" for the Green Card: West Indian Household Workers, the State and Stratified Reproduction in New York', in Roger Sanjek and Shellee Colen, eds, *At Work in Homes: Household Workers in World Perspective* (Washington DC: American Ethnological Society Monograph Series, 1990), 93.
166. Audrey Macklin, 'Foreign Domestic Worker: Surrogate Housewife or Mail Order Servant?', *McGill Law Journal*, 37: 3 (1992).
167. Phyllis Palmer, *Domesticity and Dirt: Housewives and Domestic Servants in the United States, 1920–1945* (Philadelphia: Temple University Press, 1989), 67 ff.
168. Dionne Brand, *No Burden to Carry: Narratives of Black Working Women in Ontario 1920s–1950s* (Toronto: Women's Press, 1991), 15.
169. For a consideration of the domestic workers industry internationally, see Noeleen Heyzer, Geertje Lycklama à Nijeholt and Nedra Weerakoon, eds, *The Trade in Domestic Workers: Causes, Mechanisms and Consequences of International Migration* (Kuala Lampur and London: Asian and Pacific Development Centre and Zed Books, 1994) and Parreñas, *Servants of Globalization*.
170. As of April 1992, that minimum in Ontario was $65 000 per year, about $20 000 above the national combined average annual family income. See Estanislao Oziewicz, 'Nanny Policy Called Necessary Protection', *The Globe and Mail* (29 April 1992). However, in Canada in 2000, the average gross annual income in Canada for a family employing a live-in domestic worker on the LCP has been estimated to be $100 000. Louise Langevin and Marie-Claire Belleau, *Trafficking in Women in Canada*, 22.
171. The regulations regarding foreign domestic workers' hours of work, over-time pay, minimum wage laws and the right to organize in trade unions vary between the provinces. Ontario had the earliest and widest range of protective legislation for domestic workers, followed by Quebec and BC. Not coincidentally, these are also the provinces where the largest and most effective domestic rights' organizing has taken place.
172. This pattern is analysed in more detail in Abigail B. Bakan and Daiva Stasiulis, 'Foreign Domestic Worker Policy in Canada and the Social Boundaries of Modern Citizenship', *Science and Society*, 58: 1 (Spring 1994), 7–33. See also Patricia Daenzer, *Regulating Class Privilege: Immigrant Servants in Canada 1940s–1990s* (Toronto: Canadian Scholars' Press, 1993) and Langevin and Belleau, *Trafficking in Women in Canada*.
173. Macklin, 'Foreign Domestic Worker', 691.
174. Overall, in 1974, four times as many domestics arrived in Canada on employment visas than as immigrants (Daenzer, *Regulating Class Privilege*, 92).
175. In making the distinction between private domestic service jobs and service jobs performed in restaurants, hotels, hospitals, etc., we do not want to suggest that we are glorifying the latter. Indeed, as Evelyn Nakano Glenn, points out, like domestic service, low-level service jobs offer poor wages, few or limited benefits, low rates of unionization, and in general 'subject workers to arbitrary supervision' ('From Servitude to Service Work: Historical Continuities in the Racial Division of Paid Reproductive Labor', *Signs: Journal of Women in Culture and Society*, 18: 1 (1992), 22–3). Nevertheless,

service workers 'appreciate not being personally subordinate to an employer and not having to do "their" dirty work on "their property" '(23). Further while '[r]elations with supervisors and clients are hierarchical, ... they are embedded in an impersonal structure governed by more explicit contractual obligations and limits' (23).

176. See Daenzer, *Regulating Class Privilege*, 87–108.

177. The 'Pinto case', heard by the Federal Court Trial Division, involved the appeal of a prospective Ontario employer (Pinto) of a woman from Delhi, India. The domestic worker had been refused entry into Canada under the FDM by a Canadian visa officer. (See the Federal Court of Canada, Nov. 27, 1990.) The reason given for the refusal was that the woman had insufficient experience under the policy guideline calling for one year of previous 'relevant experience'. The applicant's claim was based on the prospective employee's experience as a single mother and as a school teacher with 16 years of practice.

178. Margaret Young, 'Canada's Immigration Programme: Background Paper' (Ottawa: Minister of Supply and Services, 1994), 20–1.

179. It should be noted that the issue of what constitutes government 'consultation' with concerned constituencies regarding this policy is a subject of considerable debate. In a letter dated 3 March 1992, for e.g., Glenda P. Simms, Ph.D., then President of the Canadian Advisory Council on the Status of Women (CACSW), wrote to Bernard Valcourt, the Minister of Employment and Immigration responsible for the FDM review process. She stated that, she was 'most disappointed' that a senior governmental official meeting with the CACSW 'for the most part could not provide adequate information on your consultation review process. The group was advised that employers' letters to the Minister and employment agencies' complaints about domestic workers had been the basis for the department's consultation' (Glenda Simms, 3 March 1992). Valcourt's response to this was that 'Those consulted include domestic worker advocacy groups, other federal government departments, provincial government officials, national and municipal day care associations, employer and employment agency representatives, academics and other concerned individuals ... . In making the changes, we have aimed for a balance between the needs of domestic workers and employers' (Bernard Valcourt, 26 August 1992).

180. Young, 'Canada's Immigration Program', 20.

181. In the Operations Memorandum for the LCP, one of the key points of change is stated to be the 'legislative basis' of the new programme 'to ensure that participants possess certain qualifications pertaining to their education, training and language skills before their application for an employment authorisation can be considered'. 'Operations Memorandum' (Draft), LCP, Employment and Immigration Canada, 23 April 1992, 2.

182. Patricia M. Daenzer, 'Ideology and the Formation of Migration Policy: The Case of Immigrant Domestic Workers, 1940–1990', Ph.D. dissertation (Department of Social Work, University of Toronto, 1991), 208; Macklin 'Foreign Domestic Worker', 740; Barbara Jackman, 'Admission of Foreign Domestic Workers', (on file with authors), 1, 4.

183. Jackman, 'Admission of Foreign Domestic Workers', 3–4.

184. Unlike the *Immigration Act* and the *Immigration Regulations, 1978*, which are publicly promulgated, formal, legal instruments, the *Immigration Manual* consists of '... informal instructions addressed to bureaucrats charged with administering immigration policy ... The Preface to the Manual makes [explicit] that: "Where conflict or inconsistency exists between these guidelines (including related Operations Memoranda) and the provisions of the *Immigration Act*, Regulations and related legislation, the latter must take precedence" '. See Macklin, 'Foreign Domestic Worker', 698–9.

185. See e.g., Sedef Arat-Koc and Fely Villasin, *Caregivers Break the Silence* (Toronto: Intercede, 2001); Punam Khosa, *Review of the Situation of Women in Canada* (Toronto: National Action Committee on the Status of Women, July 1993), 16–17 and Fely Villasin, 'Domestic Workers' Struggle for Equal Rights in Canada', in Mary Ruby Palma-Bertran and Aurora Javate de Dios, eds, *Filipino Women Overseas Contract Workers: At What Cost?* (Manila: Goodwill Trading Co., 1992), 77–80.

186. Romero, *Maid in the USA*, 139–62, provides a valuable summary of these studies and an analysis of their findings and theoretical conclusions.

187. Martin and Segrave, *The Servant Problem*, 121.

188. Data collected from the Department of Citizenship and Immigration.

189. Specifically, our survey indicated that 14 of 25 West Indian domestic workers entered Canada as visitors and one claimed asylum as a refugee; only ten entered through either the FDM or LCP. In contrast, 23 of 25 Filipinas entered Canada on the FDM or LCP while only two entered as visitors. These results are further discussed in Chapter 4, and in Daiva Stasiulis and Abigail B. Bakan, 'Negotiating Citizenship: The Case of Foreign Domestic Workers in Canada', *Feminist Review*, No. 57 (Autumn 1997), 112–39.

190. See Judith Ann Warner and Helen K. Henderson, 'Latina Women Immigrants' Waged Domestic Labour: Effects of Immigration Reform on the Link Between Private Households and the International Labour Force' (American Sociological Association, paper, 1990) cited in Romero, *Maid in the USA*, 190–1, n. 29; Evelyn Nakano Glenn, *Issei, Nisei, War Bride: Three Generations of Japanese American Women in Domestic Service* (Philadelphia: Temple University Press, 1986); Anderson, *Britain's Secret Slaves*.

191. Following British conquest in the mid-seventeenth century, the Caribbean was exploited as a region rich in land and capital-generating plantation agricultural conditions. In contrast, it was an area short in the supply of labour, particularly following the near-genocide suffered by the indigenous Amerindian population. After the early failure of a movement favouring white European indentured labour, the African slave trade soared and fuelled the profits of the colonial planters, primarily through the export of sugar and related products. With emancipation in 1838, an extensive peasantry developed as freed slaves turned to private land cultivation and resisted field labour in protest at the legacy of slavery. Women played a central role in agricultural marketing, first during the plantation period for the sale of slave-grown produce, and then after emancipation. While other employment options have opened for women, this tradition has continued until the present time. See Eric Williams, *Capitalism and Slavery* (Chapel Hill: University of North Carolina Press, 1944), which remains, despite volumes of contemporary debate, the best single concise historical source on this period for the

Caribbean region. See also Janet Henshall Momsen, 'Gender Roles in Caribbean Agricultural Labour', in Malcolm Cross and Gad Hueman, eds, *Labour in the Caribbean* (London: Macmillan Caribbean, 1988), 141–58; and Janet Henshall Momsen, ed., *Women and Change in the Caribbean* (London: James Currey, 1993); Lil Despradel, 'Internal Migration of Rural Women in the Caribbean and its Effects on Their Status', in UNESCO, *Women on the Move: Contemporary Changes in Family and Society* (1984), 93–109 and Abigail B. Bakan, *Ideology and Class Conflict in Jamaica: The Politics of Rebellion* (Montreal: McGill-Queen's University Press, 1990), 18–67.

192. See e.g., C. Peach, *West Indian Migration to Britain: A Social Geography* (London: Oxford University Press, 1968).

193. See e.g., Vic Satzewich, 'Racism and Canadian Immigration Policy: The Government's View of Caribbean Migration, 1962–66', *Canadian Ethnic Studies*, XXI: 1 (1989), 77–97.

194. For an insightful account of this process, focusing on the Jamaican experience, see Trevor Munroe, *The Politics of Constitutional Decolonization, 1944–62* (Jamaica: Institute of Social and Economic Research, 1972).

195. Dennis Conway, 'Migration and Urbanisation Policies: Immediate Needs for the 21st Century', *Caribbean Affairs*, 3: 4 (October–December 1990), 73–4.

196. European Economic Commission (1973) as cited in Lil Despradel, 'Internal Migration of Rural Women in the Caribbean', 97.

197. The first figure is drawn from Gurushi Swamy, 'International Migrant Workers' Remittances: Issues and Prospects', *World Bank Working Papers*, no. 481 (Washington DC: World Bank, 1981); the second is from Hymie Rubenstein, 'The Impact of Remittances in the Rural English Speaking Caribbean', in William F. Stinner, Klaus de Albuquerque and Roy S. Bryce-Laporte, eds, *Return Migration and Remittances: Developing a Caribbean Perspective*, RILES Occasional Paper, no. 3 (Washington DC: Research Institute and Ethnic Studies, 1982). For a discussion of remittances to the region in general, and a review of the literature, see, Wilbert O. Bascom, 'Remittance Inflows and Economic Development in Selected Anglophone Caribbean Countries', in Sergio Díaz-Briquets and Sidney Weintraub, eds, *Migration, Remittances and Small Business Development: Mexico and Caribbean Basin Countries* (Boulder: Westview Press, 1991), 71–99.

198. Conway, 'Migration and Urbanisation Policies', 75.

199. A study by Multilateral Investment Fund, created in 1993, estimated that remittances to the Latin American and Caribbean region are expanding at an overall annual rate of 7–10 per cent. Stephen Fidler, 'Middle East, Latin American and Caribbean: New Migrants Spur Growth in Remittances', *Financial Times*, 17 May 2001<http://www.jubilee2000uk.org/finance/Latin_america_migrants_growth_remittances.htm>.

200. Remittances in 2000 were at 11.7 per cent of gross domestic product. Stephen Fidler, 'Middle East, Latin American and Caribbean'.

201. See Orlando Patterson, 'Reflections on the Caribbean Diaspora and its Policy Implications', in K. Hall and D. Benn, eds, *Contending with Destiny: The Caribbean in the 21st Century* (Kingston: Ian Randle), 500–10 and Anthony Weis, 'On a Precipice: Globalization and Small Farmers in Eastern Jamaica', Doctoral dissertation (Queen's University, Kingston, Ontario, 2003).

202. Despradel, 'Internal Migration of Rural Women in the Caribbean', 101;
Housewives Association of Trinidad and Tobago, *Report on Employment
Status of Household Workers in Trinidad* (Port of Spain: HATT, March 1975).
203. Janet Henshall Momsen, 'Gender Roles in Caribbean Agricultural Labour',
in Malcolm Cross and Gad Hueman, eds, *Labour in the Caribbean* (London:
Macmillan Caribbean, 1988), 147.
204. Momsen, 'Gender Roles in Caribbean Agricultural Labour', 147 and Dorian
Powell, 'Caribbean Women and their Response to Familial Experiences',
Social and Economic Studies, 35: 2 (1986), 83–127.
205. By 1970, women's paid participation rate in the Caribbean labour force overall had been superseded by work in the expanding service sector, largely
fuelled by tourism and the hotel industry. See Peggy Antrobus, 'Employment
of Women Workers in the Caribbean', in Pat Ellis, ed., *Women of the Carribean*
(New Jersey: Zed Books, 1986) and Lorna Gordon, 'Women in Caribbean
Agriculture', in Pat Ellis, ed., *Women of the Caribbean* (New Jersey: Zed Books,
1986), 31–2, and 35–40; Peggy Antrobus, 'Gender Issues in Caribbean
Development', in Stanley Lalta and Marie Freckleton, eds, *Caribbean
Economic Development: The First Generation* (Kingston, Ja.: Ian Randle
Publishers, 1993), 68–77; Joycelin Massiah, ed., 'Women in the Caribbean',
Social and Economic Studies, Special Number, Part One (vol. 35, no. 2, June
1986) and Part Two (vol. 35, no. 3, September 1986); Helen I. Safa and Peggy
Antrobus, 'Women and the Economic Crisis in the Caribbean', in Lourdes
Beneria and Shelley Feldman, eds, *Unequal Burden: Economic Crises, Persistent
Poverty, and Women's Work* (Boulder: Westview Press, 1992), 49–82 and Pat
Ellis, ed., *Women of the Caribbean* (London: Zed Press, 1986).
206. Cited in Satzewich, 'Racism and Canadian Immigration Policy', 77.
207. The policy was implemented on a limited quota basis, with 100 Caribbean
women admitted in the first year, and subsequent increases up to 280 per
year. The plan was explicitly enacted, and then extended into the 1960s, to
assuage the demands of Caribbean governments. For its part, the Canadian
government expressed explicit concern that upon achieving permanent status, sponsored relatives from the Caribbean would enter Canada and alter
the racial complexion of Canadian society. However, Canada's economic
interests in the English Caribbean, ranking third in the world after the
United States and Britain, compelled concern that some accommodation to
the region's political leaders on the immigration front were in order. See
Satzewich, 'Racism and Canadian Immigration Policy' and Daenzer,
Regulating Class Privilege, on the rise and fall of the West Indian Domestic
Scheme; see also, Agnes Calliste, 'Canada's Immigration Policy and
Domestics from the Caribbean: The Second Domestic Scheme', in Jesse Vorst
et al., eds, *Race, Class, Gender: Bonds and Barriers* (Toronto: Garamond Press,
1991) and Frances Henry, 'The West Indian Domestic Scheme in Canada',
Social and Economic Studies 17: 1 (1968). On Canada's historic economic
interests in the region, see Brian Douglas Tennyson, ed., *Canadian–Caribbean
Relations: Aspects of a Relationship* (Sydney, Nova Scotia: Centre for
International Studies, 1990); Robert Chodos, *The Caribbean Connection*
(Toronto: James Lorimer, 1977) and Abigail B. Bakan, David Cox and Colin
Leys, eds, *Imperial Power and Regional Response: The Caribbean Basin Initiative*
(Wilfrid Laurier University Press, 1993).

208. See Wolseley W. Anderson, *Caribbean Immigrants: A Socio-Demographic Profile* (Toronto: Canadian Scholars Press, 1993), 73 ff.
209. The largest single source country was Jamaica, followed by Guyana, Haiti and Trinidad. Anthony Richmond for Statistics Canada, *Current Demographic Analysis: Caribbean Immigrants* (Ottawa: Minister of Supply and Services, 1989), 3.
210. After 1973 and prior to 1981, live-in domestic workers arrived on temporary employment visas with no special provision for the attainment of permanent resident status. Shiela McLeod Arnopoulous, *Problems of Immigrant Women in the Canadian Labour Force* (Ottawa: Canadian Advisory Council on the Status of Women, January 1979): 61; 'Statistical Profiles' (November 1990); Task Force on Immigration Practices and Procedures, *Domestic Workers on Employment Authorizations* (Government of Canada, Office of the Minister of Employment and Immigration, April 1981), 48–50 and 'Foreign Domestic Workers in Canada – Where Do They Come From? How Has that Changed Over Time?', *The Moment* 2, vol. 5 (1991), 5. See also Strategic Planning and Research Directorate, Employment and Immigration Canada, 'Statistical Profiles', n.d. Table 2, 3.
211. In 1982, the number of processed contract workers from the Philippines was 314 284, compared with 598 769 in 1990. Moreover, the number of processed Filipino contract workers increased twenty-fold over a 16-year period, from just over 36 000 in 1975 to almost 700 000 in 1991. See Benjamin V. Carino, 'Migrant Workers from the Philippines', in G. Batistella and A. Paganoni, eds, *Philippine Labour Migration: Impact and Policy* (Quezon City: Scalabrini Migration Center, 1992), 7, 6.
212. See Graziano Battistella, 'Data on International Migration from the Philippines', *Asian and Pacific Migration Journal*, 4: 4 (1995), 589–99; Ramon Bultron, 'Recruitment Costs, State Exaction and Government Fees', Paper delivered at the International Migrant Conference on Labor-Export and Forced Migration amidst Globalization, Manila, 4–8 November 2001, 2.
213. International Labour Organization, Press Release, 'Female Asian Migrants: A Growing but Increasingly Vulnerable Workforce', 5 February 1996, <webinfo@ilo.org>.
214. Philippine National Statistics Office, reported in Ligaya L. McGovern, 'The Export of Labor and the Politics of Foreign Debt (The Case of Overseas Filipino Domestic Workers)', Paper presented at the International Migrant Conference on Labor Export and Forced Migration Amidst Globalization, Manila, 4–8 November 2001, 2.
215. Ludmilla Kwitko, 'Filipina Domestic Workers and the New International Division of Labour', 2; Vickers, *Women and the World Economic Crisis*, 90.
216. Antonio Tujan Jr, 'Labor Export and Forced Migration under Globalization', Paper Presented to the International Migrant Conference on Labor-Export and Forced Migration amidst Globalization, Manila, Philippines, 4–8 November 2001, 3.
217. Carino, 'Migrant Workers from the Philippines', 13.
218. Mary Ruby Palma-Beltran, 'Filipina Women Domestic Workers Overseas: Profile and Implications for Policy', *Asian Migrant*, 4: 2 (April–June 1991), 3–13.

219. Battistella, 'Data on International Migration from the Philippines', 590.
220. The emergence of massive overseas employment of Filipinos coincided with the opening of the Middle East labour market. Maruja M.B. Asis, 'The Overseas Employment Programme Policy', in G. Battistella and A. Paganoni, eds, *Philippine Labour Migration: Impact and Policy* (Quezon City: Scalabrini Migration Center, 1992), 69.
221. Ludmilla Kwitko, 'Filipina Domestic Workers and the New International Division of Labour', 8; see also Emmanuel S. de Dios and Joel Rocamora, eds, *Of Bonds and Bondage: A Reader on Philippine Debt* (Manila: Transnational Institute, Philippine Centre for Policy Studies and Freedom of Debt Coalition, 1992).
222. It is beyond the scope of this discussion to account for why the Philippines, unlike South Korea and Taiwan, with whom it shares many characteristics, did not become a Newly Industrializing Country. Angeles' account, however, is persuasive, suggesting that the role of the state, burdened by the presence of a strong landlord class, has served to block the enactment of progressive land reform and the emergence of a strong indigenous entrepreneurial class. See Leonora Angeles, 'Why the Philippines Did Not Become a Newly Industrializing Country', *Kasarinlan*, 7, 2 and 3 (1991/92), 91.
223. Kwitko, 'Filipina Domestic Workers', 8.
224. Carino, 'Migrant Workers from the Philippines', 18.
225. William J. Pomeroy, *The Philippines: Colonialism, Collaboration, and Resistance!* (New York: International Publishers, 1992), 235–6.
226. Ray Brooks, 'Why is Unemployment High in the Philippines?', IMF Working Paper (International Monetary Fund, Asia Pacific Department, 2002), <http://www.imf.org/external/pubs/ft/wp/2002/wp0223.pdf> (4 March 2002).
227. Bultron, 'Recruitment Costs, State Exaction and Government Fees', 4.
228. Pomeroy, *The Philippines*, 239.
229. Pomeroy, *The Philippines*, 238.
230. Episcopal Commission for the Pastoral Care of Migrant and Itinerant People, Reported in Ligaya L. McGovern 'The Export of Labour and the Politics of Foreign Debt', 5.
231. Vickers, *Women and the World Economic Crisis*, 89; Pomeroy, *The Philippines*, 239, McGovern, 'The Export of Labour and the Politics of Foreign Debt', 4.
232. McGovern, 'The Export of Labour and the Politics of Foreign Debt', 4.
233. Kwitko, 'Filipina Domestic Workers', 9.
234. Ka Crispin Beltran, 'Message to the International Migrant Conference', Address delivered to the International Migrant Conference on Labor-Export and Forced Migration Amidst Globalization, Manila, 4–8 November 2001, 3.
235. Interviews with the authors and CALABARZON community organizers or women workers, 3 June 1995.
236. 'CALABARZON – Where Doing Business is a Pleasure', promotional flyer, Philippines, n.d., 3.
237. Center for Women's Resources, *Economic Growth in 1994 – At Whose Expense: Facts and Figures for Filipino Women on the 1994 Philippine Economy and Politics*, February 1995, 23.
238. Kwitko, 'Filipina Domestic Workers', 90.

239. The signing into law of the May 1974 Philippines Labour Code 'signalled earnest government involvement with overseas employment'. The Code provided for the creation of the Overseas Employment Development Board (OEDB) to undertake a systematic programme for the overseas employment of land-based workers, banned direct hiring and made mandatory remittance of overseas workers' earnings. While the 1974 Code was intended to block participation of the private sector in recruitment and placement, these tasks proved too onerous for the government to handle. Thus, in 1978, the government relegated to the private sector control over recruitment and placement of Filipino workers. Asis, 'Overseas Employment Program Policy' (1992), 71–2.

240. Economists acknowledge the substantial contribution of overseas migrants' remittances in offsetting the oil bill and improving the balance of payments, especially during the mid-1980s, a period marked by massive foreign exchange problems and foreign capital flight. However, they differ in their assessments of the impact of migration on economic development in the Philippines. The most persuasive accounts conclude that overseas employment is only palliative in character, and that more lasting solutions to the country's critical development problems must address deeper structural factors. For further discussion of the impact of overseas employment on development in the Philippines, see Manolo I. Abella, 'International Migration and Development', in Batistella and Paganoni (1992); Noel Vasquez, 'Economic and Social Impact of Labour Migration', in Batistella and Paganoni (1992), 39–67; Graziano Battistella, 'Migration Opportunity or Loss?' in Batistella and Paganoni, eds, Philippine Labour Migration: Impact and Policy (Quezon City: Scalabrini Migration Center, 1992), 113–34; and Carino, 'Migrant Workers from the Philippines', 19.

241. Ruby Palma-Beltran, 'Filipina Women Domestic Workers Overseas', 46. These figures are considered to be conservative, as they do not incorporate those who depart as tourists and are therefore not registered as official overseas workers. Macklin, 'Foreign Domestic Worker', 695.

242. Manolo I. Abella, 'International Migration and Development', 30.

243. Adelle Blackett, 'Making Domestic Work Visible: The Case for Specific Regulation' (Geneva: ILO, Labour Law and Labour Relations Branch, 1998), 4, n. 15.

244. Mitter, *Common Fate, Common Bond*, 37.

245. Carino, 'Migrant Workers from the Philippines', 13–14.

246. See Parreñas, *Servants of Globalization* and Vasquez, 'Economic and Social Impact of Labour Migration', 60–62 for a discussion of the impact of overseas migration on migrants' families and communities.

247. Regarding the Philippines, Battistella notes that '[f]emale migration is concentrated on practically three sectors: domestic work, entertainment and health, which make up 82 per cent of the annual deployment of newly hired contract workers'. Battistella, 'Data on International Migration' (1995), 590.

248. Noeleen Heyzer and Vivienne Wee, 'Domestic Workers in Transient Overseas Employment: Who Benefits, Who Profits', in N. Heyzer, G. Lycklama à Nijeholt and N. Weerakoon, eds, *The Trade in Domestic Worker: Causes, Mechanisms and Consequences of International Migration* (London: Zed Books, 1992).

4 Gatekeepers in the Domestic Service Industry in Canada

249. The argument in this chapter is partially based on work developed in Abigail B. Bakan and Daiva Stasiulis, 'Making the Match: Domestic Placement Agencies and the Racialization of Women's Household Work', *Signs: Journal of Women in Culture and Society*, 20: 2 (Winter 1995) and Daiva Stasiulis and Abigail B. Bakan, 'Negotiating the Citizenship Divide: Foreign Domestic Worker Policy and Legal Jurisprudence', in Radha Jhappan, ed., *Women's Legal Strategies in Canada* (Toronto: University of Toronto Press, 2002).
250. Department of Employment and Immigration Canada, *Immigration Manual*, Appendix C. The predecessor to this agreement was called an 'Employment Contract'. The change in title suggests a deliberate attempt to make the contract unenforceable. The Operations Memorandum for the LCP abolishes the requirement for any employment agreement, stating, 'It is the responsibility of the employer and employee to set out the terms and conditions of employment in the form of a contract.' CEIC 'Operations Memorandum (Draft): Live-In Caregiver Program', 23 April 1992. The booklet on the LCP distributed by Immigration Canada to potential employers and applicants in 1992 provided a 'Sample Contract'. See Diana Bretl and Christina Davidson, 'Background Paper: Foreign Domestic Workers in British Columbia', West Coast Domestic Workers Association, Vancouver, n.d., 3.
251. Diana Bretl and Christina Davidson, 'Background Paper: Foreign Domestic Workers in British Columbia', West Coast Domestic Workers Association, Vancouver, n.d., 3.
252. *Domestic Workers Association Newsletter*, WCDWA, Vancouver, Vol. 1, no. 2, April 1987, 7. This article was written when the Federal Department of Immigration was still issuing 'Employment Contracts' as opposed to Agreements.
253. Macklin 'Foreign Domestic Worker', 723, note 192.
254. *Domestic Workers Association Newsletter*, WCDWA, Vancouver, Vol. 1, no. 16, September 1988, 4.
255. This statement appears at the bottom of the 'Sample Contract' provided by Immigration Canada in the booklet, *The Live-in Caregiver Programme: Information for Employers and Live-in Caregivers from Abroad*, Minister of Supply and Services Canada, 1992.
256. INTERCEDE, 'Improving The Ontario Employment Standards Act To Protect Domestic Workers' (Toronto: INTERCEDE, n.d.).
257. Macklin reports a case – *Khan v. Canada* (Minister of Employment and Immigration) involving Ms Khan, a Trinidadian domestic worker who was suspected of transgressing the 'live-in' requirement of the FDM. The Court ruled that immigration authorities had resorted to 'callous and unnecessary' procedures in detaining Ms Khan, who was eight months pregnant at the time of her arrest. Macklin 'Foreign Domestic Worker', 723, note 192.
258. Macklin 'Foreign Domestic Worker', 723.
259. Sedef Arat-Koc, 'In the Privacy of Our Own Home: Foreign Domestic Workers as Solution to the Crisis in the Domestic Sphere in Canada', *Studies in Political Economy* 28 (1989), 33–58, 34 ff.

260. Martha Friendly, 'Child Care and Canadian Federalism in the 1990s: Canary in a Coal Mine', in Gordon Cleveland and Michael Krashinsky, eds, *Our Children's Future: Child Care Policy in Canada* (Toronto: University of Toronto Press, 2001), 26.

261. See Claire F.L. Young, 'Child Care – A Taxing Issue?', *McGill Law Journal* 39: 3 (1994), 539–67 and Pat Armstrong and Hugh Armstrong, *The Double Ghetto: Canadian Women and Their Segregated Work*, 3rd edn (Toronto: McClelland and Stewart, 1994).

262. The federal government has largely limited its involvement in childcare to a number of funding mechanisms, such as the National Child Tax Credit and the Canada Assistance Plan (CAP). The fact that in 1990, the federal government placed limits on the annual increases to CAP has further exacerbated the regional differences in income level eligibility for child care subsidies, and the amounts of these subsidies. See Mab Oloman, 'Child Care Funding', Strategy Paper for National Child Care Conference and Lobby, Ottawa, October 1992, 4. See also The Task Force on Child Care, *Report of the Task Force on Child Care* (Ottawa: 1986); Ruth K. Abbott and R.A. Young, 'Cynical and Deliberate Manipulation? Child Care and the Reserve Army of Female Labour in Canada', *Journal of Canadian Studies* 2: 24 (Summer 1989), 22–38; Dawn Currie, 'Re-thinking What We Do and How We Do it: A Study of Reproductive Decisions', *Canadian Review of Sociology and Anthropology*, 25: 2 (May 1988), 231–53; G. Doherty, M. Friendly and M. Oloman, *Women's Support, Women's Work: Child Care in an Era of Deficit Reduction, Devolution, Downsizing and Deregulation* (Ottawa: Status of Women Canada, 1998).

263. Friendly, 'Child Care and Canadian Federalism in the 1990s', 26.

264. Jane Beach, 'A Comprehensive System of Child Care', Strategy paper for National Child Care Conference and Lobby, Ottawa, October 1992, 7.

265. Friendly, 'Child Care and Canadian Federalism in the 1990s', 26.

266. Jane Beach, 'A Comprehensive System of Child Care', Strategy Paper for National Child Care Conference and Lobby, Ottawa, October 1992, 9.

267. One of the most systematic studies in the United States conducted over a three-year period by the University of New Hampshire's Family Research Laboratory concluded in 1988 that there was no epidemic of child abuse in daycare centres in the United States, despite media claims to the contrary. In fact, private homes were cited as far more dangerous for children. See Susan Faludi, *Backlash: The Undeclared War Against American Women* (New York: Crown Publishers, 1991), 42–3. Another comparative study of childcare quality in Canada, the United States, England, Western Europe, Bermuda and New Zealand concluded that quality working conditions for childcare staff and a low child/adult ratio are the critical determinants in assessing good care. For these findings see Gillian Doherty, *Quality Matters in Child Care* (Huntsville: Jesmond Publishing, 1991).

268. The beginning of the 1990s saw the effects of a period of backlash against public childcare as an 'immoral' concession to the rights of working women, an argument that had only been partially moderated by the end of the decade. In the United States, New Right ideologues compared day care to Thalidomide treatment, and horror stories of abuse, molestation and

diseases spreading in public childcare facilities became rampant in the media. See Faludi, *Backlash;* Marilyn French, *The War Against Women* (New York: Summit Books, 1992), 137–8; Alanna Mitchell, *Globe and Mail,* Toronto, 20 April 1992; 'Our Families Come First: Why More Mothers are Choosing to Stay at Home', *Chatelaine Magazine,* February 1992 and on the backlash against the rights of women and other equity-seeking groups in Ontario, see Abigail B. Bakan and Audrey Kobayashi, *Employment Equity Policy in Canada: An Interprovincial Comparison* (Ottawa: Status of Women Canada, 2000). The ideological backlash against public day care has also been accompanied by horror stories of the untrustworthy nanny. One of the most popular movies released in the winter of 1992 was *The Hand that Rocks the Cradle* (Hollywood Pictures, directed by Curtis Hanson), which featured a psychopathic nanny who attempts to murder her employer and kidnap the children. It should be noted that the nanny portrayed in the movie was atypically upper class, and was motivated by revenge for her husband's suicide. But the true story of the death of three-month-old Kristie Fischer, whose Swiss nanny, 20-year-old Olivia Riner was charged by police for murder and arson in the Thornwood New York home, could only increase the fears of parents regarding the quality of live-in childcare (Ames *et al.,* 27 January 1992, 50). One company, Brown–McComas Child Care Management Resources, based in Duncanville, Texas markets a 'Child Care Screening System' to domestic placement agencies that includes a software programme called the Child Abuse Inventory Potential (CAP). The system is advertised to measure 'an applicant's attitudes that exhaustive research and theory have proven to be associated with physical abuse'. Brochure produced by Brown–McComas Child Care Management Resources, n.d.
269. Louise Langevin and Marie-Claire Belleau, *Trafficking in Women in Canada, A Critical Analysis of the Legal Framework Governing Immigrant Live-in Caregivers and Mail Order Brides* (Ottawa: Status of Women Canada, October 2000), 22.
270. For an insightful summary of the problems of universalizing household labour, and the alternative value of viewing household work 'historically, locally and contextually within a world capitalist system', see Shellee Colen and Roger Sanjek, 'At Work in Homes II: Directions', in Roger Sanjek and Shellee Colen, eds, *At Work in Homes: Household Workers in World Perspective* (Washington DC: American Ethnological Society Monograph Series, 1990), 176–88.
271. Additionally, the authors observed several national and international meetings and conferences organized by placement agencies, and consulted a wide variety of policy documents and secondary sources. The domestic placement agency industry is extremely volatile. As small, often single family or single employee businesses, agencies open and close frequently, particularly in times of economic instability. At the time of the interviews, Ontario was one of the few Canadian provinces that required licences for placement agencies. (Under the Employment Standards Act (2000) passed into law under the Ontario Progressive Conservative government, agencies were no longer required to be licensed, though certain standards were enacted into the law.) The agencies selected for interviewing in this case study were all licensed, reputable and well-established agencies with two or more years of successful operation in the industry. While all of the agencies

interviewed did some overseas recruitment, in light of recessionary conditions they also placed foreign domestics already resident in Canada on temporary status employment authorizations. All serviced the area of Toronto
and vicinity, where the largest concentration in the country of in-home
legally documented foreign domestics is employed. At the time of the interviews however, numerous unlicensed agencies were operating within
Ontario, as well as Quebec and BC, the other provinces that required licensure. This could be witnessed by a glance at any daily newspaper across
Canada. See 'Newspaper Ads Photocopies File: 1988–92', compiled by Judy
Richards.
272. For a discussion of the value of 'intensive' qualitative methods such as structural and causal analysis, participant observation and/or informal and inter-
active interviews, see Andrew Sayer, *Method in Social Science: A Realist
Approach* (London: Hutchison, 1984), 221 ff.
273. Interview, 2 October 1991, A. Bakan with Agency 'C'.
274. Interview, 6 October 1992, A. Bakan with Agency 'K'.
275. Agencies are not, of course, the only group with an interest in careful
screening. Parent support movements and childcare advocates similarly
argue for careful selection processes to be followed, in part in response to
the low status normally assigned to in-home childcare. See Barbara Kaiser
and Judy Sklar Rasminsky, *The Daycare Handbook: A Parents' Guide to Finding
and Keeping Quality Daycare in Canada* (Toronto: Little, Brown and Co.,
1991), 34–50; 'Nanny Placement Practices in America: Preliminary Survey
Results', *National Nanny Newsletter*, 3: 4 (Fall 1988), 8–11 and Gordon
Cleveland and Michael Krashinsky, eds, *Our Children's Future: Child Care
Policy in Canada* (Toronto: University of Toronto Press, 2001).
276. Interview, 22 November 1991, A. Bakan with Agency 'G'.
277. Ibid.
278. Ibid.
279. Interview, 1 October 1991, A. Bakan with Agency 'C'. All of the placement
agencies interviewed routinely referred to the domestic workers as 'girls',
regardless of their actual age, while female employers were never referred to
using this term. The class and racially specific gender stereotyping in this
linguistic differentiation is obvious. On the role of linguistic deference in
the domestic–employer relationship, see Judith Rollins, *Between Women:
Domestics and Their Employers* (Philadelphia: Temple University Press, 1985),
158 ff.
280. Interview, 23 October 1991, A. Bakan with Agency 'E'.
281. Interview, 22 November 1991, A. Bakan with Agency 'G'.
282. Interview, 6 November 1991, A. Bakan with Agency 'F'.
283. Macklin, 'Foreign Domestic Worker', 681. There is evidence to suggest a
fairly extensive mail-order bride service currently in operation, drawing particularly among Filipino women in search of permanent residency in
Canada. This practice exists in the netherworld between legal and illegal
immigration activities. Once legal marriage is intended, a Canadian citizen
can apply legally to sponsor their spouse to enter the country as a landed
immigrant, or permanent resident. However, the 'arrangement' of such
marriages is usually mediated by coercive measures, at a price, by illegal
mediators. In some countries, such as Japan, the entry of Filipino women

under such circumstances is largely controlled by the criminal underworld. See Naomi Hosoda, 'Filipino Women in the Japanese Entertainment Industry: The International Division of Labour and the Commodification of Female Sexuality' (Masters Thesis, Queen's University, 1994) and Langevin and Belleau, *Trafficking in Women in Canada*.

284. Interview, 26 September 1991, A. Bakan with Agency 'B'.

285. Interview, 16 September 1991, A. Bakan with Marna Martin, spokesperson for Canadian Coalition for In-Home Child and Domestic Care, Canada.

286. Barbara Bush, *Slave Women in Caribbean Society* (Kingston: Heinemann Publishers Caribbean, 1990), 12–13.

287. See Sedef Arat-Koc, 'From "Mothers of the Nation" to Migrant Workers', in Abigail B. Bakan and Daiva K. Stasiulis, eds, *Not One of the Family: Foreign Domestic Workers in Canada* (Toronto: University of Toronto Press, 1997), 55, 61–6.

288. Enloe, *Bananas, Beaches and Bases*, 177–94.

289. Nancy Rose Hunt, 'Domesticity and Colonialism in Belgian Africa: Usumbura's Foyer Social, 1946–1960', *Signs: Journal of Women in Culture and Society*, 5, 31: 447–74.

290. See e.g., Deborah Gaitskell, 'Housewives, Maids or Mothers: Some Contradictions of Domesticity for Christian Women in Johannesburg, 1903–39', *Journal of African History*, 24: 2 (1983), 241–56 and ' "Christian Compounds for Girls": Church Hostels for African Women in Johannesburg, 1907–1970', *Journal of African Studies*, 6: 1 (1979), 44–69; Audrey Wipper, 'The Maendeleo ya Wanawake Movement in the Colonial Period: The Canadian Connection, Mau Mau, Embroidery and Agriculture', *Rural Africana*, 29 (Winter 1975–76), 195–214; Margaret Strobel, 'African Women: A Review', *Signs: Journal of Women in Culture and Society*, 8: 1 (Autumn 1982), 109–31; Elizabeth Jelin, 'Migration and Labor Force Participation of Latin American Women: The Domestic Servants in the Cities', *Signs: Journal of Women in Culture and Society*, 3: 1 (Autumn 1977), 129–41; E. Chaney and M. Garcia Castro, eds, *Muchachas No More: Household Workers in Latin America and the Caribbean* (Philadelphia: Temple University Press, 1989); B.W. Higman, 'Domestic Service in Jamaica Since 1750', in B. Higman, ed., *Trade, Government and Society in Caribbean History 1700–1920* (Kingston: Heinemann Educational Books Caribbean Ltd, 1983); Patricia Mohammed, 'Domestic Workers', in Pat Ellis, ed., *Women of the Caribbean* (London: Zed Books, 1985), 41–6.

291. A thorough exploration of class relations in plantation America as they relate to racialized gender roles can be found in Elizabeth Fox-Genovese, *Within the Plantation Household: Black and White Women in the Old South* (Chapel Hill: University of North Carolina Press, 1988). See also Sutherland (1981), who summarizes: 'The southern mammy was the symbol of the perfect nursemaid and the model of faithful service throughout the nineteenth century' (142). Regarding the British Caribbean experience, see Bush, *Slave Women in Caribbean Society*.

292. Unidentified newspaper advertisement, cited in John Ashton, *Social Life in the Reign of Queen Anne Taken from Original Sources* (Chatto and Windus, 1882), I 81 and Peter Fryer, *Staying Power: The History of Black People in Britain* (London: Pluto Press, 1984), 63.

293. J.D. Brierley, R.H. Fryer and E. Goldschmeid, *A Future for Nursery Nursing: Report of the Panel of Inquiry Appointed by the National Nursery Examination Board*

(London: NNEB, n.d.(circa 1980)), 7, 22. This work puts the number of NNEB colleges at 146. The higher figure is for 1992. Interview, A. Bakan with Maureen Smith, Senior Assistant Director, NNEB, St Albans, England, 16 July 1992.
294. Interview, 16 July 1992, A. Bakan with Maureen Smith.
295. The National Nursery Examination Board NNEB, *The Diploma and Preliminary Diploma in Nursery Nursing – Modular Scheme: An Overview, 1992* (St Albans: NNEB, 1992). The NNEB is an intensive programme of two years of full time study, involving health, educational and socio-cultural issues in the curriculum. Notably, the current syllabus includes training in 'understanding of a child's developing awareness and experience of race, gender and disability, the possible outcomes of membership of any group open to discrimination and the need to avoid stereotyping' (NNEB, *The Diploma* (1992), 12 ff.)
296. RG 76 83/84/349, Vol. 150, File 5850–6–4–533 Part 6, Department of Manpower and Immigration. Memorandum to W.K. Bell, Director, Programme and Procedures, as cited in Patricia M. Daenzer, 'Ideology and the Formation of Migration Policy: The Case of Immigrant Domestic Workers, 1940–1990', Ph.D. dissertation (Department of Social Work, University of Toronto, 1991), 208, n. 15.
297. See Daenzer, 'Ideology and the Formation of Migration Policy', 190–1.
298. See Fudge, 'Little Victories and Big Defeats', 119–45.
299. Interview, 23 October 1991, A. Bakan with Agency 'E'.
300. Interview, 12 December 1991, A. Bakan with Agency 'H'.
301. Interview, 6 November 1991, A. Bakan with Agency 'F'.
302. See Timothy Appleby, 'Crime Story: The Jamaican Connection', in three parts, *The Globe and Mail* (10, 11 and 13 July 1992). See also Frances Henry, *The Caribbean Diaspora in Toronto: Learning to Live with Racism* (Toronto: University of Toronto Press, 1994); Michael Ornstein, *Ethno-racial Inequality in the City of Toronto: An Analysis of the 1996 Census* (Toronto: Canadian Social Justice Foundation for Research and Education, 2002).
303. Interview, 15 October 1991, A. Bakan with Agency 'D'.
304. Interview, 21 May 1991, A. Bakan and D. Stasiulis with Agency 'I'.
305. Interview, 15 October 1991, A. Bakan with Agency 'D'.
306. Interview, 26 September 1991, A. Bakan with Agency 'B'.
307. Interview, 23 October 1991, A. Bakan with Agency 'E'.
308. Citizenship and Immigration Canada, Facts and Figures (Ottawa: 1998), 101. We would like to thank Deirdre McKay for pointing out recent changes in gender distribution in the LCP.
309. Department of Employment and Immigration, Report from Statistical Review of FDM Program, *Persons Entering the Foreign Domestic Program by Year and Gender, 1982–1989* and Arat-Koc, *Studies in Political Economy*, 34.
310. Interview, 23 October 1991, A. Bakan with Agency 'E'.
311. Interview, 21 May 1991, A. Bakan and D. Stasiulis with Agency 'I'.
312. Interview, 1 October 1991, A. Bakan with Agency 'C'.
313. Interview, 23 October 1991, A. Bakan with Agency 'E'. It should be noted that it was made clear in this interview that 'the garbage' referred to those considered to be unqualified nannies, not unscrupulous placement agents.
314. Interview, 15 October 1991, A. Bakan with Agency 'D'.
315. Interview, 15 October 1991, A. Bakan with Agency 'D'.
316. Interview, 6 October 1992, A. Bakan with Agency 'K'. It is, of course, formally illegal for any employment agency to bias its placement policies

towards one specific applicant cohort on the basis of race, nationality or ethnicity. However, at the time of the interview this agency was licensed in Ontario and operating a highly successful business primarily dependent upon personal referrals for its clientele.

317. Interview, 6 October 1992, A. Bakan with Agency 'K'.
318. Interview, 6 November 1991, A. Bakan with Agency 'F'.
319. Interview, 15 October 1991, A. Bakan with Agency 'D'.

5   Marginalized and Dissident Non-Citizens: Foreign Domestic Workers

320. Sections of this chapter are drawn from Daiva Stasiulis and Abigail B. Bakan, 'Negotiating Citizenship Globally: Migrant Domestic Workers as a Case Study', *Feminist Review*, no. 57, London, UK, Autumn 1997.
321. The 50 interviews took place between 1994 and 1995, after the new LCP legislation was enacted. Some of the interviewees arrived in Canada under the previous FDM and others by means elaborated further in the chapter. We would like to acknowledge the research assistance of Maria Leynes, Marcia Williams and Claudine Charley in conducting interviews for this study.
322. For purposes of security and confidentiality we did not interview the employers of the domestic workers in this survey, upon whom the interviewees depended for their very livelihood and residence in Canada. Interviews with placement agencies documented in the previous chapter provide a reasonable profile of their clients, the employers of domestic workers in Canada. This methodology also applied to the nursing interviews. See Chapter 6.
323. Respondents identified Trinidad and Tobago, Jamaica, Barbados and Guyana as the countries of origin among West Indian domestic workers participating in the survey.
324. The reference 'Q' followed by a number refers to the question number of the interview schedule. This chapter is an interpretation of selected findings, relevant to the wider analysis of negotiating citizenship rights. The survey questionnaire is available on request from the authors.
325. See Abigail B. Bakan, 'The International Market for Female Labour and Individual Deskilling: West Indian Women Workers in Toronto', *North/South: Canadian Journal of Latin American and Caribbean Studies* (1987), vol. 12, no. 24.
326. See Parreñas, *Servants of Globalization*.
327. According to the Department of Citizenship and Immigration Canada (CIC): 'An important requirement of the Programme is that employees must live in the employer's home. The Live-in Caregiver Program exists only because there is a shortage of Canadians to fill the need for live-in care work. There is no shortage of Canadian workers available for caregiving positions where there is no live-in requirement.' See CIC, LCP website, <http://www.cic.gc.ca/english/visit/caregi_e2.html#2>.
328. See e.g., Arat-Koc and Villasin, *Caregivers Break the Silence*.
329. See Romero, *Maid in the USA*; Grace Chang, *Disposable Domestics: Immigrant Women in the Global Economy* (Cambridge, Mass.: South End Press, 2000);

Ximena Bunster and Elsa M. Chaney, *Sellers and Servants: Working Women in Lima Peru* (Granby, Mass: Bergin and Garvey, 1989) and Noeleen Heyzer, Geertje Lycklama à Nijeholt and Nedra Weerakoon, eds, *The Trade in Domestic Workers.*

330. 'Operations Memorandum' (Draft), LCP Employment and Immigration Canada, 23 April 1992.

331. See Department of CIC, LCP website, <http://www.cic.gc.ca/english/visit/caregi_e2.html#2>.

332. According to the CIC; 'Any live-in caregiver who decides to live out, or who accepts any other type of employment, can be disqualified from the Program.' However, during time off from work, CIC also states that: 'Off-duty time is yours to spend as you wish: your employer cannot insist that you spend your own time in his or her house.' See: <http://www.cic.gc.ca/english/visit/caregi_e2.html#2>.

333. Question 4A2A1.

334. The CIC guidelines are silent in regard to house cleaning. However, there is the recommendation of a written contract between the employee and the employer upon acceptance of a job in Canada on the LCP, with the proviso that the federal government has no authority for enforcement and that labour standards vary across the provinces. In the CIC's Sample Contract, 'Housekeeping Responsibilities' are, however listed, under the heading of 'Care Responsibilities/Duties', and accompanied by two boxes, 'Yes' and 'No'. Then there is room in the sample contract under the heading 'Describe', to explain the specific duties expected. See CIC, 'The Live-in Caregiver Program: Information for Employers and Live-in Caregivers from Abroad', Ottawa, February 1999, <http:www.cic.gc.ca/English/visit/caregi_e2.html>.

335. See e.g., Chang, *Disposable Domestics.*

336. The Ontario Employment Standards Act was amended in 2000, but it continues to permit employers the option to give workers time off in lieu of pay for overtime worked. The law specifies that such an arrangement must be agreed upon by the employee and must be met within 12 weeks after the pay is earned. Ontario, *Employment Standards – Fact Sheet: 'Domestic Workers'*, <http://www.gov.on.ca/LAB/es/dome.htm>, 2001.

337. See Fudge, 'Little Victories and Big Defeats', 119–45.

338. INTERCEDE conducted a study in 1989 of live-in domestic workers, which revealed that fully 65 per cent of the 576 workers surveyed, reported they were regularly required to work overtime, but only 33 per cent who were so required received the legal compensation; 43.7 per cent of those required to work overtime received no compensation whatever. (Sedef Arat-Koc and Fely Villasin, *Report and Recommendations on the Foreign Domestic Movement Program*, INTERCEDE report for submission to the Ministry of Employment and Immigration, 1990, 5–7.)

339. This was based on results from Q4A12A, Q4A12B and Q4A12C, where respondents paid weekly, bi-weekly or monthly, respectively, provided their regular earnings over the appropriate time period. These figures were averaged according to the number of respondents, and divided into hourly units according to the average working week for West Indian and Filipino workers.

340. The Ontario NDP government raised the minimum wage from $5.40 per hour to $6.85 per hour on 1 January 1995. Interviews were conducted both before and after this date. The Ontario minimum wage has not been increased since this time.
341. CIC, 'The Live-in Caregiver Program: Employers and Live-in Caregivers from Abroad', Ottawa, February 1999, <http:www.cic.gc.ca/English/visit/caregi_e2.html#1>, 5.
342. CIC, 'The Live-in Caregiver Program: 7.
343. Ontario, *Employment Standards – Fact Sheet*, <http://www.gov.on.ca/LAB/es/dome.htm>, 2001.
344. In some provinces and territories, the employer is required to pay the cost of belonging to Canada's national health insurance system, while in others the worker is responsible for paying these costs. See Citizenship and Immigration Canada, 'The Live-in Caregiver Program Employers and Live-in Caregivers from Abroad', Ottawa, February 1999, <http:www.cic.gc.ca/English/visit/caregi_e2.html#1>, 4.
345. For instance, the Immigration booklet for the Live-in Caregiver lists employment standards that 'may' be accessible to domestic workers, depending on provincial/territorial standards as including days off, vacation time with pay, paid public holidays, overtime pay, minimum wage, equal pay, equal benefits, pregnancy leave and notice of employment termination, employment insurance, Canada pension plan and old age security. See Citizenship and Immigration, 'The Live-in Caregiver Program: 4.
346. Peter Stalker, *The Work of Strangers* (Geneva: International Labour Organisation, 1994), 126.
347. See Heyzer, Nijeholt and Weerakoon, eds, *The Trade in Domestic Workers*.
348. See e.g., Elizabeth Uy Eviota, *The Political Economy of Gender: Women and the Sexual Division of Labour in the Philippines* (New Jersey: Zed Books, 1992); Momsen, ed., *Women and Change in the Caribbean*.
349. Linda Miller Mattei, 'Gender and International Labor Migration: A Networks Approach', *Social Justice*, vol. 23, no. 3 (1996), 38–54.
350. See Rina Cohen, 'The Work Conditions of Immigrant Women Live-in Domestics: Racism, Sexual Abuse, and Invisibility', *Resources for Feminist Research*, 16: 1 (1987), 36–8.
351. Young, 'The "Mistress" and the "Maid" in the Globalized Economy', 315–16.

6   Marginalized and Dissident Citizens: Nurses of Colour

352. Glenn, 'From Servitude to Service Work', 1–43.
353. Kathryn McPherson, *Bedside Matters: The Transformation of Canadian Nursing, 1900–1990* (Toronto: University of Toronto Press, 1996), 17.
354. McPherson, *Bedside Matters*, 118, 211–14; Agnes Calliste, 'Women of "Exceptional Merit": Immigration of Caribbean Nurses to Canada', *Canadian Journal of Women and the Law*, 6: 1 (1993), 85–102.
355. Calliste, 'Women of "Exceptional Merit" ', 94.
356. Pat Armstrong and Hugh Armstrong, *Wasting Away: The Undermining of Canadian Health Care* (Toronto: Oxford University Press, 1996), 108.

357. Kathy Hardill, 'Discovering Fire Where the Smoke is: Racism in the Health Care System', *Towards Justice in Health* (Summer 1993); Agnes Calliste, 'Antiracism Organizing and Resistance in Nursing: African Canadian Women', *Canadian Review of Sociology and Anthropology*, 33: 3 (August 1996), 361–90; Tania das Gupta, 'Racism in Nursing' in *Racism and Paid Work* (Toronto: Garamond Press, 1996) and 'Anti-Black Racism in Nursing in Ontario', *Studies in Political Economy*, 51 (Fall 1996), 97–116.
358. For instance, in the 1990s, Black, Filipino and white nurses and community activists formed the NAFAD movement in order to challenge cases of racial discrimination against nurses. Interview. Cathy Holliday, 15 March 2000, Toronto.
359. Darlene Clark Hine, *Black Women in White: Racial Conflict and Cooperation in the Nursing Profession, 1890–1950* (Bloomington: Indiana University Press, 1989), 191.
360. As hospitals are the single largest item in public health care, the cost-reduction strategies of governments have focused on cutting hospital expenditures. Armstrong and Armstrong, *Wasting Away*, 173.
361. Mike Harris resigned as Premier and leader of the Ontario Progressive Conservative Party in 2002. In the spring of that year, a leadership convention saw the election of Ernie Eves, who subsequently became the new Conservative Party Premier of Ontario. On the impact of Mike Harris's policies, see Bill Murnighan, *Selling Ontario's Health Care: The Real Story on Government Speding and Public Relations*, Technical Paper no. 11, Ontario's Alternative Budget (Ontario: Canadian Centre for Policy Alternatives, 2001).
362. Pat Armstrong, 'Women's Health Care Work: Nursing in Context', in P. Armstrong, J. Choiniere and Elaine Day, eds, *Vital Signs: Nursing in Transition* (Toronto: Garamond Press, 1993), 40, 48; Armstrong and Armstrong, *Wasting Away*, 213. In 1999, Pat Armstrong and Hugh Armstrong have found that staff nurses in long-term care facilities saw their workloads double – from a ratio of one nurse for every 20 patients to one per 40, with a further rise to one per 80 projected for the year 2000. See April Lindgren, 'Health Care Cuts Hit Women Hardest: Report', *Citizen*, Ottawa, 4 December 1999, A4.
363. Leslie Papp, 'Seven Nurses Get Award in "Landmark" Rights Case', *Toronto Star*, 13 May 1994.
364. Ali Shariff, 'Hospital Colour Code: Six Fired Black Nurses at Northwestern Hospital Have Raised the Curtain on Systemic Racism', *Now* Toronto, 7–13 January 1993, 23.
365. Calliste, 'Anti racism Organizing', 371.
366. 'End the Silence on Racism and Health Care: A Conference for Black Nurses and Other Health Care Workers.' Sponsored by the Congress of Black Women in Canada, Toronto Chapter, Ontario Institute for the Studies of Education, 25–26 May 1995, Toronto. Observers' Notes, A. Bakan.
367. Chang, *Disposable Domestics*, 131.
368. Chang, *Disposable Domestics*, 110.
369. Lily Ann Beldago, National Philippines Nurses Association, Interview, A. Bakan and D. Stasiulis with Lily Ann Balgago, Vice-President, Philippine Nursing Association, Manila, 8 June 1995.

370. New immigration regulations that accompanied the IRPA that came into effect in June 2002 should theoretically make it easier for foreign-trained nurses to migrate as independent immigrants to Canada insofar as they place greater emphasis on education and previous work experience rather than being based on 'labour shortage'.

371. Besides passing the Canadian nursing exam, foreign-trained nurses must have completed an acceptable programme, as determined by the regulatory body for nursing in each province and territory, provided evidence of work experience within the past five years, speak either French or English, and have proof of citizenship or landed immigrant status before being registered as a nurse in each province or territory. Katherine Harding, 'Nursing is Different Here', *Globe and Mail*, Toronto, 8 January 2003.

372. One Filipino nurse explained the difficulty of passing the Canadian exam in terms of its culturally specific standard of care and terminology. Harding, 'Nursing is Different Here'.

373. The FNSG is run out of the Philippine Women's Centre, which had established a prior record of organizing and advocating on behalf of Filipino domestics. The Centre conducts community-based research and education in order to elucidate the reality and root causes of the Filipino migrant presence in Canada. Organization of migrant nurses also assists individual nurses to navigate their way through the obstacles imposed by a network of public and private nursing gatekeepers. Thus, as of October 2000, the FNSG had supported 20 nurses from the Philippines to meet all accreditation requirements and obtain their nursing registration. In addition, the FNSG has publicized the fact that many qualified and fully accredited nurses continue to be imprisoned by the restrictions of the LCP, thus disabling them to practice in their profession. FNSG, Media Release, Vancouver, 18 October 2000; Cecilia Dioscon, 'Filipino Women's Identity: Social, Cultural and Economic Segregation in Canada', Presented to the 'Towards the Transformation of Race and Gender' conference organized by the Race and Gender Teaching Advisory Group, University of British Columbia, May 2001.

374. For an account of the experiences of Filipino nurses who first worked in Canada as nannies, see 'Memoirs of the Invisible Nurse', *Pinoy Sa Canada* (Fall 1992), 4–5. In our survey of 49 nurses, only one Filipino nurse and one West Indian nurse had entered Canada under the foreign domestic worker programme. Most of these women, however, had immigrated to Canada on average 15 years prior and our reports of nurses migrating to Canada as domestic workers suggest that this phenomenon has become more common in the 1980s and 1990s. The estimates from nursing placement agency owners of Filipino nurses who had migrated to Canada as domestic workers ranged from 30 per cent to 90 per cent. Interviews, D. Stasiulis with: Fredelina Brueckner, Owner, Alba Nursing Services, 19 October 1992; Desi Crisoftomo, Mayfair Nursing Personnel Ltd, 1 October 1992; Norma Marcos, Owner, MS Employment Consultant Ltd, 15 October 1992.

375. Implications of the immigration statuses assigned to migrant and immigrant nurses will be explored later in this chapter.

376. Glenn, 'From Servitude to Service Work', 23.

377. McPherson, *Bedside Matters*, 6–9; Robert D. Hiscott, *Career Paths of Nursing Professionals: A Study of Employment Mobility* (Ottawa: Carleton University Press, 1998), 3–6.

378. Nurses have fought layoffs, often staging illegal strikes, in Alberta (1988, 1994), Ontario (1996) and Quebec (1999). See Elaine Day, 'The Unionization of Nurses', in Pat Armstrong, Jacqueline Choiniere and Elaine Day, eds, *Vital Signs: Nursing in Transition* (Toronto: Garamond Press, 1993), 89–109. Robert Sheppard, 'Nurses at the Ready', *Globe and Mail*, 15 August 1999, A7; Tu Thanh Ha, 'Quebec Strike a Litmus Test for Fall Talks', *Globe and Mail*, Toronto, 3 July 1999, A4.

379. One completed interview was eliminated from the West Indian sample when it was found that this nurse had been born in Canada.

380. Repeated requests for interviews with the ONA were declined. However, there was an exchange of information and correspondence with the authors regarding the activities of ONA in regard to nurses of colour. See correspondence, ONA, Marwynne Parke, Manager, Employee Services, ONA to A. Bakan, 10 July 2001.

381. Calliste, 'Women of "Exceptional Merit" ', and 'Antiracism Organizing', 361–90; das Gupta, 'Racism in Nursing', and 'Anti-Black Racism in Nursing in Ontario', 97–116; Wilson Head, *An Exploratory Study of Attitudes and Perceptions of Minority and Majority Group Healthcare Workers* (Toronto: Ontario Ministry of Labour 1985).

382. Calliste, 'Antiracism Organizing', 363, 368; das Gupta, 'Racism in Nursing', 'Anti-Black Racism in Nursing in Ontario'.

383. Indeed, during the 1900s, small numbers of Canadian nurses migrated to mission fields in China and India, where the skills of trained nurses were actively sought. McPherson, *Bedside Matters*, 53.

384. Alfonso Mejia, Helena Pizurki and Erica Royston, *Physician and Nurse Migration: Analysis and Policy Implications*, Report of a WHO Study (WHO, Geneva, 1979), 34.

385. Calliste, 'Women of "Exceptional Merit" ', 98.

386. Hine, *Black Women in White*, xix, 189.

387. Mejia, Pizurki and Royston, *Physician and Nurse Migration*, 44.

388. Government of the Philippines, Report of the Senate Committee on Health, *Where the Nurses Are* (Manila, 1989), 21.

389. Philippine Women's Centre, Briefing Note, Vancouver, 10 September 1999, 2.

390. Philippine Women's Centre, 2.

391. Erlinda L. Ortin, 'The Brain Drain as Viewed by an Exporting Country', *International Nursing Review*, 37: 5 (1990), 340–4. A Philippine government pamphlet established that 'The most frequent reason why nurses migrate is the low salaries they receive'. While Philippine nurses earned a mininum monthly wage of 3102 pesos, or about US$60 a month (according to January 2002 exchange rates) the prevailing wages in the United States were between US$2000 and $3000 a month and in the Middle East US$400–$600 a month plus free accommodations, meals and airline tickets to the Philippines. Government of the Philippines, Report of the Senate Committee on Health, 22–3. A registered nurse from the Philippines was reported to have left her $3-a-week job in a Philippine government hospital

to work as a live-in domestic worker for minimum wages in Vancouver so as to be able to send money home to her family. Brenda Jones, 'System Racist, Nurse Charges', *Vancouver Echo* (19 May 1999), 14.

392. Interview, A. Bakan and D. Stasiulis with Lily Ann Balgago, Vice-President, Philippine Nursing Association, Manila, 8 June 1995.
393. McPherson, *Bedside Matters*, 208.
394. A February 2001 survey of Ontario registered nurses who had migrated, primarily to the United States, found that a large majority (62.7 per cent of 1051 respondents) cited downsizing or lack of employment opportunities as the major reason for their departure. Registered Nurses Association of Ontario, 'Earning Their Return: When and Why Ontario RNs Left Canada, and What Will Bring Them Back', Toronto, 23 February 2001. According to Sarah Jane Growe, '[t]he Canada–US free trade agreement now makes it easier for nurses to get temporary work visas in the United States, where private multi-million-dollar health-care businesses offer annual salaries 33 per cent higher, night shift differentials as high as five dollars a shift (Ontario hospitals pay their night nurses an extra forty cents), subsidized and fully paid tuition'. Sarah Jane Growe, *Who Cares: The Crisis in Canadian Nursing* (Toronto: McClelland & Stewart, 1991), 66.
395. Calliste, 'Women of "Exceptional Merit" ', 96.
396. McPherson, *Bedside Matters*, 213.
397. Calliste, 'Women of "Exceptional Merit" ', 94–8. For a discussion of the deskilling of migrant Caribbean women in Canada, see Abigail Bakan, 'The International Market for Female Labour and Individual Deskilling', 69–85.
398. 'Interview with Sally Quan, President of Filipino Nurses Association, Pinoy Sa Canada', Summer 1992, 3.
399. Interview, D. Stasiulis with Virginia Levesque, Ottawa, 26 June 1991.
400. Brenda Jones, 'System Racist, Nurse Charges', 9.
401. Interview, D. Stasiulis with Virginia Levesque.
402. Robert D. Hiscott, *Career Paths of Nursing Professionals*, 7.
403. Interview, D. Stasiulis with Mohammed Doma, Manager of Human Resources, Northwestern General Hospital, 21 October 1992.
404. Interview, D. Stasiulis with Treva McCumber, Director of Nursing Recruitment, Toronto Hospital, 19 October 1992.
405. Interview with Treva McCumber.
406. Interview with Mohammed Doma.
407. Interview with Treva McCumber.
408. Sally Quan, 'Interview', 3.
409. 'Memoirs of the Invisible Nurse', 4.
410. Hiscott, *Career Paths of Nursing Professionals*, 2, 7.
411. Armstrong and Armstrong, *Wasting Away*, 66.
412. D. Vincent, 'Hospital Nursing Cuts Bite Deep', *Toronto Star*, 26 January 1997, A14, cited in Hiscott, *Career Paths of Nursing Professionals*, 9.
413. Hiscott, *Career Paths of Nursing Professionals*, 7.
414. Interview with Mohammed Doma.
415. Interviews with Treva McCumber, Mohammed Doma.
416. Interview, D. Stasiulis with Marilyn Gaul, Manager, Recruitment, Human Resources, Mount Sinai Hospital, 21 December 1992.

417. Armstrong and Armstrong, *Wasting Away*, 175.

418. D. Vincent, 'Hospital Nursing Cuts Bite Deep', A14.

419. Hiscott, *Career Paths of Nursing Professionals*, 11. In October 1992, Toronto Hospital's Director of Nursing Recruitment contrasted the profile of nursing staff in October 1992 with less than a year earlier: 'In December 1991, we had 33% RNs with 8–10 years experience, 33% RNs with 3–6 years experience, and 33% new graduates. Now, about 30% of the nurses I bring in are RNs with at least 5 years experience, and about 70% are graduate nurses, with about 15% of that 70% from abroad, and 55% Canadian new graduate nurses, with their last training here.' Interview with Treva McCumber. The shift from RNs to graduate nurses represented substantial savings as registered nurses earned between $17.00 and $27.00 an hour in 1996, in comparison with the maximum rate of $15.00 an hour for graduate nurses. J. Coutts, 'Hospitals Replace Registered Nurses: Less-skilled Take Over Tasks', *Globe and Mail* (23 May 1996), A1, A8.

420. Armstrong and Armstrong, *Wasting Away*, 176; Hiscott, *Career Paths of Nursing Professionals*, 3.

421. Valerie MacDonald, Co-ordinator, Employment Relations Services, ONA, Toronto, Ontario. Letter to Ms Linda Ackroyd, Regional Manager, OHRC, Toronto, 2 June 1995 (copy on file with authors).

422. Growe, *Who Cares?*, 91.

423. Interview, D. Stasiulis with Fredelina Brueckner, Owner, Alba Nursing Services Ltd, Toronto, 19 October 1992.

424. Calliste, 'Antiracism Organizing and Resistance', 369.

425. The new Canadian immigration legislation that came into effect in June 2002 has reduced the period of legal and financial dependence of sponsored immigrants on their sponsors from ten years to three.

426. Alma Estable, 'Immigrant Women in Canada – Current Issues'. A Background Paper for the Canadian Advisory Council on the Status of Women (Ottawa, 1986). Monica Boyd, 'Immigrant Women in Canada', in Rita J. Simon and Caroline Brettel, eds, *International Migration: The Female Experience* (Ottawa: Rowman and Allenheld, 1986), 47–75.

427. Daenzer, *Regulating Class Privilege*; Vic Satzewich, 'The Canadian State and the Racialization of Caribbean Migrant Farm Labour, 1947–1966', *Ethnic and Racial Studies*, 11: 3 (1988), 282–304.

428. Philippine Women's Centre, 'Project proposal: Breaking the Barriers, Gaining Strength for Further Development', Vancouver, 1999, 5.

429. According to Sarah Jane Growe, by the early 1990s, more than 80 per cent of RNs working within Canada had graduated with diplomas, either from a hospital-based school or a community college. The percentage of nurses with university degrees almost doubled between 1971 and 1986. Growe, *Who Cares?*, 158.

430. Pomeroy, *The Philippines*.

431. See Bakan, Cox and Leys, *Imperial Power and Regional Trade*.

432. Lutz, 'The Limits of European-ness', 98.

433. This point is developed in greater detail in Chapter 3.

434. Not a single Filipino nurse had mentioned knowledge of other cultures as something they had gained in migrating to Canada, perhaps reflecting the

tremendous cultural, ethnic and racial diversity and hybridity that exists within the Philippines.

435. Chris Mullard, 'Multiracial Education in Britain: From Assimilation to Cultural Pluralism', in J. Tierney, ed., *Race, Migration and Schooling* (London: Holt, Rinehart and Winston, 1982).

436. One such critic is dub poet and journalist Joseph Clifton who evocatively questions, 'Why would, and yeah, why should the non-French and non-English communities who have contributed valiantly to the development of Canada ultimately settle for the subordinate position under some fabled jive of the two "(lost/&) found(ing) races"?' Clifton Joseph. 'On Your Mark! Get Set! Go Multi-culti', *This Magazine*, 28, no. 5 (January–February 1995), 28. For analyses of the depoliticization of issues of racism within Canadian multiculturalism state policies, see Daiva Stasiulis, 'The Symbolic Mosaic Reaffirmed: Multiculturalism Policy', in K. Graham, ed., *How Ottawa Spends, 1988–89* (Ottawa: Carleton University Press, 1988), 81–111; 'Symbolic Representation and the Numbers Game: Tory Policies on "Race" and Visible Minorities', in Frances Abele, ed., *How Ottawa Spends, 1990–91: The Politics of Fragmentation* (Ottawa: Carleton University Press, 1991), 229–68; Frances Henry and Carol Tator, 'State Policy and Practices as Racialized Discourse: Multiculturalism, The Charter and Employment Equity', 88–115 in Peter S. Li, ed., *Race and Ethnic Relations in Canada*, 2nd edn (Toronto: Oxford University Press, 1999).

437. Darlene Barnes, President, Local 97, ONA, Toronto General Hospital, 'End the Silence on Racism and Health Care: A Conference for Black Nurses and Other Health Care Workers', Sponsored by the Congress of Black Women in Canada, Toronto Chapter, Ontario Institute for the Studies of Education, Toronto, 25–26 May 1995.

438. das Gupta, 'Racism in Nursing', 79.

439. The perception that Filipino nurses are uncomplaining in doing the dirtiest and heaviest work was found to prevail in a successful class action suit concluded March 1999 against a health care centre in Missouri won by 65 Filipino nurses who were paid half the wage rate of American-born RNs. The lawyer for the regional Equal Employment Opportunity Commission Robert Johnson commented that 'It's not unusual for nursing homes to make use of foreign nurses, especially Filipino nurses because they speak English and are trained in the same way as nurses here. *They're seen as being able to be pushed around and paid less without complaining about it*'. Rachelle Q. Ayuyang, 'Nursing the Dream', *Filipinas*, May 1999, 39 (italics added).

440. Doris Marshall Institute and Arnold Minors and Associates, 'Equality for All', Final Report, Appendices, Consultants' Report to Northwestern General Hospital (Toronto, March 1994).

441. Calliste, 'Antiracism Organizing', 368–69.

442. Shariff, 'Hospital Colour Code', 12.

443. Shariff, 'Hospital Colour Code', 12.

444. Shariff, 'Hospital Colour Code', 12; Hardill, 'Discovering Fire', 18.

445. Hardill, 'Discovering Fire', 18.

446. Calliste, 'Antiracism Organizing', 370.

447. Interview with Mohammed Doma.

448. Doris Marshall Institute and Arnold Minors & Associates, 'Equality for All', 34.
449. This matches the finding of the OHRC investigation into Northwestern General that 'policies requiring that doctor's notes be provided by nurses returning from sick days were arbitrarily applied to black nurses and not other nurses'. Hardill, 'Discovering the Fire', 18.
450. Nursing survey.
451. Calliste, 'Antiracism Organizing and Resistance', 371.
452. Nursing survey.
453. These were the findings of the OHRC in its investigation of racism in Northwestern General Hospital. Sharrif, 'Hospital Colour Code', 12; see also Calliste, 'Antiracism Organizing', and das Gupta, 'Racism in Nursing'.
454. Nursing survey.
455. Nursing survey.
456. Shariff, 'Hospital Colour Code', 12; Calliste, 'Antiracism Organizing', 371.
457. Calliste, 'Antiracism Organizing', 379.
458. Ibid., 380–3.
459. Agnes Calliste provides an informative analysis of the antiracist movement in health care during the early to mid-1990s. See Calliste, 'Antiracism Organizing'.
460. Leslie Papp, 'Seven Nurses get Award in "Landmark" Rights Case'.
461. Statements of nurses involved in the Northwestern General Hospital Ontario Human Rights Case (Vlada Christian and unidentified others), 'End the Silence on Racism and Health Care: A Conference for Black Nurses and Other Health Care Workers', Sponsored by the Congress of Black Women in Canada, Toronto Chapter, Ontario Institute for the Studies of Education, Toronto, 25–26 May 1995. Statements of nurses involved in the Northwestern General Hospital Ontario Human Rights Case.
462. See the leaflet put out by the NAFAD, n.d.; Maureen O'Halloran of the ONA, quoted in Shariff, 'Hospital Colour Code', 23.
463. Holloway Sparks, 'Dissident Citizenship: Democratic Theory, Political Courage, and Activist Women', *Hypatia* 12: 4 (Fall 1997), 74–110.
464. Harding, 'Nursing'.
465. 'Nursing and Feminism: The Uneasy Relationship', Conference sponsored by Queen's University School of Nursing, Queen's University, 12–13 November 1991, Observers' Notes, A. Bakan; and Rebecca Priegert Coulter, 'Alberta Nurses and the "Illegal" Strike of 1988', in Linda Briskin and Patricia McDermott, eds, *Women Challenging Unions: Feminism, Democracy and Militancy* (Toronto: University of Toronto Press, 1993), 44–61.
466. Meeting with Filipino nurses who work as live-in caregivers, Philippine Women's Centre, Daiva Stasiulis notes, Vancouver, 5 November 1999.
467. Telephone interview, D. Stasiulis with Mark Davidson, Policy Branch, Citizenship and Immigration, 8 September 1999.
468. These immigration reforms are meant to ease the movement of highly skilled workers to Canada in order to enhance Canada's global competitiveness. While the points system was a feature of the old immigration policy, the new points system places greater emphasis on 'transferable skill sets' that have applicability to many different occupations and workplaces. This change reflects the notion of the desirable 'flexible' economic immigrant

who can shift seamlessly from one job and locality to another as labour market needs change in the new global economy. See Abu-Laban and Gabriel, *Selling Diversity*, 79.

469. Lisa Little, Health Human Resources Consultant, Canadian Nurses Association, D. Stasiulis, e-mail correspondence with Anne Kerr, 27 September 2002.

470. College of Nurses of Ontario, 'College of Nurses Welcomes Baccalaureate Requirement for Registered Nurses', News Release, 12 April 2000, <http://www.cno.org/index.new.html>.

471. According to a recent report by the government of British Columbia, nurses who graduate from BC schools make up less than half the number of nurses needed to replace those who retire annually. Several of the hospitals in the province that had closed beds and operating rooms due to nursing short-ages are attempting to recruit English-speaking nurses from Hong Kong, Malaysia and Great Britain. Robert Matas, 'B.C. Looking Overseas to Hire More Nurses', *Globe and Mail*, Toronto (5 November 1999), A10.

7   The Global Citizenship Divide and the Negotiation of Legal Rights

472. Davia Stasiulis and Abigail B. Bakan, 'Negotiating the Citizenship Divide: Foreign Domestic Worker Policy and Legal Jurisprudence', in Radha Jhappan, ed., Women's Legal Strategies in Canada (Toronto: University of Toronto Press, 2002), 237–94.

473. Anderson, *Doing the Dirty Work?*, 175.

474. Sparks, 'Dissident Citizenship', 75.

475. Sparks, 'Dissident Citizenship', 75.

476. See Richard Falk, 'The Making of Global Citizenship', in *Global Visions: Beyond the New World Order* (Montreal: Black Rose Books, 1993), 39–52. In their recent discussion of the transnationalization of popular movements contesting corporate-led forms of globalization, Wilson and Whitmore define popular movements as 'citizen's groups' and as representing 'ordinary citizens', thus suggesting that transnational activists in fact possess the juridical citizenship status of the state in which they engage politically. Maureen G. Wilson and Elizabeth Whitmore, *Seeds of Fire: Social Development in an Era of Globalization* (Halifax: Fernwood Publishing, 2000), 47.

477. Riva Kastoryano, 'Settlement, Transnational Communities and Citizenship', *International Social Science Journal*, 165 (September 2000), 311.

478. Stasiulis and Bakan, 'Negotiating Citizenship', 126.

479. In her study of Chicana household workers, Mary Romero found that these workers would reject their employer's definitions of them as 'one of the family'. These workers retained a separation between the tasks completed for their employers and 'works of love' given to their own families. Romero, *Maid in the U.S.A.*, 157.

480. Sparks, 'Dissident Citizenship', 75. According to Sparks (75), unconventional political practices include 'marches, protest, and picket lines; sit-ins, slow-downs, and cleanups, speeches, strikes and street theater' whereas conventional practices include voting, lobbying and petitioning.

481. Andrea Timoll, 'Foreign Domestic Servants in Canada', Honours Research Essay (Department of Political Science, Carleton University, September 1989), 57–8.
482. Macklin, 'Foreign Domestic Worker', 734.
483. *Lodge v. M.M.I* (1979) 1 F.C., 775.
484. Barbara Jackman, 'Admission of Foreign Domestic Workers', 2. For various accounts of this struggle, see Anne Bayefsky, 'The Jamaican Women Case and the Canadian Human Rights Act: Is Government Subject to the Principle of Equal Opportunity?' (1980) 18 *U.W.O.L. Rev.*, 461–7; Ronnie Leah and Gwen Morgan, 'Immigrant Women Fight Back; The Case of the Seven Jamaican Women', *Resources for Feminist Research*, 7: 3 (1979), 23–4; Macklin, 'Foreign Domestic Worker', 734–5.
485. *Fernanadez* (14 March 1989), Vancouver 9530-01-5955 (Bd Inquiry) in Macklin, 'Foreign Domestic Worker', 707.
486. *Fernandez*, 1989.
487. The WCDWA reports on the practice of agencies in the home countries of domestic applicants advising them to lie about their marital status and dependents on the grounds that 'they have a better chance of being admitted as domestics if they say they are single and have no dependants. Although Immigration denies that this is true, in 1988, of the 24 000 new work visas issued, fewer than 2000 were issued to women who admitted they were married. In other words, Immigration discriminates against women who are married or have children'. *Domestic Workers Association Newsletter*, WCDWA, Vancouver, vol. 2, no. 10 (October 1989), 3.
488. *Domestic Workers Association Newsletter*, 3.
489. Correspondence of R. Jankowski, Canadian Immigration Centre, Vancouver to West Coast Domestic Workers' Association, 17 January 1990; *Domestic Workers Association Newsletter*, WCDWA, Vancouver, vol. 3, no. 8 (August 1990), 5.
490. Deborah Cheney, 'Valued Judgments?: A Reading of Immigration Cases', in Anne Bottomley and Joanne Conaghan, eds, *Feminist Theory and Legal Strategy* (Oxford: Blackwell, 1993), 24.
491. *Eugenio v. Canada (Minister of Citizenship and Immmigration)* (1997) 38 Imm. L.R. (2d) 165 (Immigration and Refugee Board [Appeal Division]).
492. *Eugenio v. Canada*, 170.
493. *Eugenio v. Canada*, 171.
494. *Eugenio v. Canada*, 172.
495. Cheney, 'Valued Judgments?', 23.
496. *Bernardez v. Canada (Minister of Citizenship and Immigration)* (1995) 31 Imm. L.R. (2d) 90.
497. *Bernardez v. Canada*, 1995, 90.
498. *Bernardez v. Canada*, (italics added for emphasis).
499. *Bernardez v. Canada*, 1995, 5.
500. *Turingan v. Canada (Minister of Employment and Immigration)* (1993) 24 Imm. L.R. (2d) 113.
501. *Bernardez*, 6, emphasis added.
502. In viewing the reasoning in *Bernardez* as reflecting a 'contextualised' approach, we are not suggesting that the court has gone as far as the 'contextualised approach to Charter sexual equality' pursued by the legal women's rights association, the Legal Education and Action Fund (LEAF)

which, since 1985 has sought to use the law to effective progressive social change, especially for women. Since 1992, in response to criticisms of its own gender essentialism, LEAF has pursued legal strategies that recognize and attempt to ameliorate complex and intersecting forms of equality, including those of race, class, immigrant status, disability and sexual orientation. In contrast, none of the judicial rulings on domestic worker cases discussed here make reference to the discrimination experienced by household workers, stemming from their positions in relations of race, class or gender. For discussions of the development of LEAF's contextualized approach to sex equality, see Lise Gotell, 'Towards a Democratic Practice of Feminist Litigation? LEAF's Changing Approach to *Charter* Equality', in Radha Jhappan, ed., *Women's Legal Strategies in Canada* (Toronto: University of Toronto, 2002), 135–74.

503. See Rachel Epstein, 'Domestic Workers: The Experience in B.C.', in Linda Briskin and Lynda Yanz, eds, *Union Sisters* (Toronto: Women's Press, 1983), 222–37; Fudge, 'Little Victories and Big Defeats', 125.

504. Such cases include *Turingan v. Canada (Minister of Employment and Immigration)*, 24 Imm. L.R. (2d); *Caletana v. Canada (Solicitor General)* (1994) (F.C.T.D.) 23 Imm. L.R. (2d); and *Peje v. Canada (Minister of Citizenship and Immigration* (1997) (F.C.T.D.) 37 Imm. L.R. (2d). For an analysis of these cases, see Stasiulis and Bakan, 'Negotiating the Citizenship Divide'.

505. Leon Benoit, M.P., 'Last Chance for Leticia Cables, The Nanny That Worked Too Hard', press release, 29 February 2000, Ottawa.

506. *Baker v. Canada (Minister of Citizenship and Immigration)* [1999] 2 S.C.R. 817 (hereafter *Baker*).

507. *Baker v. Canada*, 827. Original upper case.

508. *Baker v. Canada*, 830.

509. *Baker v. Canada*, 860.

510. *Baker v. Canada*, 866.

511. Justice Claire L'Heureux-Dubé was quoting from R. Sullivan, Driedger on the Construction of Statutes (3rd edn 1994), 330.

512. As this legislation fails to mention the LCP, it again leaves the policy on foreign domestic workers to Immigration Regulations and thus subject to wide bureaucratic discretion. See Canadian Council for Refugees, 'Brief – Bill C-11'.

513. United Nations, General Assembly, 45th Session, Third Committee *Report of the Open-Ended Working Group on the Drafting of the International Convention on the Protection of the Rights of all Migrant Workers and Members of their Families.*, UN Doc.A/c.3/45/1 (21 June 1990).

514. *Sarmini Mustaji v. Khi Yoeng Tjin and Rosna Elly Tjin* (1996) (Court of Appeal for British Columbia), Court of Appeal Registry.

515. Kim Bolan, ' "Virtual prisoner" awarded $250 000', *Vancouver Sun*, 14 January 1995, A4.

516. Margaret E. Keck and Kathryn Sikkink, *Activists Beyond Borders: Advocacy Networks in International Politics* (Ithaca: Cornell University Press, 1998), 16.

517. The absence of legal challenge to the federal government's LCP and past domestic worker programmes must be questioned given the long-standing consensus among domestic worker associations regarding the unfairness and discrimination inherent in the LCP's imposition of the temporary

status and mandatory live-in condition. Part of the explanation for this absence of a constitutional challenge lies in the historical reticence of domestic worker associations. Until recently, these organizations had decided strategically to attack the objectionable conditions of the domestic worker programmes, especially the temporary visa and the mandatory live-in requirement, rather than the programmes themselves. Domestic advocates had feared that openly arguing for the abolition of the programme would jeopardize an important means for legal entry of women from Third World countries such as the Philippines. A significant deterrent was the question of available remedies should the court have found the LCP to be in violation of the *Canadian Charter of Rights and Freedoms*. Asking the Court to replace the LCP, or certain offensive parts of the policy, would be beyond its jurisdiction. Domestic worker legal advocates may therefore have refrained from legally challenging the LCP and past domestic worker immigration policies because they feared the consequences of the entire shut down of the programme. During the last few years, however, many domestic worker associations have grown impatient with the lack of meaningful reform to the programme and have openly called for its elimination, while some legal feminists have continued to endorse a reformed temporary worker programme that would mitigate (though not remove) the worst aspects of the programme. The Philippine Women Centre of British Columbia, for instance, has been especially outspoken against the programme for its racism and anti-woman biases. The *Association des Aides Familiaux du Québec*, based in Montreal, has made similar arguments. The National Action Committee for the Status of Women, the umbrella organization for women's organizations in Canada, also stated its support for the elimination of the programme during a hurried consultation process held by the Immigration department in Spring 1998. INTERCEDE's submission on *Bill C-31*, the Liberal government's proposed *Immigration and Refugee Protection Act*, clearly stated the recommendation that domestic workers and caregivers 'be admitted as permanent residents in accordance with experience, educational and skills criteria that are appropriate and practical to their occupation'. A coalition led by more legally inclined women's groups, which included the National Association of Women and the Law, West Coast Domestic Workers Association, *La Table féministe francophone de concertation provinciale de l'Ontario* and the National Organisation of Immigrant and Visible Minority Women of Canada, while supporting the admission of foreign domestic workers as landed immigrants, offered legislative amendments to *Bill C-31*, that would continue to permit caregivers to enter under temporary employment authorizations.

518. Philip L. Bryden, 'Fundamental Justice and Family Class Immigration: The Example of *Pangli v. Minister of Employment and Immigration*', *University of Toronto Law Journal* 4 (1991), 516–17.

519. Thus, Bryden argues that refugee cases, including Madame Justice Wilson's decision in *Singh et al. v. Minister of Employment and Immigration* [1985] 17 D.L.R. (4) 422, have been treated differently than immigration cases. In extending *Charter* protections to non-citizen refugee applicants, the courts have viewed refugee protection to be a more urgent matter than the protection of the rights of immigrant visa applicants. Bryden, 'Fundamental Justice', 514.

520. Chantal Tie, 'Only Discriminating Visa Officers Need Apply: Visa Officer Decisions, the *Charter* and *Lee v. Canada (Minister of Citizenship and Immigration)*', unpublished manuscript, (on file with authors), 4.
521. Barbara Jackman, 'Admission of Foreign Domestic Workers'. Immigration law 'has the reputation among people interested in administrative law as a sort of wasteland in which judges have been loath to apply the legal principles we normally associate with a sense of justice in Canadian public administration'. Bryden, 'Fundamental Justice and Family Class Immigration', 484.
522. Cheney, 'Valued Judgments?', 122, 24. Deborah Cheney is here describing British immigration law, but her characterization of immigration legislation is equally applicable to Canada.
523. Susan George, George Manbiot *et al.*, *Anti-Capitalism: A Guide to the Movement* (London: Bookmarks Publications, 2001); Abigail B. Bakan, 'Capital, Marxism and the World Economy: APEC and the MAI', in Abigail B. Bakan and Eleanor MacDonald, eds, *Critical Political Studies: Debates and Dialogues from the Left* (Kingston and Montreal: McGill-Queen's University Press, 2002).

8 Dissident Transnational Citizenship: Resistance, Solidarity and Organization

524. See Basch, Schiller and Blanc, *Nations Unbound*; Labelle and Midy, 'Rereading citizenship and the transnational practices of immigrants', 213–32; and Kastoryano, 'Settlement, Transnational Communities and Citizenship'.
525. Basch *et al.*, *Nations Unbound*, 6.
526. Every administration in the Philippines since Marcos has encouraged return migration of the *balikbayan* (homecomers), luring them with special airfares, reduced visa requirements, warm Christmas welcomes and the promise of voting rights for Filipinos who have taken citizenship elsewhere. Basch *et al.*, *Nations Unbound*, 256–8.
527. Kastoryano, 'Settlement, Transnational Communities and Citizenship'.
528. See James Walker, *A History of Blacks in Canada* (Hull, Quebec: Minister of Supply and Services, 1980); Daiva Stasiulis, 'Race, Ethnicity, and the State: The Political Structuring of South Asian and West Indian Communal Action in Combating Racism'. Ph.D. dissertation (University of Toronto, Department of Sociology, 1982); Henry, *The Caribbean Diaspora in Toronto*; Brian Douglas Tennyson, ed., *Canadian–Caribbean Relations* (Sydney, N.S.: Centre for International Studies, University College of Cape Breton, 1990).
529. Merciditas Cruz, quoted in Grace Chang, *Disposable Domestics*, 143.
530. M. Rodriguez, 'Migrant Heroes', 345.
531. M. Rodriguez, 'Migrant Heroes', 354.
532. Filipino Nurses Support Group, Press Release, 10 November 2000.
533. Filipino Nurses Support Group, 'BC Nurses' Union Position on Foreign Worker Recruitment Program Violates Democratic Rights of Workers', Press Release, 9 April 2002, <http://www.kalayaancentre.org/content/pressrelease/April/FNGS_benuviolates.htm>.
534. Chang, *Disposable Domestics*, 143.
535. R. M. Rodriguez, 'Migrant Heroes', 352.
536. R. M. Rodriguez, 'Migrant Heroes', 351.

537. R. M. Rodriguez, 'Migrant Heroes', 353.
538. See for example, Daiva Stasiulis and Abigail B. Bakan, 'Flor Contemplacion: A Study in Non-Citizenship', *Public Policy*, Manila, Philippines (April–June 1999), 1–41.
539. See Press Releases of the Philippine Women's Centre, 6 November 2000; 30 November 2000; 18 January 2001.
540. R. M. Rodriguez, 'Migrant Heroes', 354.
541. For a discussion of the concept of 'reproductive citizenship', see Bryan S. Turner, 'The Erosion of Citizenship', *British Journal of Sociology*, 52: 2 (June 2001), 196–8.
542. Pauline Hwang, 'Racism, Sexism and Canadian Immigration', Colours of Resistance website, <http://www.tao.ca/~colours/hwang.html>.
543. 'Campaign to Stop the Expulsion of Melca Salavador', Montreal, 13 August 2000, <http://pages.infini.net.ugay/melca/statement/htm>.
544. 'Campaign to Stop the Expulsion of Melca Salavador'.
545. Philippine Women's Centre, 'Celebrating Gains, Continuing the Resistance', 11 May 2001.
546. Nicholas Rose, 'Government and Control', *British Journal of Criminology*, 40: 321–39, (2000).
547. As of January 2003, the UN Convention on the Rights of Migrants and Members of Their Families had received its twentieth state signature with the signing by East Timor, a former province of Indonesia and newly independent country. Twenty signatures are the minimum required for ratification of a UN treaty. The long delay in receiving this degree of state support reflects significant opposition among migrant-receiving states to a form of transnational citizenship that would impinge on states' rights to control their borders.
548. Jacqueline Bhabha, 'Belonging in Europe: Citizenship and Post-national Rights', *International Social Science Journal*, 159 (1999), 12.

Bibliography

Abbott, Ruth K. and R.A. Young. 'Cynical and Deliberate Manipulation? Child Care and the Reserve Army of Female Labour in Canada', *Journal of Canadian Studies*, 2: 24 (Summer 1989), 22–38.

Abella, Manolo. 'International Migration and Development', in G. Batistella and A. Paganoni, eds, *Philippine Labour Migration: Impact and Policy* (Quezon City: Scalabrini Migration Center, 1992).

Abu-Laban, Yasmeen. 'Reconstructing an Inclusive Citizenship for a New Millennium', *International Politics*, 37: 4 (December 2000).

Abu-Laban, Yasmeen and Christina Gabriel. *Selling Diversity: Immigration, Multiculturalism, Employment Equity and Globalization* (Peterborough: Broadview Press, 2002).

Amerfoort, H. and R. Pennix. 'Regulating Migration in Europe: The Dutch Experience, 1960–92', *Annals of the American Academy*, 534 (1994), 132–46.

Amnesty International. *Brief on Bill C-11: An Act Respecting Immigration to Canada and the Granting of Refugee Protection to Persons who are Displaced, Persecuted or in Danger* (March 2001), http://www.amnesty.ca/Refugee/Bill_C-11.PDF.

Anderson, Bridget. *Doing the Dirty Work? The Global Politics of Domestic Labour* (London: Zed Books, 2000).

——. *Britain's Secret Slaves: An Investigation into the Plight of Overseas Domestic Workers* (United Kingdom: Anti-Slavery International and Kalayaan, 1993).

Anderson, Wolseley W. *Caribbean Immigrants: A Socio-Demographic Profile* (Toronto: Canadian Scholars Press, 1993).

Angeles, Leonora. 'Why the Philippines Did Not Become a Newly Industrializing Country', *Kasarinlan*, 7: 2, 3 (1991/92).

Antrobus, Peggy. 'Gender Issues in Caribbean Development', in Stanley Lalta and Marie Freckleton, eds, *Caribbean Economic Development: The First Generation* (Kingston, Ja.: Ian Randle Publishers, 1993), 68–77.

——. 'Employment of Women Workers in the Caribbean', in Pat Ellis, ed., *Women of the Caribbean* (New Jersey: Zed Books, 1986).

Appadurai, Arjun. 'Cities and Citizenship', *Public Culture*, 8 (1996), 187–204.

Appleby, Timothy. 'Crime Story: The Jamaican Connection', in three parts, *The Globe and Mail* (10, 11 and 13 July 1992).

Arat-Koc, Sedef. From ' "Mothers of the Nation" to Migrant Workers', in Abigail B. Bakan and Daiva K. Stasiulis, eds, *Not One of the Family: Foreign Domestic Workers in Canada* (Toronto: University of Toronto Press, 1997), 53–80.

——. 'In the Privacy of Our Own Home: Foreign Domestic Workers as Solution to the Crisis in the Domestic Sphere in Canada', *Studies in Political Economy*, 28 (1989), 33–58.

Arat-Koc, Sedef and Fely Villasin. *Caregivers Break the Silence* (Toronto: Intercede, 2001).

——. *Report and Recommendations on the Foreign Domestic Movement Program* (INTERCEDE report for submission to the Ministry of Employment and Immigration, Ottawa, 1990).

Armstrong, Pat. 'Restructuring Public and Private: Women's Paid and Unpaid Work', in Susan B. Boyd, ed., *Challenging the Public/Private Divide* (Toronto: University of Toronto Press, 1997), 37–61.

——. 'Women's Health Care Work: Nursing in Context', in P. Armstrong, J. Choiniere and Elaine Day, eds, *Vital Signs: Nursing in Transition* (Toronto: Garamond Press, 1993).

Armstrong, Pat and Hugh Armstrong. *Wasting Away: The Undermining of Canadian Health Care* (Toronto: Oxford University Press, 1996).

——. *The Double Ghetto: Canadian Women and Their Segregated Work*, 3rd edn (Toronto: McClelland and Stewart, 1994).

Arnopoulous, Sheila McLeod. *Problems of Immigrant Women in the Canadian Labour Force* (Ottawa: Canadian Advisory Council on the Status of Women, January 1979).

Ashton, John. *Social Life in the Reign of Queen Anne Taken from Original Sources* (n.d.: Chatto and Windus, 1882).

Asis, Maruja M.B. 'The Overseas Employment Program Policy', in G. Batistella, and A. Paganoni, eds, *Philippine Labour Migration: Impact and Policy* (Quezon City: Scalabrini Migration Center, 1992).

Ayuyang, Rachelle Q. 'Nursing the Dream', *Filipinas*, May 1999.

Bacon, D. 'For an Immigration Policy Based on Human Rights', *Social Justice*, 23: 3 (1996), 137–53.

Bakan, Abigail B. 'Capital, Marxism and the World Economy: APEC and the MAI', in Abigail B. Bakan and Eleanor MacDonald, eds, *Critical Political Studies: Debates and Dialogues from the Left* (Kingston and Montreal: McGill-Queen's University Press, 2002).

——. *Ideology and Class Conflict in Jamaica: The Politics of Rebellion* (Montreal: McGill-Queen's University Press, 1990).

——. 'The International Market for Female Labour and Individual Deskilling: West Indian Women Workers in Toronto', *North/South: Canadian Journal of Latin American and Caribbean Studies*, 12: 24 (1987).

Bakan, Abigail B., David Cox and Colin Leys, eds. *Imperial Power and Regional Response: The Caribbean Basin Initiative* (Wilfrid Laurier University Press, 1993).

Bakan, Abigail B. and Audrey Kobayashi. *Employment Equity Policy in Canada: An Interprovincial Comparison* (Ottawa: Status of Women Canada, 2000).

Bakan, Abigail B. and Eleanor MacDonald, eds. *Critical Political Studies: Debates and Dialogues from the Left* (Kingston and Montreal: McGill-Queen's University Press, 2002).

Bakan, Abigail B. and Daiva Stasiulis. 'Structural Adjustment, Citizenship, and Foreign Domestic Labour: The Canadian Case', in Isabella Bakker, ed., *Rethinking Restructuring: Gender and Change in Canada* (University of Toronto Press, 1996), 217–42.

——. 'Making the Match: Domestic Placement Agencies and the Racialization of Women's Household Work', *Signs: Journal of Women in Culture and Society*, 20: 2 (Winter 1995), 303–5.

——. 'Foreign Domestic Worker Policy in Canada and the Social Boundaries of Modern Citizenship', *Science and Society*, 58: 1 (Spring 1994), 7–33.

Balibar, Etienne. '*Es Gibt Keinen Staat in Europa*: Racism and Politics in Europe Today', *New Left Review* (March–April 1991).

Barclay, Glen St. J. 'The European Union and the Maghreb: A Clash of Civilisations', *Australia and World Affairs*, 25 (Winter 1995), 5–17.

Barlow, Maude and Tony Clarke. *Global Showdown* (Toronto: Stoddart, 2001).

Basch, L., N.G. Schiller and C.S. Blanc. *Nations Unbound: Transnational Projects, Postcolonial Predicaments, and Deterritorialized Nation-States* (Amsterdam: Gordon and Breach, 1994).

Bascom, Wilbert O. 'Remittance Inflows and Economic Development in Selected Anglophone Caribbean Countries', in Sergio Díaz-Briquets and Sidney Weintraub, eds, *Migration, Remittances and Small Business Development: Mexico and Caribbean Basin Countries* (Boulder: Westview Press, 1991), 71–99.

Battistella, Graziano. 'Data on International Migration from the Philippines', *Asian and Pacific Migration Journal*, 4: 4 (1995), 589–99.

——. 'Migration: Opportunity or Loss?' in G. Batistella, and A. Paganoni, eds, *Philippine Labour Migration: Impact and Policy* (Quezon City: Scalabrini Migration Center, 1992), 113–34.

Bayefsky, Anne. 'The Jamaican Women Case and the Canadian Human Rights Act: Is Government Subject to the Principle of Equal Opportunity?' *U.W.O.L. Rev.*, 18 (1980), 461–7.

Beach, Jane. 'A Comprehensive System of Child Care', Strategy Paper for National Child Care Conference and Lobby, Ottawa, October 1992.

Beltran, Ka Crispin. 'Message to the International Migrant Conference', Address Delivered to the International Migrant Conference on Labor-Export and Forced Migration Amidst Globalization, Manila, 4–8 November 2001.

Benoit, Leon M.P. 'Last Chance for Leticia Cables, The Nanny That Worked Too Hard', press release, 29 February 2000, Ottawa.

Bhabha, Jacqueline. 'Enforcing the Human Rights of Citizens and Non-Citizens in the Era of Maastricht: Some Reflections on the Importance of States', *Globalization and Identity: Dialectics of Flow and Closure* (Oxford: Blackwell, 1999).

——. 'Belonging in Europe: Citizenship and Post-national Rights', *International Social Science Journal*, 159 (1999).

——. 'Embodied Rights, Gender Persecution, State Sovereignty, and Refugees', *Public Culture*, 9 (1996), 3–32.

Blackett, Adelle. 'Making Domestic Work Visible: The Case for Specific Regulation' (Geneva: ILO, Labour Law and Labour Relations Branch, 1998).

A. Borowski, A. Richmond, J. Shu and A. Simmons. 'The International Movements of Peoples', in H. Adelman *et al.* eds, *Immigration and Refugee Policy: Australia and Canada Compared*, Vol. 1 (Toronto: University of Toronto Press, 1995).

Boyd, Monica. 'Immigrant Women in Canada', in Rita J. Simon and Caroline B. Brettell, eds, *International Migration: The Female Experience* (Totowa, NJ: Rowman and Allenheld, 1986), 47–75.

Boyd, Susan. 'Challenging the Public/Private Divide: an Overview', in S. Boyd, ed., *Challenging the Public/Private Divide* (Toronto: University of Toronto Press, 1997).

Brand, Dionne. *No Burden to Carry: Narratives of Black Working Women in Ontario 1920s–1950s* (Toronto: Women's Press, 1991).

Bretl, Diana and Christina Davidson. 'Background Paper: Foreign Domestic Workers in British Columbia' (West Coast Domestic Workers Association, Vancouver, n.d.).

Brierley, J.D., R.H. Fryer and E. Goldschmeid. *A Future for Nursery Nursing: Report of the Panel of Inquiry Appointed by the National Nursery Examination Board* (London: NNEB, n.d.).

Broadbent, Edward. 'Citizenship Today: Is There a Crisis?' in Dave Broad and Wayne Antony, eds, *Citizens or Consumers? Social Policy in a Market Society* (Halifax: Fernwood Press, 1999).

Brodie, Janine. 'Citizenship and Solidarity: Reflections on the Canadian Way', *Citizenship Studies*, 6: 4 (December 2002), 377–94.

——. 'The Politics of Social Policy in the Twenty-First Century', in D. Broad and W. Antony, *Citizens or Consumers? Social Policy in a Market Society* (Halifax: Fernwood Press, 1999).

Brooks, Ray. 'Why is Unemployment High in the Philippines?', IMF Working Paper (International Monetary Fund, Asia Pacific Department, 2002), <http://www.imf.org/external/pubs/ft/wp/2002/wp0223.pdf>.

Brubaker, R. 'Commentary: Are Immigration Control Efforts Really Failing?' in W.A. Cornelius, P.L. Martin and J.F. Hollifield, eds, *Controlling Immigration: A Global Perspective* (Stanford: Stanford University Press, 1994).

Bryden, Philip L. 'Fundamental Justice and Family Class Immigration: The Example of *Pangli v. Minister of Employment and Immigration*', *University of Toronto Law Journal* 4 (1991), at 516–17.

Bultran, Ramon. 'Recruitment Costs, State Exaction and Government Fees', Paper delivered at the International Migrant Conference on Labor-Export and Forced Migration Amidst Globalization, Manila, 4–8 November 2001.

Bunster, Ximena and Elsa M. Chaney. *Sellers and Servants: Working Women in Lima Peru* (Granby, Mass: Bergin and Garvey, 1989).

Bush, Barbara. *Slave Women in Caribbean Society* (Kingston: Heinemann Publishers Caribbean, 1990).

Calavita, K. 'U.S. Immigration and Policy Responses: The Limits of Legislation', in W.A. Cornelius, P.L. Martin and J.F. Hollifield, eds, *Controlling Immigration: A Global Perspective* (Stanford: Stanford University Press, 1994), 55–82.

Calliste, Agnes. 'Antiracism Organizing and Resistance in Nursing: African Canadian Women', *Canadian Review of Sociology and Anthropology*, 33: 3 (August 1996), 361–90.

——. 'Women of "Exceptional Merit": Immigration of Caribbean Nurses to Canada', *Canadian Journal of Women and the Law*, 6: 1 (1993), 85–102.

——. 'Canada's Immigration Policy and Domestics from the Caribbean: The Second Domestic Scheme', in Jesse Vorst *et al.*, eds, *Race, Class, Gender: Bonds and Barriers* (Toronto: Garamond Press, 1991), 133–65.

Canada, Citizenship and Immigration Canada. *Facts and Figures* (Ottawa, 1998).

——. 'Citizenship: Fact Sheet', June 1997, available at <http://www.cic.gc.ca/english/newcomer.fact_09e.html>.

——. Live-in Caregiver Program website, <http://www.cic.gc.ca/english/visit/caregi_e2.html#2>.

——. 'The Live-in Caregiver Program: Information for Employers and Live-in Caregivers from Abroad', Minister of Supply and Services, Canada, 1992.

Canada, Employment and Immigration Canada. 'Operations Memorandum' (Draft), Live-in Caregiver Program, Employment and Immigration Canada, (Ottawa, 23 April 1992).

——. 'Report from Statistical Review of FDM Program: Persons Entering the Foreign Domestic Program by Year and Gender, 1982–1989' (Ottawa, 1990).

Canada Employment and Immigration Canada. Task Force on Immigration Practices and Procedures, *Domestic Workers on Employment Authorizations* (Ottawa: Office of the Minister, Employment and Immigration, April 1981).

Canada, House of Commons. Bill C-11, 'Immigration and Refugee Protection Act', <http://www.parl.gc.ca/37/1/parlbus/chambus/house/bills/government/C-11/C-11_3/90141bE.html#1>.

Canada, Immigration and Refugee Board. *Guidelines on Women Refugees Fleeing Gender-Related Persecution* (Ottawa, 1993).

Canada, Statistics Canada. *Current Demographic Analysis: Caribbean Immigrants* (Ottawa: Minister of Supply and Services, 1989).

Canadian Council for Refugees. 'Canadian Council for Refugees Reacts to Publication of Immigration Regulations', 11 June 2002, <http://www.web.net/~ccr/regsrelease.html>.

——. 'Bill C-11 Brief', Ottawa, 25 March 2001.

——. 'Comments on Bill C-31: An Act Respecting Immigration to Canada and the Granting of Refugee Protection to Persons who are Displaced, Persecuted or in Danger', Montreal, July 2000.

Carens, Joseph H. 'Aliens and Citizens: The Case For Open Borders', *The Review of Politics*, 49 (1987), 251–73.

Carino, Benjamin V. 'Migrant Workers from the Philippines', in G. Batistella and A. Paganoni, eds, *Philippine Labour Migration: Impact and Policy* (Quezon City: Scalabrini Migration Center, 1992).

Chaney, E. and M. Garcia Castro, eds. *Muchachas No More: Household Workers in Latin America and the Caribbean* (Philadelphia: Temple University Press, 1989).

Chang, Grace. *Disposable Domestics: Immigrant Women in the Global Economy* (Cambridge, Mass.: South End Press, 2000).

Chant, Sylvia. *Women and Survival in Mexican Cities: Perspectives on Gender, Labor Markets and Low-income Households* (New York: Manchester University Press, 1991).

Cheney, Deborah. 'Valued Judgments?: A Reading of Immigration Cases', in Anne Bottomley and Joanne Conaghan, eds, *Feminist Theory and Legal Strategy* (Oxford: Blackwell, 1993).

Chodos, Robert. *The Caribbean Connection* (Toronto: James Lorimer, 1977).

Churchill, Ward. *A Little Matter of Genocide: Holocaust and Denial in the Americas 1492 to the Present* (San Francisco: City Lights Books, 1997).

Chussodovksy, Michel. *The Globalisation of Poverty: Impacts of IMF and World Bank Reforms* (New Jersey: Zed Books, 1999).

Clark-Lewis, Elizabeth. 'This Work had a End ... ', in Carol Groneman and Mary Beth Norton, eds, *'To Toil the Livelong Day': America's Women at Work 1780–1980* (Ithaca: Cornell University Press, 1987).

Cleveland, Gordon and Michael Krashinsky, eds, *Our Children's Future: Child Care Policy in Canada* (Toronto: University of Toronto Press, 2001).

Cleveland, Gordon and Michael Krashinsky. 'Introduction', in Gordon Cleveland and Michael Krashinsky, eds, *Our Children's Future: Child Care Policy in Canada* (Toronto: University of Toronto Press, 2001).

Cohen, Rina. 'The Work Conditions of Immigrant Women Live-in Domestics: Racism, Sexual Abuse, and Invisibility', *Resources for Feminist Research*, 16: 1 (1987), 36–8.

Cohen, Robin. *The New Helots: Migrants and the International Division of Labor* (Vermont: Gower Publishing Co., 1987).

Colen, Shellee. ' "Housekeeping" for the Green Card: West Indian Household Workers, the State and Stratified Reproduction in New York', in Roger Sanjek and Shellee Colen, eds, *At Work in Homes: Household Workers in World Perspective* (Washington DC: American Ethnological Society Monograph Series, 1990).

Colen, Shellee and Roger Sanjek. 'At Work in Homes II: Directions', in Roger Sanjek and Shellee Colen, eds, *At Work in Homes: Household Workers in World Perspective* (Washington DC: American Ethnological Society Monograph Series, 1990), 176–88.

College of Nurses of Ontario, 'College of Nurses Welcomes Baccalaureate Requirement for Registered Nurses', News Release, 12 April 2000, <http://www.cno.org/index.new.html>.

Conway, Dennis. 'Migration and Urbanisation Policies: Immediate Needs for the 21st Century', *Caribbean Affairs*, 3: 4 (October–December 1990).

Coulter, Rebecca Priegert. 'Alberta Nurses and the "Illegal" Strike of 1988', in Linda Briskin and Patricia McDermott, eds, *Women Challenging Unions: Feminism, Democracy and Militancy* (Toronto: University of Toronto Press, 1993).

Coutts, J. 'Hospitals Replace Registered Nurses: Less-skilled Take Over Tasks', *Globe and Mail*, 23 May 1996, A1, A8.

Currie, Dawn. 'Re-thinking What We Do and How We Do it: A Study of Reproductive Decisions', *Canadian Review of Sociology and Anthropology*, 25: 2 (May 1988), 231–53.

Daenzer, Patricia. *Regulating Class Privilege: Immigrant Servants in Canada 1940s–1990s* (Toronto: Canadian Scholars' Press, 1993).

——. 'Ideology and the Formation of Migration Policy: The Case of Immigrant Domestic Workers, 1940–1990', Ph.D. dissertation (Department of Social Work, University of Toronto, 1991).

Danaher, Kevin, ed. *Democratizing the Global Economy* (Philadelphia: Common Courage Press, 2001).

das Gupta, Tania. 'Racism in Nursing', in *Racism and Paid Work* (Toronto: Garamond Press, 1996).

——. 'Anti-Black Racism in Nursing in Ontario', *Studies in Political Economy*, 51 (Fall 1996), 97–116.

Day, Elaine. 'The Unionization of Nurses', in Pat Armstrong, Jacqueline Choiniere and Elaine Day, eds, *Vital Signs: Nursing in Transition* (Toronto: Garamond Press, 1993), 89–109.

de Dios, Emmanuel S. and Joel Rocamora, eds. *Of Bonds and Bondage: A Reader on Philippine Debt* (Manila: Transnational Institute, Philippine Centre for Policy Studies, and Freedom of Debt Coalition, 1992).

Denis, Claude. ' "Government Can Do Whatever it Wants": Moral Regulation in Ralph Klein's Alberta', *Canadian Review of Sociology and Anthropology*, 32: 3 (1995), 365–83.

Denitch, B. 'Democracy and the New World Order: Dilemmas and Conflicts', *Social Justice*, 23: 1–2 (1996), 21–38.

Despradel, Lil. 'Internal Migration of Rural Women in the Caribbean and its Effects on Their Status', in UNESCO, *Women on the Move: Contemporary Changes in Family and Society* (1984), 93–109.

Diamond, S. 'Right-wing Politics and the Anti-Immigration Cause', *Social Justice*, 23: 3 (1996), 159.

Dioscon, Cecilia. 'Filipino Women's Identity: Social, Cultural and Economic Segregation in Canada', Presented to the 'Towards the Transformation of Race and Gender' conference organized by the Race and Gender Teaching Advisory Group, University of British Columbia, May 2001.

Doherty, Gillian. *Quality Matters in Child Care* (Huntsville: Jesmond Publishing, 1991).

Doherty, G., M. Friendly and M. Oloman. *Women's Support, Women's Work: Child Care in an Era of Deficit Reduction, Devolution, Downsizing and Deregulation* (Ottawa: Status of Women Canada, 1998).

Doris Marshall Institute and Arnold Minors & Associates. 'Equality for all', Final Report, Appendices, Consultants' Report to Northwestern General Hospital (Toronto, March 1994).

Ellis, Pat, ed. *Women of the Caribbean* (London: Zed Press, 1986).

Elson, Diane. 'Male Bias in Macro-economics: The Case of Structural Adjustment', in Diane Elson, ed., *Male Bias in the Development Process* (New York: Manchester University Press, 1991).

Enloe, Cynthia. *Bananas, Beaches and Bases: Making Feminist Sense of International Politics* (Berkeley: University of California Press, 1989).

Epstein, Rachel. 'Domestic Workers: The Experience in B.C.', in Linda Briskin and Lynda Yanz, eds, *Union Sisters* (Toronto: Women's Press, 1983), 222–37.

Estable, Alma. 'Immigrant Women in Canada – Current Issues'. A Background Paper for the Canadian Advisory Council on the Status of Women (Ottawa, 1986).

Eviota, Elizabeth Uy. *The Political Economy of Gender: Women and the Sexual Division of Labour in the Philippines* (New Jersey: Zed Books, 1992).

Falk, Richard. 'The Making of Global Citizenship', in *Global Visions: Beyond the New World Order* (Montreal: Black Rose Books, 1993), 39–52.

Falk, Richard, Lester Edwin J. Ruiz and R.B. Walker. 'Introduction: The International and the Challenge of Speculative Reason', in Richard Falk, Lester Edwin J. Ruiz and R.B. Walker, eds, *Reframing the International* (New York: Routledge, 2002).

Faludi, Susan. *Backlash: The Undeclared War Against American Women* (New York: Crown Publishers, 1991).

Filipino Nurses Support Group. Media Release, Vancouver, 18 October 2000.

Fox-Genovese, Elizabeth. *Within the Plantation Household: Black and White Women in the Old South* (Chapel Hill: University of North Carolina Press, 1988).

Friendly, Martha. 'Child Care and Canadian Federalism in the 1990s: Canary in a Coal Mine', in Gordon Cleveland and Michael Krashinsky, eds, *Our Children's Future: Child Care Policy in Canada* (Toronto: University of Toronto Press, 2001).

French, Marilyn. *The War Against Women* (New York: Summit Books, 1992).

Fryer, Peter. *Staying Power: The History of Black People in Britain* (London: Pluto Press, 1984).

Fudge, Judy. 'Little Victories and Big Defeats: The Rise and Fall of Collective Bargaining Rights for Domestic Workers in Ontario', in A. Bakan and D. Stasiulis, eds, *Not One of the Family: Foreign Domestic Workers in Canada* (Toronto: University of Toronto Press, 1997), 119–45.

Gaitskell, Deborah. 'Housewives, Maids or Mothers: Some Contradictions of Domesticity for Christian Women in Johannesburg, 1903–39', *Journal of African History*, 24: 2 (1983), 241–56.

———. ' "Christian Compounds for Girls": Church Hostels for African Women in Johannesburg, 1907–1970', *Journal of African Studies*, 6: 1 (1979), 44–69.

George, Susan. *The Debt Boomerang: How Third World Debt Hurts Us All* (Boulder: Westview Press, 1992).

George, Susan, George Manbiot *et al*. *Anti-Capitalism: A Guide to the Movement* (London: Bookmarks Publications, 2001).

Giddens, Anthony. *Profiles and Critiques in Social Theory* (London: Macmillan, 1982).

Glenn, Evelyn Nakano. 'From Servitude to Service Work: Historical Continuities in the Racial Division of Paid Reproductive Labor', *Signs: Journal of Women in Culture and Society*, 18: 1 (1992), 1–43.

———. *Issei, Nisei, War Bride: Three Generations of Japanese American Women in Domestic Service* (Philadelphia: Temple University Press, 1986).

Gordon, Lorna. 'Women in Caribbean Agriculture', in Pat Ellis, ed., *Women of the Caribbean* (New Jersey: Zed Books, 1986).

Gotell, Lise. 'Towards a Democratic Practice of Feminist Litigation? LEAF's Changing Approach to *Charter* Equality', in Radha Jhappan, ed., *Women's Legal Strategies in Canada* (Toronto: University of Toronto, 2002), 135–74.

Government of the Philippines, Report of the Senate Committee on Health, *Where the Nurses Are* (Manila, 1989).

Growe, Sarah Jane. *Who Cares: The Crisis in Canadian Nursing* (Toronto: McClelland & Stewart, 1991).

Ha, Tu Thanh. 'Quebec Strike a Litmus Test for Fall Talks', *Globe and Mail*, Toronto, 3 July 1999, A4.

Halfmann, Jost. 'Citizenship Universalism, Migration and the Risks of Exclusion', *British Journal of Sociology*, 49: 4 (1998).

Hardill, Kathy. 'Discovering Fire Where the Smoke is: Racism in the Health Care System', *Towards Justice in Health* (Summer 1993).

Harding, Katherine. 'Nursing is different here', *Globe and Mail*, Toronto, 8 January 2003.

Harris, Nigel. *The New Untouchables: Immigration and the New World Worker* (Harmondsworth: Penguin Books, 1995).

Harrison, Paul. *Inside the Third World* (Harmondsworth: Penguin Books, 1993).

Head, Wilson. *An Exploratory Study of Attitudes and Perceptions of Minority and Majority Group Healthcare Workers* (Toronto: Ontario Ministry of Labour, 1985).

Held, David. *Democracy and the Global Order: From the Modern State to Cosmopolitan Governance* (Cambridge: Cambridge University Press, 1995).

Henderson, James (Sákéj). '*Sui Generis* and Treaty Citizenship', *Citizenship Studies*, 6: 4 (December 2002), 415–40.

Henry, Frances. *The Caribbean Diaspora in Toronto: Learning to Live with Racism* (Toronto: University of Toronto Press, 1994).

———. 'The West Indian Domestic Scheme in Canada', *Social and Economic Studies*, 17: 1 (1968).

Henry, Frances and Carol Tator. 'State Policy and Practices as Racialized Discourse: Multiculturalism, The Charter and Employment Equity', in Peter S. Li, ed., *Race and Ethnic Relations in Canada*, 2nd edn. (Toronto: Oxford University Press, 1999), 88–115.

Heyzer, Noeleen and Vivienne Wee. 'Domestic Workers in Transient Overseas Employment: Who Benefits, Who Profits', in N. Heyzer, G. Lycklama à Nijeholt and N. Weerakoon, eds, *The Trade in Domestic Worker's: Causes, Mechanisms and Consequences of International Migration* (London: Zed Books, 1994), 31–102.

Heyzer, Noeleen, Geertje Lycklama à Nijeholt and Nedra Weerakoon, eds. *The Trade in Domestic Workers: Causes, Mechanisms and Consequences of International Migration* (Kuala Lampur and London: Asian and Pacific Development Centre and Zed Books, 1994).

Higman, B.W. 'Domestic Service in Jamaica Since 1750', in B. Higman, ed., *Trade, Government and Society in Caribbean History 1700–1920* (Kingston: Heinemann Educational Books Caribbean Ltd, 1983).

Hindess, Barry. 'Neo-liberal Citizenship', *Citizenship Studies* 6: 4 (June 2002), 127–44.

Hine, Darlene Clark. *Black Women in White: Racial Conflict and Cooperation in the Nursing Profession, 1890–1950* (Bloomington: Indiana University Press, 1989).

Hiscott, Robert D. *Career Paths of Nursing Professionals: A Study of Employment Mobility* (Ottawa: Carleton University Press, 1998).

Hollifield, J.F. 'Immigration and Republicanism in France: The Hidden Consensus', in W.A. Cornelius, P.L. Martin and J.F. Hollifield, eds, *Controlling Immigration: A Global Perspective* (Stanford: Stanford University Press, 1994).

Holston, James and Arjun Appadurai, 'Cities and Citizenship', *Public Culture*, 8 (1996), 187–204.

Holton, Robert J. *Globalization and the Nation-State* (London: Palgrave, 1998).

Hosoda, Naomi. 'Filipino Women in the Japanese Entertainment Industry: The International Division of Labour and the Commodification of Female Sexuality' (Masters Thesis, Queen's University, 1994).

Housewives Association of Trinidad and Tobago. *Report on Employment Status of Household Workers in Trinidad* (Port of Spain: HATT, March 1975).

Human Rights Watch, 'Refugees and Displaced Persons', <http:www.hr.org/refugees/>.

Hunt, Nancy Rose. 'Domesticity and Colonialism in Belgian Africa: Usumbura's Foyer Social, 1946–1960', *Signs: Journal of Women in Culture and Society*, 31: 5, 447–74.

Hwang, Pauline. 'Racism, Sexism and Canadian Immigration', Colours of Resistance Website, <http://www.tao.ca/~colours/hwang.html>.

INTERCEDE. 'Improving the Ontario Employment Standards Act to Protect Domestic Workers' (Toronto: INTERCEDE, n.d.).

International Labour Organization. Press Release, 'Female Asian Migrants: A Growing but Increasingly Vulnerable Workforce', 5 February 1996, webinfo@ilo.org.

International Organization for Migration. *World Migration Report* (New York: United Nations, 2000).

Isbister, J. 'Are Immigration Controls Ethical?' *Social Justice*, 23: 3 (1996), 54–67.

Human Rights Watch U.S. 'We Are Not the Enemy', <http:///www.hrw.org/us/indix.php>.

Jackman, B. 'Admission of Foreign Domestic Workers', unpublished manuscript.

Jacobsen, David. *Rights Across Borders: Immigration and the Decline of Citizenship* (Baltimore: Johns Hopkins University Press, 1996).

Jelin, Elizabeth. 'Migration and Labor Force Participation of Latin American Women: The Domestic Servants in the Cities', *Signs: Journal of Women in Culture and Society*, 3: 1 (Autumn 1977), 129–41.

Jenson, Jane. 'Fated to Live in Interesting Times: Canada's Changing Citizenship Regimes', *Canadian Journal of Political Science*, XXX: 4 (December 1997).

Jenson, Jane, and Susan Phillips. 'Regime Shift: New Citizenship Practices in Canada', *International Journal of Canadian Studies*, 14 (1996), 111–35.

Jonas, S. 'Rethinking Immigration Policy and Citizenship in the Americas: A Regional Framework', *Social Justice*, 23: 3 (1996).

Jones, Brenda. 'System Racist, Nurse Charges', *Vancouver Echo* (19 May 1999), 14.

Joppke, C. 'Review of Thomas Faist, David Jacobsen and Marco Martiniello', *Contemporary Sociology*, 26: 1 (1997).

Joseph, Clifton. 'On Your Mark! Get Set! Go Multi-culti', *This Magazine*, 28: 5 (January–February 1995).

Kastoryano Riva. 'Settlement, Transnational Communities and Citizenship', *International Social Science Journal*, 165 (September 2000).

Keck, Margaret E. and Kathryn Sikkink. *Activists Across Borders: Advocacy Networks in International Politics* (Ithaca: Cornell University Press, 1998).

Khosa, Punam. *Review of the Situation of Women in Canada* (Toronto: National Action Committee on the Status of Women, July 1993).

Koc, Mustafa. 'Globalization as a Discourse', in Alessandro Bonnan *et al.*, eds, *From Columbus to ConAgra: The Globalization of Agriculture and Food* (Lawrence: University Press of Kansas, 1994).

Kwitko, Ludmilla. 'Filipina Domestic Workers and the New International Division of Labour', Paper presented at the Asia in the 1990s: Making and Meeting a New World Conference (Queen's University, Kingston, 1993).

Labelle, Micheline and Midy Franklin. 'Re-reading Citizenship and the Transnational Practices of Immigrants', *Journal of Ethnic and Migration Studies*, 25: 2 (April 1999), 213–32.

Langevin, Louise and Marie-Claire Belleau. *Trafficking in Women in Canada: A Critical Analysis of the Legal Framework Governing Immigration Live-in Caregivers and Mail-Order Brides* (Ottawa: Status of Women Canada, October 2000).

Leah, Ronnie and Gwen Morgan. 'Immigrant Women Fight Back; The Case of the Seven Jamaican Women', *Resources for Feminist Research*, 7: 3 (1979), 23–4.

Lim, L. 'Women's Work in Export Factories: The Politics of a Cause', in I. Tinker, ed., *Persistent Inequalities* (New York: Oxford University Press, 1990).

Lindgren, April. 'Health care cuts hit women hardest: report', *Citizen*, Ottawa, 4 December 1999, A4.

Linklater, Andrew. 'Cosmopolitan Citizenship', in Kimberley Hutchings and Roland Dannreuther, eds, *Cosmopolitan Citizenship* (Houndmills, UK: Macmillan Press, 1999).

Lutz, Helma. 'The Limits of European-ness: Immigrant Women in Fortress Europe', *Feminist Review*, 57 (Autumn 1997), 93–111.

Macklin, Audrey. 'Foreign Domestic Worker: Surrogate Housewife or Mail Order Servant?' *McGill Law Journal*, 37: 3 (1992), 681–760.

Marshall, T.H. *Citizenship and Social Class* (Cambridge: Cambridge University Press, 1950).

Martin, Linda and Kelly Segrave. *The Servant Problem: Domestic Workers in North America* (Jefferson, N.C.: McFarland, 1985).

Martin, P.L. 'The United States: Benign Neglect Towards Immigration', in W.A. Cornelius, P.L. Martin and J.F. Hollifield, eds, *Controlling Immigration: A Global Perspective* (Stanford: Stanford University Press, 1994).

Martiniello, M., ed. *Migration, Citizenship and Ethnic Minorities in the European Union* (Aldershot: Avebury, 1995).

Massiah, Joycelin, ed. 'Women in the Caribbean', *Social and Economic Studies*, Special Number, Part One (Vol. 35, No. 2, June 1986) and Part Two (Vol. 35, No. 3, September 1986).

Matas, Robert. 'B.C. Looking Overseas to Hire More Nurses', *Globe and Mail*, Toronto, 5 November 1999, A10.

Mattei, Linda Miller. 'Gender and International Labor Migration: A Networks Approach', *Social Justice*, 23: 3 (1996), 38–54.

McAfee, Kathy. *Storm Signals: Structural Adjustment and Development Alternatives in the Caribbean* (London: Zed Books and Oxfam America, 1991).

McGovern, Ligaya L. 'The Export of Labor and the Politics of Foreign Debt (The Case of Overseas Filipino Domestic Workers)', Paper Presented at the International Migrant Conference on Labor Export and Forced Migration Amidst Globalization, Manila, 4–8 November 2001.

McPherson, Kathryn. *Bedside Matters: The Transformation of Canadian Nursing, 1900–1990* (Toronto: University of Toronto Press, 1996).

Meekosha, Helen and Leanne Dowse. 'Enabling Citizenship: Gender, Disability and Citizenship in Australia', *Feminist Review*, 57 (Autumn 1997), 49–72.

Mejia, Alfonso, Helena Pizurki and Erica Royston. *Physician and Nurse Migration: Analysis and Policy Implications*, Report of a WHO Study (World Health Organization, Geneva, 1979).

Menzies, Robert, Robert Adamoski and Dorothy Chunn. 'Rethinking the Citizen in Canadian Social History', in Robert Adamoski, Dorothy Chunn and Robert Menzies, eds, *Contesting Canadian Citizenship* (Peterborough, Ontario: Broadview Press, 2002), 11–42.

Miliband, Ralph. 'The New World Order and the Left', *Social Justice*, 23: 1–2, (1996) 15–20.

Mitchell, Alanna. 'Our Families Come First: Why More Mothers are Choosing to Stay at Home', *Chatelaine Magazine*, February 1992.

——. *Globe and Mail*, Toronto, 20 April 1992.

Mitter, Swasti. *Common Fate, Common Bond: Women in the Global Economy* (London: Pluto Press, 1986).

Mohammed, Patricia. 'Domestic Workers', in Pat Ellis, ed., *Women of the Caribbean* (London: Zed Books, 1985), 41–6.

Momsen, Janet Henshall, ed. *Women and Change in the Caribbean* (London: James Currey, 1993).

——. 'Gender Roles in Caribbean Agricultural Labour', in Malcolm Cross and Gad Hueman, eds, *Labour in the Caribbean* (London: Macmillan Caribbean, 1988), 141–58.

Money, Jeannette. *Fences and Neighbors: The Political Geography of Immigration Control* (Ithaca: Cornell University Press, 1999).

Mullard, Chris. 'Multiracial Education in Britain: From Assimilation to Cultural Pluralism', in J. Tierney, ed., *Race, Migration and Schooling* (London: Holt, Rinehart and Winston, 1982).

Murphy, Michael and Siobhán Harty. 'Reconstructing Citizenship: Self-Determination in a Post-National Era', Paper Presented at the Annual Meeting of the American Political Science Association, San Francisco, 3 August–2 September 2001.

Munroe, Trevor. *The Politics of Constitutional Decolonization, 1944–62* (Jamaica: Institute of Social and Economic Research, 1972).

Murnighan, Bill. *Selling Ontario's Health Care: The Real Story on Government Spending and Public Relations*, Technical Paper no. 11, Ontario's Alternative Budget (Ontario: Canadian Centre for Policy Alternatives, 2001).

National Nanny Newsletter. 'Nanny Placement Practices in America: Preliminary Survey Results', *National Nanny Newsletter*, vol. 4 (Fall 1988), 8–11.

National Nursery Examination Board (NNEB). *The Diploma and Preliminary Diploma in Nursery Nursing – Modular Scheme: An Overview, 1992* (St Albans: NNEB, 1992).

Niessen, Jan. 'Third-country Nationals and the Legal Basis for Community Action Against Discrimination', MGP [Migration Policy Group] – EP Hearing on anti-discrimination', E:\WPDOC\AUDITION\2000\23–24 mail\Contributions\ EXPERTS\ Speech – Niessen EN.doc, 17 May 2000.

Nyers, Peter. 'Forms of Cosmopolitan Dissent', Paper Delivered at the Citizenship Studies Symposium, York University, 15 January 2003.

Oakly, Annie. *Subject Women* (New York: Pantheon Books, 1981).

Oloman, Mab. *Women's Support, Women's Work: Child Care in an Era of Deficit Reduction, Devolution, Downsizing and Deregulation* (Ottawa: Status of Women Canada, 1998).

——. 'Child Care Funding', Strategy Paper for National Child Care Conference and Lobby, Ottawa, October 1992.

Ong, Aihwa. *Flexible Citizenship: The Cultural Logics of Transnationality* (Durham: Duke University Press, 1999).

Ontario. *Employment Standards – Fact Sheet: 'Domestic Workers'*, <http://www. gov.on.ca/LAB/es/dome.htm> 2001.

Ornstein. Michael. *Ethno-racial Inequality in the City of Toronto: An Analysis of the 1996 Census* (Toronto: Canadian Social Justice Foundation for Research and Education, 2002).

Ortin, Erlinda L. 'The Brain Drain as Viewed by an Exporting Country', *International Nursing Review*, 37: 5 (1990), 340–4.

Overbeek, H. 'Towards A New International Migration Regime: Globalization', in D. Thranhardt and R. Miles, eds, *Migration and European Integration: The Dynamics of Inclusion and Exclusion* (London: Pinter, 1995).

Oziewicz, Estanislao. 'Nanny Policy Called Necessary Protection', *The Globe and Mail* (29 April 1992).

Palma-Beltran, Mary Ruby. 'Filipina Women Domestic Workers Overseas: Profile and Implications for Policy', *Asian Migrant*, 4: 2 (April–June 1991).

Palmer, Phyllis. *Domesticity and Dirt: Housewives and Domestic Servants in the United States, 1920–1945* (Philadelphia: Temple University Press, 1989).

——. 'Housewife and Household Worker: Employer–Employee Relationships in the Home, 1928–1941', in Carol Groneman and Mary Beth Norton, eds, *'To Toil the Livelong Day': America's Women at Work 1780–1980* (Ithaca: Cornell University Press, 1987).

Papp, Leslie. 'Seven Nurses Get Award in "Landmark" Rights Case', *Toronto Star*, 13 May 1994.

Parreñas, Rhacel Salazar. *Servants of Globalization: Women, Migration, and Domestic Work* (Stanford: Stanford University Press, 2001).

Peach, C. *West Indian Migration to Britain: A Social Geography* (London: Oxford University Press, 1968).

Pellerin, Hélène. 'The Global Governance of International Migration in the 1990s', in C. Turenne Sjolander and J.F. Thibault, eds, *On Global Governance* (Ottawa: University of Ottawa, forthcoming).

———. 'The Cart Before the Horse? The Coordination of Migration Policies in the Americas and the Neo-liberal Economic Project of Integration', *Review of International Political Economy*. 6: 4 (Winter 1999).

Pellerin, Hélène and Henk Overbeek, 'Neo-Liberal Regionalism and the Management of People's Mobility', in A. Bieler and A.D. Morton, eds, *Social Forces in the Making of the New Europe* (Basingstoke: Palgrave, 2001).

Philippine Women's Centre, 'Project Proposal: Breaking the Barriers, Gaining Strength for Further Development' (Vancouver, 1999).

Pomeroy, William J. *The Philippines: Colonialism, Collaboration, and Resistance!* (New York: International Publishers, 1992).

Powell, Dorian. 'Caribbean Women and their Response to Familial Experiences', *Social and Economic Studies*, 35: 2 (1986), 83–127.

Powell, Martin. 'The Hidden History of Social Citizenship', *Citizenship Studies*, 6: 3 (2002), 229–44.

Rapoport, Rhonda and Robert Rapoport. 'Work and Family in Contemporary Society', in John N. Edwards, ed., *The Family and Change* (New York: Knopf, 1969), 385–408.

Rasminsky, Sklar. *The Daycare Handbook: A Parents' Guide to Finding and Keeping Quality Daycare in Canada* (Toronto: Little, Brown and Co., 1991).

Richmond, Anthony. *Global Apartheid: Refugees, Racism and the New World Order* (Toronto: Oxford University Press, 1994).

Ringer, Benjamin B. *We the People and Others* (New York and London: Routledge, 1983).

Roche, M. 'Citizenship, Social Theory and Social Change', *Theory and Society*, 16 (1987), 363–99.

Rodriguez, N. 'The Battle for the Border: Notes on Autonomous Migration, Transnational Communities and the State', *Social Justice*, 23: 3 (1996), 21–37.

Rodriguez, Robyn M. 'Migrant Heroes: Nationalism, Citizenship and the Politics of Filipino Migrant Labor', *Citizenship Studies*, 6: 3 (2002), 341–56.

Romanow, Roy. *Building on Values: The Future of Health Care in Canada*, Commissioner (Ottawa: Government of Canada, 2001), <http://publications. gc.ca/control/publicHomePage?lang = English%20>.

Rollins, Judith. *Between Women: Domestics and Their Employers* (Philadelphia: Temple University Press, 1985).

Romero, Mary. *Maid in the USA* (New York: Routledge, 1992).

Rose, Nicholas. 'Government and Control', *British Journal of Criminology*, 40: 2000, 321–39.

Rubenstein, Hymie. 'The Impact of Remittances in the Rural English Speaking Caribbean', in William F. Stinner, Klaus de Albuquerque and Roy S. Bryce-Laporte, eds, *Return Migration and Remittances: Developing a Caribbean Perspective*, RILES Occasional Paper, no. 3 (Washington DC: Research Institute and Ethnic Studies, 1982).

Safa, Helen I. and Peggy Antrobus. 'Women and the Economic Crisis in the Caribbean', in Lourdes Beneria and Shelley Feldman, eds, *Unequal Burden: Economic Crises, Persistent Poverty, and Women's Work* (Boulder: Westview Press, 1992), 49–82.

Salt, J. 'The Future of International Labor Migration', *International Migration Review*, 26: 4 (1993).

Sassen, Saskia. *Losing Control? Sovereignty in an Age of Globalization* (New York: Columbia University Press, 1996).

Sassen-Koob, Saskia. 'Labour Migrations and the New International Division of Labour', in June Nash and Maria Patricia Fernandez-Kelly, eds, *Women, Men and the International Division of Labour* (Albany: State University of New York Press, 1983), 175–204.

Satzewich, Vic. 'Racism and Canadian Immigration Policy: The Government's View of Caribbean Migration, 1962–66', *Canadian Ethnic Studies*, XXI: 1 (1989), 77–97.

———. 'The Canadian State and the Racialization of Caribbean Migrant Farm Labour, 1947–1966', *Ethnic and Racial Studies*, 11: 3 (1988), 282–304.

Sayer, Andrew. *Method in Social Science: A Realist Approach* (London: Hutchison, 1984).

Schreuer, Christoph. 'The Waning of the Sovereign State: Toward a New Paradigm for International Law?' *European Journal of International Law*, 4 (1993).

Schuk, Peter H. and Roger M. Smith. *Citizenship Without Consent: Illegal Aliens in the American Polity* (New Haven: Yale University Press, 1985).

Schuster, Liza and John Solomos. 'Rights and Wrongs Across European Borders: Migrants, Minorities and Citizenship', *Citizenship Studies*, 6: 1 (March 2002), 37–54

Schwarz, Peter. 'Vote for National Front Leader Heightens Political Crisis in France', <http://www.wsws.org/articles/2002/apr2002/fran-a23.shtml>.

Shariff, Ali. 'Hospital colour code: six fired black nurses at Northwestern hospital have raised the curtain on systemic racism', *Now* Toronto, 7–13 January 1993.

Sheppard, Robert. 'Nurses at the Ready', *Globe and Mail*, 15 August 1999, A7.

Shohat, Ella and Robert Stam. *Unthinking Eurocentrism: Multiculturalism and the Media* (London: Routledge, 1994).

Siltanen, Janet. 'Paradise Paved? Reflections on the Fate of Social Citizenship in Canada', *Citizenship Studies*, 6: 4 (2002), 397–414.

Simpson, J. 'Conservatism by any other name', *Globe and Mail*, Toronto (29 March 1997), D4.

Soysal, Yasemin Nuhoglu. 'Changing Citizenship in Europe: Remarks on Post-national Membership and the National State', in D. Cesarini and M. Fulbrook, eds, *Nationality and Migration in Europe* (London: Routledge, 1996).

———. *Limits of Citizenship: Migrants and Post-national Membership in Europe* (Chicago: University of Chicago Press, 1994).

Sparks, Holloway. 'Dissident Citizenship: Democratic Theory, Political Courage, and Activist Women', *Hypatia*, 12: 4 (Fall 1997), 74–110.

Sparr, Paula, ed. *Mortgaging Women's Lives* (London: Zed Books, 1994).

Stalker, Peter. *The No-Nonsense Guide to International Migration* (Toronto: New Internationalist Publications, 2001).

———. *Workers Without Frontiers: The Impact of Globalization on International Migration* (Boulder, Colo.: Lynne Rienner Publishers, 2000).

———. *The Work of Strangers* (Geneva: International Labour Organization, 1994).

Stasiulis, Daiva. 'Symbolic Representation and the Numbers Game: Tory Policies on "Race" and Visible Minorities', in Frances Abele, ed., *How Ottawa Spends, 1990–91: The Politics of Fragmentation* (Ottawa: Carleton University Press, 1991), 229–68.

Stasiulis, Daiva. 'The Symbolic Mosaic Reaffirmed: Multiculturalism Policy', in K. Graham, ed., *How Ottawa Spends, 1988–89* (Ottawa: Carleton University Press, 1988), 81–111.
———. 'Race, Ethnicity, and the State: The Political Structuring of South Asian and West Indian Communal Action in Combatting Racism', Ph.D. dissertation (University of Toronto, Department of Sociology, 1982).
Stasiulis, Daiva and Abigail B. Bakan. 'Negotiating the Citizenship Divide: Foreign Domestic Worker Policy and Legal Jurisprudence', in Radha Jhappan, ed., *Women's Legal Strategies in Canada* (Toronto: University of Toronto Press, 2002), 237–94.
———. 'Flor Contemplacion: A Study in Non-Citizenship', *Public Policy*, Manila, Philippines (April–June, 1999), 1–41.
———. 'Negotiating Citizenship: The Case of Foreign Domestic Workers in Canada', *Feminist Review*, No. 57 (Autumn 1997), 112–39.
Stasiulis, Daiva and Nira Yuval-Davis, eds. *Unsettling Settler Societies: Articulations of Gender, Race, Ethnicity and Class* (London: Sage, 1995).
Strange, Susan. *The Retreat of the State: The Diffusion of Power in the World Economy* (Cambridge: Cambridge University Press, 1996).
Strauss, Andrew L. 'Overcoming the Dysfunction of the Bifurcated Global System: The Promise of a People's Assembly', in Richard Falk, Lester Edwin J. Ruiz and R.B.J. Walker, eds, *Reframing the International: Law, Culture, Politics* (New York: Routledge, 2002), 83–106.
Strobel, Margaret. 'African Women: A Review', *Signs: Journal of Women in Culture and Society*, 8: 1 (Autumn 1982), 109–31.
Sutherland, Donald E. *America and Their Servants: Domestic Service in the United States from 1800 to 1920* (Baton Rouge: Louisiana University Press, 1981).
Swamy, Gurushi. 'International Migrant Workers' Remittances: Issues and Prospects', *World Bank Working Papers*, no. 481 (Washington DC: World Bank, 1981).
Tambini, Damian. 'Post-national Citizenship', *Ethnic and Racial Studies*, vol. 24 (2001), 195–217.
Task Force on Child Care. *Report of the Task Force on Child Care* (Ottawa: 1986).
Tennyson, Brian Douglas. ed. *Canadian–Caribbean Relations: Aspects of a Relationship* (Sydney, Nova Scotia: Centre for International Studies, 1990).
———, ed., *Canadian–Caribbean Relations* (Sydney, N.S.: Centre for International Studies, University College of Cape Breton, 1990).
Tie, Chantal. 'Only Discriminating Visa Officers Need Apply: Visa Officer Decisions, the *Charter* and *Lee v. Canada (Minister of Citizenship and Immigration)*', unpublished manuscript.
Tilly, L.A. and J.W. Scott. *Women, Work and Family* (New York: Holt, Rinehart, and Winston, 1978).
Timoll, Andrea. 'Foreign Domestic Servants in Canada', Honours research essay (Department of Political Science, Carleton University, September 1989).
Truong Thanh-Dam. *Sex, Money and Morality: Prostitution and Tourism in South-East Asia* (London: Zed Books,1990).
Tujan Jr, Antonio. 'Labor Export and Forced Migration under Globalization', Paper Presented to the International Migrant Conference on Labor-Export and Forced Migration Amidst Globalization, Manila, Philippines, 4–8 November 2001.

Turner, Bryan S. 'The Erosion of Citizenship', *British Journal of Sociology*, 52: 2 (June 2001), 189–209.

——. 'Outline of a Theory of Citizenship', *Sociology*, 24: 2 (May 1990).

United Nations, General Assembly, 45th Session, Third Committee, *Report of the Open-Ended Working Group on the Drafting of the International Convention on the Protection of the Rights of All Migrant Workers and Members of Their Families*, UN Doc.A/c.3/45/1 (21 June 1990).

Vasquez Noel. 'Economic and Social Impact of Labour Migration', in G. Batistella and A. Paganoni, eds, *Philippine Labour Migration: Impact and Policy* (Quezon City: Scalabrini Migration Center, 1992), 39–67.

Vickers, Jeanne. *Women and the World Economic Crisis* (London: Zed Books, 1991).

Villasin, Fely. 'Domestic Workers' Struggle for Equal Rights in Canada', in Mary Ruby Palma-Bertran and Aurora Javate de Dios, eds, *Filipino Women Overseas Contract Workers: At What Cost?* (Manila: Goodwill Trading Co., 1992), 77–80.

Vincent, D. 'Hospital nursing cuts bite deep', *Toronto Star*, 26 January 1997, A14.

Walker, James. *A History of Blacks in Canada* (Hull, Quebec: Minister of Supply and Services, 1980).

Wallach, Lori and Michelle Sforza. *The WTO: Five Years of Reasons to Resist Corporate Globalization* (New York: Seven Stories Press, 1999).

Ward, Kathryn, ed. *Women Workers and Global Restructuring* (Ithaca: Cornell University Press, 1990).

West Coast Domestic Workers Association, *Domestic Workers Association Newsletter*, Vancouver, 3: 8, August 1990.

——. *Domestic Workers Association Newsletter*, Vancouver, 2: 10, October 1989.

——. *Domestic Workers Association Newsletter*, Vancouver, 1: 16, September 1988.

White, Melanie. 'Neo-Liberalism and the Rise of the Citizen as Consumer', in D. Broad and W. Antony, *Citizens or Consumers? Social Policy in a Market Society* (Halifax: Fernwood Press, 1999).

Williams, Eric. *Capitalism and Slavery* (Chapel Hill: University of North Carolina Press, 1944).

Wipper, Audrey. 'The Maendeleo ya Wanawake Movement in the Colonial Period: The Canadian Connection, Mau Mau, Embroidery and Agriculture', *Rural Africana*, 29 (Winter 1975–76), 195–214.

Whitney, Craig. 'Criticism of bill angers French', *Globe and Mail*, 26 February 1997, A13A.

Wilson, Maureen G. and Elizabeth Whitmore. *Seeds of Fire: Social Development in an Era of Globalization* (Halifax: Fernwood Publishing, 2000).

Wood, Ellen Meiksins. *Democracy Against Capitalism* (Cambridge UK: Cambridge University Press, 1995).

Working Group on the WTO/MAI, 'A Citizens' Guide to the World Trade Organization', July 1999.

Young, Brigitte. 'The "Mistress" and the "Maid" in the Globalized Economy', in Leo Panitch and Colin Leys, eds, *Socialist Register, 2001: Working Classes, Global Realities*, (London: Merlin Press, 2001).

Young, Claire F.L. 'Child Care – A Taxing Issue?' *McGill Law Journal*, 39: 3 (1994), 539–67.

Young, Margaret. 'Canada's Immigration Program: Background Paper' (Ottawa: Minister of Supply and Services, 1994).

Index

childcare, ix, 3, 5, 23–4, 42–3, 46, 50,
64, 66–8, 71–4, 78, 81–2, 94–5,
137, 166, 191
Chinese refugees, 32
Chirac, Jacques, 34
citizenship, viii
denial of, 14
dissident, 7–8, 141, 159, 167
global, 13–14, 37–8, 140–56
hierarchical nature, 11
implications, 60–2
modern, 11–12, 15
national, 1, 13, 16–18, 36
post-national, 15, 37–8
racialized basis for inclusion, 18
rights, 1, 3, 8, 15, 159
social and legal differentiation, 2
terms and conditions of, 2
transnational practices, 160–5
type of participation, 15
universalism of, 16
'citizenship regime', 172
Cohen, Rina, 105, 180, 198
Congress of Black Women of Canada
in 1995, 112
Corazon, Aquino, 57

Dallas, Texas, 4
das Gupta, T., 113, 199, 201, 204–5
Debré, Jean-Louis, 34
deportation, 5, 14, 30, 38, 49, 52, 55,
65–6, 78, 89, 91–2, 124, 144–5,
147–55, 164–5, 167, 177
deskilling, 110, 120
Dioscon, C., 116, 200
domestic service industry, 4, 42
gatekeepers, 63–85
domestic workers, viii, 12, 86, 92
sexist stereotyping of, 82

Elson, D., 41, 181
employers, 5–6, 42, 48–50, 61, 65–6,
68–70, 98–101, 106, 111, 115,
117, 135, 142, 148–50, 154–5
citizen, 6, 14, 87–8, 94
crisis of childcare, 66–73, 78–80,
82–4, 87–92
power of, 52
English language tests, 117

Enloe, C., 27, 175, 181, 194, 218
Estrada, J.E., 163
Europe, 14, 30, 33, 55, 61, 165
European Domestics, 48, 55
European Union (EU), 36

FDM *see* Foreign Domestic Movement
Federal Court of Canada (Trial
Division), 152
females
care workers, 12
citizens, 25, 42
domestic workers, 54, 63–4, 70,
75–6, 95, 102–5
migrant workers, 1, 14, 44–5, 51,
56, 61, 70, 112
nurses, 121
feminism, 68
Fernandez, 145
Filipino
domestic workers, 6, 55–6, 80, 86,
96, 100, 126
migrant nurses, 7, 115, 128–36
migrant workers, 56, 60, 159
nurses, 4, 111, 122, 126
women workers, 3, 106
Filipino Nurses Association, 112
Filipino Nurses Support Group
(FNSG), 111
First World countries, 41, 61
'fit nanny', 6
Foreign Domestic Movement
(FDM), 49–51, 64–5, 70, 77,
88–9, 93, 100, 144, 146, 150,
154
foreign domestic worker policy
(currently the LCP), 42, 150
foreign domestic workers, 5, 86, 93–4,
136–7, 141, 143
deficits in rights, 136
immigration legislation, 141
recruiting, 93, 138
working conditions, wages and
benefits, 94
foreign-trained nurses, 137–8
France, 22, 33
Free Trade Area of the Americas
(FTAA), 21, 156
Friendly, M., 67, 191